ALFRED KAZIN

God and the American Writer

Alfred Kazin was born in Brooklyn in 1915. His first book of criticism, *On Native Grounds* (1942), was a groundbreaking study of American literature that changed radically our way of looking at it, and established him overnight as a major figure. In a series of books of his own since then, and in many critically edited texts of classic American literary works, he established himself as our preeminent man of letters. He taught widely at Harvard, Smith, Amherst, Hunter College, the Graduate Center of the City University of New York, and elsewhere. In 1996 he received from the Truman Capote Literary Trust its first Lifetime Achievement Award in Literary Criticism (in memory of Newton Arvin). He died in June of 1998.

Books by ALFRED KAZIN

God and the American Writer

A Lifetime Burning in Every Moment:
From the Journals of Alfred Kazin

Writing Was Everything

Our New York (WITH DAVID FINN)

A Writer's America: Landscape in Literature

Bright Book of Life:
American Novelists and Storytellers from Hemingway to Mailer

An American Procession

On Native Grounds

Starting Out in the Thirties

The Inmost Leaf

New York Jew

Contemporaries

A Walker in the City

EDITOR

The Viking Portable Blake

F. Scott Fitzgerald: The Man and His Work

The Stature of Theodore Dreiser (WITH CHARLES SHAPIRO)

Herman Melville, *Moby-Dick*

Emerson: A Modern Anthology (WITH DANIEL AARON)

The Works of Anne Frank (WITH ANN BIRSTEIN)

The Open Form: Essays for Our Time

Selected Short Stories of Nathaniel Hawthorne

Henry James, *The Ambassadors*

Walt Whitman, *Specimen Days*

GOD &
THE
AMERICAN
WRITER

ALFRED KAZIN

GOD &
THE
AMERICAN
WRITER

VINTAGE BOOKS

A Division of Random House, Inc.

New York

FIRST VINTAGE BOOKS EDITION, NOVEMBER 1998

Some of the material in this book first appeared, in slightly different form, in
The New York Review of Books, The Princeton University Library Chronicle,
and the 1989 Conference on Faulkner and Religion published by the University Press of Mississippi.

The Library of Congress has cataloged the Knopf edition as follows:
Kazin, Alfred.
God and the American writer / Alfred Kazin.—1st ed.
p. cm.
Includes index.
ISBN 0-394-54968-6
1. American literature—History and criticism. 2. Christianity and
literature—United States. 3. Puritan movements in literature. 4. Religion
and literature. 5. Theology in literature. 6. God in literature. I. Title.
PS166.K39 1997 97–2993
810.9'382—dc21
CIP

Vintage ISBN: 0-679-73341-8

www.randomhouse.com

FOR AN ABSENT FRIEND

RICHARD HOFSTADTER

(1916–1970)

I have sometimes asked Americans whom I chanced to meet in their own country or in Europe whether in their opinion religion contributes to the stability of the State and the maintenance of law and order. They always answered, without a moment's hesitation, that a civilized community, especially one that enjoys the benefit of freedom, cannot exist without religion. In fact, an American sees in religion the surest guarantee of the stability of the State and the safety of individuals. This much is evident even to those least versed in political science. Yet there is no country in the world in which the boldest political theories of the eighteenth-century philosophers are put so effectively into practice as in America. Only their anti-religious doctrines have never made any headway in that country, and this despite the unlimited freedom of the press.

ALEXIS DE TOCQUEVILLE
The Old Regime and the French Revolution

Contents

GOD &
THE
AMERICAN
WRITER

Prelude: These Strange Minds

We thank thee, Father, for these strange minds that enamor us against thee.
EMILY DICKINSON

IN THE BEGINNING at New England our writers were Calvinists, absolutely sure of God and all His purposes. He created man to glorify Him forever. But never sure of his obedience, distrustful of his innate disposition to sin, God kept man forever under His eye. Each claimed to know the other because there was a covenant between them, a contract. Each was eternally watchful of the other, each apparently needed the other. Nothing in the world around a Calvinist counted so much as his dependence on God, his knowledge of God, his standing with God. And God was as eternally occupied with man as man was with God. They were so bound to each other that to the Romantic poets and scientific rationalists who came in with the Age of Reason, God and man seemed born of each other. No wonder that the Puritans in the wilderness, lacking everything but God, were confident to the last that they knew God's mind.

The people who were soon to distance themselves from primitive New England, to call themselves "Americans" and to expand until they were all over the continent, had to be restless optimists, boosters and boasters always on the go. The writers who stood slightly apart inherited Calvinism with their distrust of human nature. They were Puritans—certain of the next world but never sure of man in this one—thus inaugurating a split between writers occupied with humankind's self-deceiving ways and a populace afraid of too much self-questioning.

Calvinism held to the unquestioned omnipotence of God and so to belief in predestination. While the latter could make you anxious about your chance for salvation, the former gave you assurance that God was always there. This was behind the individual's high sense of himself so famous in the American character. "By nourishing in every individual the highest raptures and ecstasies of devotion," David Hume observed of Scotland under Calvinism, "it consecrated, in a manner, every individual; and in his own eyes, bestowed a character on him much superior to what forms and ceremonious institutions could confer."

In his own eyes, at least, the Protestant had special authority. Increase Mather (son of Richard Mather, father of Cotton Mather) confidently wrote in "The Mystery of Israel's Salvation":

> Consider . . . that some of us are under special advantage to understand these mysterious truths of God; that is to say, such of us as are in an exiled condition in this wilderness. . . . God hath led us into a wilderness, and surely it was not because the Lord hated us but because he loved us that he brought us hither into this Jeshimon [a desert or barren waste].

Although he was in England on behalf of the colonists when hysteria over witchcraft began, Increase Mather was frequently held responsible for fomenting the Salem witchcraft trials. In the spring and summer of 1692, 19 persons were hanged; one man was pressed to death; 55 were frightened or tortured into confessions of guilt; 150 were imprisoned; and more than 200 were named as deserving arrest. In his book *Cases of Conscience Concerning Evil Spirits* (1693) Increase Mather disapproved of the court's emphasis on spectral evidence and seemed to believe that it was better for a guilty witch to die than for an innocent man to escape.

It was his son Cotton Mather, much occupied with devils, who roundly affirmed the justice of the trials—the punishment to be fasting and prayer. In *The Wonders of the Invisible World* (1693) Cotton declared, "The New Englanders are a people of God settled in those, which were once the devil's territories; and it may easily be supposed that the devil was exceedingly disturbed when he perceived such a people here accomplishing the promise of old made unto our blessed Jesus, that He should have the utmost parts of the earth for His possession."

The Mathers were endlessly productive scholars, writers of remarkable intensity, fervently sure of their place in this world and the next. They knew the Hebrew Bible so well that it was never any trouble for them to find everywhere in it anticipations of themselves as the new and better Israel (thanks to Christ) in a wilderness primitive as old Canaan.

The Mathers were such fierce apologists and polemicists, always writing, sermonizing, and heading institutions, that they dominate our image of the early Church in New England. Only scholars, specialists in the Puritan period, burrow into the mountains of their published works. For the rest of us they are names irritably exercising Authority. I used to think of this in connection with Edmund Wilson, our last great man of letters (he thought so himself), who was on his maternal side descended from the Mathers. There were also Presbyterian ministers among his forebears. Wilson often told me, during summers on Cape Cod, "We must simply live without religion." Whenever the word itself came up in conversation, Wilson could get prickly and dogmatic, denouncing it with the freedom of H. L. Mencken in the 1920s (but without Mencken's laughter). Yet the same man was proud of having taught himself Hebrew from his grandfather's old grammar at Princeton's Theology School, had more than any other "journalist" (as Wilson liked to call himself) popularized our knowledge of the Dead Sea Scrolls, and had investigated the caves where they had been found. Were these interests not connected with religion? No, learning new languages "was like beginning a love affair," and his scholarly curiosity in the 1950s was as aroused by the recovery of the Dead Sea Scrolls as in the 1930s it had been by going to Russia, learning Russian, and devouring its literature. In his last years he learned Hungarian and was interested in Yiddish.

Happily, Puritan New England in the seventeenth century had one delightful poet, Anne Bradstreet (c. 1612–1672), and one intensely gifted poet, Edward Taylor (c. 1644–1729), who did not want his "poetical works" published. They were discovered and published in 1937 after being withheld by his grandson, Ezra Stiles (1727–1795) of Yale. Stiles was supposed to be the most learned man of his time in America. When asked why he studied Hebrew so assiduously, he explained that on his arrival in heaven he would be able to converse with God in His native language.

Anne Bradstreet has come down to us as a delightful, very womanly poet who was mocked for writing poetry "when my hand a needle better fits" and who did not take her verses seriously when a friend got her first published in England without her knowledge—*The Tenth Muse Lately Sprung Up in America* (1650). Married at sixteen and eventually the mother of eight, she came with husband Simon and father Thomas

Dudley (future governors of the colony) in 1630 on the *Arbella*. They were among the founders of the Massachusetts Bay Colony under John Winthrop. For all the charming diffidence of her poetry, she was absolute in the "spirit" as against the "flesh":

> *Sisters we are, yea, twins we be,*
> *Yet deadly feud 'twixt thee and me;*
> *For from one father are we not,*
> *Thou by old Adam wast begot,*
> *But my arise is from above,*
> *Whence my dear Father I do love.*
> *Thou speak'st me fair, but hat'st me sore,*
> *Thy flatt'ring shews Ile trust no more.*

Her faith, she wrote, would withstand the disasters of life in child-bearing, losing everything to the fire that destroyed her house, fear that an early death would leave her much loved husband alone.

In *Homage to Mistress Bradstreet* (1956) the tragic poet John Berryman was fascinated by the hardiness of her life, and pictured her "before a fire at, bright eyes on the Lord, / all the children still." As she reads a poem aloud, "Outside the New World winters in grand dark / white air lashing high thro' the virgin stands / foxes down foxholes sigh, / surely the English heart quails, stunned." Simon's "rigour for your poetry" is like the way he stands up to "this blast, that sea." In this storm, this wilderness, the loving husband and wife have only their love for each other. Berryman to Bradstreet: "it seems I find you, young. I come to check." The poem flickers like the fire warming the Bradstreet hut. Now bravely, now with deliberate, desperate contractions and inversions (Berryman's way of muddling through when the incoherence of his life was the subject), the poem comes and goes between joy in the recovered seventeenth-century scene and our contemporary poet's self-conflict: "I am a man of griefs & fits / trying to be my friend." He tremblingly brings God into the Bradstreet hut: "God awaits us (but I am yielding) who Hell wars." "Hell" was more familiar to John Berryman internally than it was to Anne Bradstreet, the loyal Puritan always being warned of hell: "sin cross & opposite, wherein I survive / nightmares of Eden." Berryman was haunted all his life by his own father's suicide. Determined to follow his father in death. Three hundred years have passed since Bradstreet bewailed the ruins of her house, everything destroyed:

> *Then streight I 'gin my heart to chide,*
> *And did thy wealth on earth abide*
> *Didst fix thy hope on mouldring dust,*
> *The arm of flesh didst make thy trust?*
> *Raise up thy thoughts above the skye*
> *That dunghill mists away may fly.*

Berryman—"I cannot feel myself God waits. He flies / nearer a kindly world; or else he is flown."

Edward Taylor wrote poems not for publication but to bear witness to the fact that he was alone and positively possessed by God. Herbert and Donne, his great Anglican contemporaries back in England, were intimately involved with the nobility. Crashaw, the Puritan turned Catholic, was a favorite of Catholics reigning in France and Italy. Milton was in his own way the poet of the English revolution, Cromwell's Latin secretary for communication with the European powers, and the great epic poet of the Reformation. Taylor was a pastor and physician in Westfield, on the Massachusetts frontier.

Like Bradstreet, he was as much a product of the solitude on the frontier as he was of Calvinism—softer and more florid in poetry than Jonathan Edwards was to reveal himself in the more personal prose of the next century. Taylor, in typical seventeenth-century style, regards himself as matter for God to make use of as He likes:

> *Make me, O Lord, thy Spining Wheele compleate;*
> *Thy Holy Worde my Distaff make for mee.*
> *Make mine Affections thy Swift Flyers neate,*
> *And make my Soule thy Holy Spoole to bee.*
> *My conversation maker to be thy Reele,*
> *And reele the yarn thereon spun of thy Wheele.*

God was so omnipotent to Taylor that the poet feels himself effaced:

> *His hand hath made this noble worke which Stands*
> *His Glorious Handywork not made by hands*

> *Who spake all things from nothing;*
> *And with ease*
> *Can speake all things to nothing, if he please.*

Such "naïve" devotion on the part of God-enraptured solitaries in a society still colonial could not absorb what Alfred North Whitehead called "the century of genius"—the scientific revolution of the seventeenth century taking place in their old homeland. In the next century Thomas Paine, "that dirty little atheist," as Theodore Roosevelt called him, was so imbued with the Enlightenment and the belief that reason would always prevail that he actually wrote *The Age of Reason* (1793–95) from a prison cell in Paris during the Reign of Terror. He was in France to support the Revolution but was not radical enough for the Jacobins. Addressing himself to "my fellow citizens of the United States," Paine was proud of having "liberally religious" friends in Franklin, Jefferson, and Joel Barlow. The sweet reasonableness of *The Age of Reason* makes one want to call it "Common Sense," after the great pamphlet Paine wrote in support of the American Revolution. Newton proved that Nature is harmony, law and order, and man has finally learned to read it accurately. But man could not invent and make a universe—he could not invent nature. The universe is governed by laws. When we look through nature up to Nature's God, we are on the right road to happiness. The creation is the Bible of the Deist.

Paine was not always at home in a post-Revolutionary America too conservative for an untiring rebel. He would have fled back to his native England if he had been subjected to America's official piety at the end of the twentieth century. "Soon after I had published the pamphlet *Common Sense*, in America, I saw the exceeding probability that a revolution in the system of government would be followed by a revolution in the system of religion." Paine called the connection of church and state "adulterous." Like the ill-fated Trotsky, Paine believed in permanent revolution. The perfect state was always just over the horizon.

Jefferson did not push the connection between revolution in government and revolution in religion as Paine did. In this respect he was more the private citizen, the aristocratic thinker, the scientist. Jefferson upheld what Immanuel Kant had defined as "religion within the limits of reason alone." He ended the Declaration of Independence "with a firm reliance on the protection of divine Providence" and in his first inaugural as president dutifully honored "a supreme ruler" over the universe he believed to be self-regulating. The lingering spirit of the Enlightenment, refreshed by the success of the American Revolution, fostered a Virginia patrician's scattered individual heresies. His obstinate enthusiasm for the strident anticlericalism in the French Revolution led many Americans to consider him an atheist. The Enlightenment in Virginia would not survive the hysterical support of slavery. Lincoln, who considered Jefferson his intellectual teacher, was outraged when Southerners mocked Jefferson's writing into the Declaration of Independence that "all men are created equal" was a self-evident truth. Of course this was a hope, not existing reality anywhere in America. Jefferson was full of hope for the future because he thought he could create it.

The main force behind the establishment of the University of Virginia, Jefferson also devised its curriculum. To which he added:

> And how much more encouraging to the achievements of science and improvement is thus, than the desponding view that the condition of man cannot be ameliorated, that what has been must ever be, and that to secure ourselves where we are, we must tread with awful reverence in the footsteps of our fathers. This doctrine is the genuine fruit of the alliance between Church and State; the tenants of which, finding themselves but too well in their present condition, oppose all advances which might unmask their usurpations, and monopolies of honors, wealth, and power, and fear every change, as endangering the comforts they now hold.

Jefferson in 1786 had been instrumental in helping to disestablish the Anglican Church in Virginia. In his proposal for revising the law, he began by expressing the highest optimism for an enlightened age:

> The opinions and beliefs of men . . . follow involuntarily the evidence proposed to their minds; that Almighty God hath created the mind free, and manifested his supreme will that free it shall remain by making it altogether insusceptible of restraint; that all attempts to influence it by temporal punishments, or burthens, or by civil incapacitations, tend only to beget habits of hypocrisy and

meanness, and are a departure from the plan of the holy author of
our religion, who being lord both of body and mind, yet chose not
to propagate it by coercions on either, . . . but to extend it by its influence on reason alone.

This is as magnificent as the bow to "Nature and Nature's God" in
the preamble to the Declaration of Independence, a document that was
assigned to Jefferson, said John Adams, "because of his peculiar felicity
in expression." Jefferson's literary felicity was so great on a vast number
of subjects—like his professed abhorrence of slavery and his unwaver-
ing attachment to the French Revolution—that we forget how little influence it often had. There was no lasting transmission of his Deism
and religious ideals to the American people. Like Tolstoy after him, he
made a personal arrangement of the Gospels that eliminated everything
he believed Jesus had never said. This work is known only to Jefferson
specialists. Jefferson's plans and projects for civil society were so radical
and libertarian in the abstract that the leading apologists for slavery professed all admiration for Jefferson while mocking the equality of all men
written into the Declaration. And in the name of Jefferson's partiality to
a yeoman democracy of small independent holders, the "Fugitives" of
I'll Take My Stand in the 1930s, deeply conservative southern men of
letters, idealized an imaginary South that was without tenant farmers
and so without blacks.

If in many respects Jefferson's intended revolution in religion ended
with himself, this was also true of Jonathan Edwards, and after him, of
Emerson, Whitman, and Lincoln. Their offerings in matters of the
spirit were all personal, orphic, literary, inspired. It may seem strange to
attach our "personalist" tradition in American writing on religion to so
assiduous and systematic a theologian as Edwards. But this truly last
Puritan and greatest of American Calvinist thinkers was a phenomenon
not just in his precocity (at ten he was writing on the immortality of the
soul; at twelve he was describing the habits of the "flying spider"; at
fourteen he was influenced by Locke's *Essay Concerning Human Understanding*). In his ecstatic devotion to the absolute reality and rule of
God, he trembles with raging eloquence in *Sinners in the Hands of an
Angry God* even as he refuses to except children from hellfire. We are all
depraved.

The God that holds you over the pit of hell, much as one holds a spider, or some loathsome insect over the fire, abhors you, and is dreadfully provoked; his wrath towards you burns like fire; he looks upon you as worthy of nothing else, but to be cast into the fire; he is of purer eyes than to bear to have you in his sight; you are ten thousand times more abominable in his eyes, than the most hateful venomous spider is in ours.

Yet he was so naturally open and of a lyric temperament that in his *Personal Narrative* he wins our hearts by confessing, "I spent most of my time in thinking of divine things, year after year: often walking alone in the woods, and solitary places, for meditation, soliloquy, and prayer, and converse with God; and it was always my manner, at such time, to sing forth my contemplations." We feel his own throbbing as he describes his intense absorption in the idea of God's *will* throbbing through the universe. In *A Careful and Strict Enquiry into the Modern Prevailing Notions, of that Freedom of Will which is supposed to be Essential to Moral Agency, Vertue [sic] and Vice, Reward and Punishment, Praise and Blame* Edwards spelled out his belief that since any effect must have a cause, all volitions, being events, are determined by what is strongest in the mind and most agreeable to it. The *direction* of what is most agreeable is determined entirely without independent activity on the part of the individual will. God has already planted in us the common and natural sense of what is most agreeable. By attributing everything to God and denying all freedom of the will, Edwards in a way ended the tradition he sought to reinforce. Once belief in God's absolute will receded, the idea of necessity became the mechanism explaining the universe. In a famous passage describing his fear of being locked in by doctrines of "necessity" reminiscent of Calvinism, William James said, "My first act of free will shall be to believe in free will." James, not Edwards, was the future.

Edwards had many descendants and disciples. One of his grandsons was the ambitious rogue Aaron Burr, vice president of the United States in Jefferson's first term, who killed Alexander Hamilton in a duel and was later tried for treason after joining the conspiracy to detach Trans-Appalachia from the United States in the interests of foreign powers. He is fondly pictured as a charming cynic in Gore Vidal's *Burr*

(1973), and in Harriet Beecher Stowe's novel *The Minister's Wooing* (1859), which describes the decline of Calvinism in New England after the Revolutionary War, Burr is briefly pictured as a trifler and a sophisticated flirt unconcerned with the religious interests of the community. Edwards's disciple Samuel Hopkins, who in life was said to "out-Edwards Edwards" by holding that the willingness to be damned for the glory of God was the test of true regeneration, is the kindly elderly minister in Stowe's novel. Always at his books, he is unsuitably engaged to a young woman who has given up her true love because the young man admits to skepticism. In the end he sees the true light and Hopkins releases his fiancée to the satisfaction of all concerned.

In *The Minister's Wooing* Calvinism is a lingering atmosphere, a convention. Mrs. Stowe is able to introduce a certain latitude into the end of the eighteenth century because she is writing from the nineteenth century. The nineteenth century was seen by many writers as the last great battleground over faith. On this subject they were variously at war with their past, the Church, and themselves. There were so many choices to be made, and conversions were so rife, that the French novelist Joris-Karl Huysmans (*À rebours*, 1884) was not the only one to think that one must end up either on the scaffold or at the foot of the cross. The future Cardinal Newman said that he was just returning to Origen and the doctors of the early church when he left the Church of England for Rome. "Believing where we cannot prove," Tennyson determinedly opened the future *In Memoriam*. Dostoevsky said, "If someone proved to me that Christ is outside the truth, and that *in reality* the truth were outside of Christ then I should prefer to remain with Christ than with the truth." "One cannot live so! One cannot live so!" Tolstoy said before his turn to a deeply personal religion caused him to be excommunicated by the Holy Russian Synod.

The hysterical revival meetings in the second quarter of the eighteenth century, the Great Awakening, had a lingering effect on the general religiosity of the American people. Every fresh batch of immigrants seemed to produce religious factions within their old European churches and to spawn new churches. Before long the Mormons, driven from Illinois to the Great Salt Lake in Utah, created on their own territory the first wholly native American religion, with their own Bible and their own saints.

The first evangelical zeal of the Reformation was re-created in America with a vengeance—convert, propagate, but above all remain separate! A masterful all-pervading Protestantism that was to exfoliate into innumerable sects was split on every doctrinal issue except its hostility to Catholicism, the Whore of Babylon. In New England the former Transcendentalist and Brook Farm fellow-utopian Orestes Brownson turned Catholic, followed by Isaac Hecker, who in time founded the Paulist order. But such regression to dogma and obedience to clerical authority, as it seemed to these old friends, hardly interested the descendants and opponents of Calvinism in New England under the leadership of William Ellery Channing, the leading spokesman for Unitarianism in America. Starting from their abhorrence of the doctrine of the Trinity, Unitarians became the most liberal and rational church in America, gathering the intelligentsia into its fold and taking over the Divinity School at Harvard (and the rest of Harvard, too). They were now the body of the elect in the name of what Channing called "unremitting appeals to the reason and conscience."

A church founded on separatism could not long keep Emerson, who was so instinctively and forthrightly a believer exclusively on his own terms that he could not abide the church of which he was a minister. Nine generations of Emersons before him had all been ministers, which gave Emerson his much relished chance to attack all organized religion, all systematic theology, and to make the self-sufficiency of the individual the key to *all* things identifiably American. But who was that individual when he was not Waldo Emerson himself? Emerson was an original and gifted writer; he was such a genius at expressing his intuitions of the divine that in the creative ecstasy of his first great manifesto, *Nature* (1836), and the lectures that became the Divinity School Address, "Self-Reliance," and "The Over-Soul," he raptly projected his identity upon his audience and wrote as if the future, like his reading of the universe, were already sublime. Only Emerson in his own time would have declared his central doctrine to be "the infinitude of the private mind." He built on the infinite as if it were within the reach of a single sentence. He led readers then (and now) to believe that all the world was as easy to capture as it was to him. Emerson began as a religion but ended as literature. Given the hunger for religious certainty that suffused this period, Christians no longer in the fold saw no difference between them. In our corporate time Emerson's private infinitude in religion can still so madden the orthodox that I once heard the Southern critic Cleanth Brooks charge that "Emerson led to Hitler."

Emerson was too priggish to understand fiction. He privately said Hawthorne's romances were "good for nothing." It tickled me to open my book with "Hawthorne and His Puritans" and to close it with "Faulkner: God over the South." While seventeenth-century Massachusetts was controlled by religion and Mississippi is still deep in religion, neither Hawthorne nor Faulkner was personally a believer. I am interested not in the artist's professions of belief but in the imagination he brings to his tale of religion in human affairs. Hawthorne was hardly conventional; he became startlingly rebellious on the few occasions when he felt it necessary to define his Christianity. But as a "mere storyteller," as he pretended to think of himself by contrast with the Puritan forebears he imagined shaking their heads over him, he was so obsessed that he wrote *The Scarlet Letter* and fables like "Young Goodman Brown" as if warding off a curse.

The "power of darkness," the fatality in human character that Melville saw in Hawthorne's work, relieved Melville's creative isolation. It led him to love Hawthorne as America's only other genius, when Melville in 1850–51 was writing *Moby-Dick*. Melville rhapsodically called Hawthorne another of "God's spies." But unlike Hawthorne, Melville did believe in personal belief. As Hawthorne saw when they met again in Liverpool in 1856—Hawthorne was the American consul, Melville on his way to the Holy Land—Melville could neither believe nor be happy in his disbelief. He was torn enough to hope that the Holy Land would tide him over his religious anxieties. What he could never get over was the unlimited power of divinity on a cosmic scale which he had torrentially poured into *Moby-Dick*. At Melville's death (1891) in his native New York, Elizabeth Melville found no takers for her husband's vast collection of theology. Hawthorne, in the preface to *Mosses from an Old Manse*, scorned the many wearisome tomes of theology he found in the manse, and called "impertinent" their portentous explanations of human life and its destiny.

Melville's fellow New Yorker Whitman was the opposite of him in religion—so easily loving of his fellow man and affectionately leaning on one creed or another to proclaim the satisfaction with his own existence necessary to his "message." And what a message it was. "I do not despise you priests, all time, the world over, / My faith is the greatest of faiths and the least of faiths, / Enclosing worship ancient and modern." Whitman was so natural and spontaneously a believer, of the earth earthly, and worshiping the power of sex, that unlike so many of my nineteenth-century characters, he owed practically nothing to any church and eventually became (in England) a sort of church himself.

Emily Dickinson never read Whitman but was told he was "disgraceful." And of course he never had a chance even to hear of her. America! In any event, she could not have put any matter of faith so baldly and oratorically as he did. She was pierced by what lies in the middle between man and God, what is truly *between* them. The most penetrating literary intelligence honored in this book, she explained the religious quest better than anyone, and with justice to all, when she tossed off in a letter, "It is true that the unknown is the largest need of intellect, although for this no one thinks to thank God." God was not a convenient presence for her to write about. God was a property of the human mind inquiring into the infinity of our relationships. Although she was a recluse in far-off Amherst entirely involved with her own thought, she could not escape the Civil War as the bodies of young men she had known were being returned from the battlefield. Perhaps she did not pay attention when Abraham Lincoln, another lonely nineteenth-century thinker like herself, delivered his second inaugural address, on March 4, 1865. His reflections on the mercy and justice of God in regard to slavery are as intricate and far-reaching as her poems.

Slavery is a central concern of this book, and not just in the pages of Emerson, Thoreau, John Brown, Hawthorne, William Lloyd Garrison, Harriet Beecher Stowe, Lincoln, Melville, Mark Twain, Faulkner, and others. Lincoln said in the Second Inaugural Address, "These slaves constituted a peculiar and powerful interest. All knew that this interest was, somehow, the cause of the war." A friend notes, "The War (and slavery) is really the reason for the awful fascination of the whole subject of God in America. You put this *unforgivingly*." The "awful fascination" of black servitude once led writers to justify God's supposed approval, to appeal to God, to deny God. On this terrible subject all true and ancient believers outdo the Biblical Jacob—they wrestle with Him forever.

Mark Twain, straddling the nineteenth and twentieth centuries, is our contemporary—he is outside the world he sees as mechanism. But like so many nineteenth-century characters who had been severely raised in an orthodoxy he soon escaped, he kept up a grudge against God. In his last years he wrote and wrote feverishly, satirizing everything about God's justice and church tales of heavenly rewards he had been forced to swallow in childhood. But of course he was afraid to antagonize his doting public by saying any heresies aloud. He lamely excused himself on the ground that "only dead men tell the truth." Mark Twain in his last years would have been alarmed to discover that he was a naturalist in the spirit of Theodore Dreiser's *Sister Carrie* (1900) and Stephen Crane's fiction—and especially Crane's poems jeering at the disappearance of God, *The Black Riders* (1895)—and Frank Norris's *McTeague* (1899).

These writers a century ago saw the new urban world with a devastating iciness and brutality. They had all been hardened by the contrast between the forced orthodoxy of their childhoods and the heartlessness of the cities they learned about too well as reporters. Dreiser's father was a fanatical German Catholic immigrant. Crane's father was a leading Methodist minister and his mother a founder of the Women's Christian Temperance Union. The writers could have been in perfect sympathy with Harvard's William James, one of the first experimental psychologists to demonstrate what really drives human beings instead of the soul.

Yet for James the "soul" remained, if only as a metaphor for the subconscious longing for something "more" in the universe which James called "the will to believe" and which he tried to justify in exploring the case histories that make up *The Varieties of Religious Experience*. This book could have been called "The *Ability* to Believe," an ability that James candidly denied in his own case. He stopped at the threshold beyond which was God. Religion was just the experience of a particular temperament.

Not so, T. S. Eliot would have replied if he had not missed James at Harvard and only once bothered to comment on James at all. (He actually reviewed James on immortality in *The New Statesman*, September 8, 1917.) Eliot was of course exactly the kind of anxious temperament (like James himself) that James made the center of the *Varieties*. But like so many of the converts in the book, Eliot was repelled by liberalism and insisted that there is no Christianity without the Incarnation. Eliot traveled far from the Unitarianism of his childhood in St. Louis. He became a British subject and as a freshly baptized Anglican became a sternly conservative Anglo-Catholic and political Tory. In 1922, with *The Waste Land*, Eliot mesmerized the literary world with his poem of a world intellectually vacant and spiritually self-destructive. There was even a guided tour of the poem in his scholarly references following the text. But the "religious" warnings of dissolution ending the poem in thunder meant less to Eliot's admirers than to him.

The contest between Robert Frost and Wallace Stevens (as two old men they farcically came to blows) was of course more in Frost's mind than in Stevens's. Frost was the most self-absorbed and combative writer I ever knew. He could not open his mouth without seeking to advance his cause as America's great poet. And this he was. Essentially a Darwinian, he saw life as a battleground between winners and losers. God was somewhere offstage, waiting for Frost to summon Him and be argued with about the eternal injustice. Frost did not love God (few of the moderns ever do) but never lost sight of His force over the universe. The manifest distortions of Providence were so much on Frost's mind that he makes me recall Maxim Gorky's description of Tolstoy's arduous relation to God—"two bears in the same den."

The "losers" Frost brought to life with such starkness in "The Death of the Hired Man," the monologue of "A Servant to Servants," and other great pieces stand out in our modern poetry and shame its abundantly trivial subject matter. Frost's Swedenborgian mother taught him there were "other worlds," but he did not believe it any more than Henry James believed *his* Swedenborgian father on this score. Life for both James and Frost was here and now. But not being a novelist of society, Frost was haunted by the separateness of people (beginning with himself in *A Boy's Will*). This was a state of mind, as with Emily Dickinson, a human dilemma just about to be solved but which never is. It could be worked out only in a *succession* of poems that pursued the argument into the autonomous drama of human relationships. Frost is our only great poet of marriage. The passion behind it, and that can twist out of recognition, is always there.

There are no losers—or winners—in Wallace Stevens and not many perceptible man-and-woman relationships. *His* relationship to this strange world of appearances is what counts for him, never people vying with one another. There is no struggle for existence, only a leisurely choice of perspective on this world of appearances. All begins in thought, speculation, irony, playing with the sounds and colors provided by language. Stevens's poetry is first a poetry of pleasure, of Epicurean murmurings of delight and of satisfaction. I met him once, a portly benign figure, at the Harvard Club in Boston. He looked thoroughly at ease with life. No wonder that in time spared from the Hartford Accident and Indemnity Company he wrote poetry as if on holiday. And so he was. Since everything was realized and named only in thought, anything in this whimsical perspective became a "fiction." A fiction was not unreal, just made up, as ultimately everything is made by the mind. "Reality" was a fiction for Stevens even in his external daily life as a lawyer; the poetry that described things as fictions was another. And "God" was the supreme fiction. In "Sunday Morning" (1915) Stevens wrote the great modern poem of absenting oneself from church forever, of leaving religion for the pleasure of playing out to oneself the origin and death of God.

> *Why should she give her bounty to the dead?*
> *What is divinity if it can come*
> *Only in silent shadows and in dreams?*
> *Shall she not find in comforts of the sun,*
> *In pungent fruit and bright, green wings, or else*
> *In any balm or beauty of the earth,*
> *Things to be cherished like the thought of heaven?*
> *Divinity must live within herself.*

What I always carry away from this favorite poem is not any great involvement on Stevens's part with God, but the perfect rendition of the senses in

> *Passions of rain, or moods in falling snow;*
> *Grievings in loneliness, or unsubdued*
> *Elations when the forest blooms; gusty*
> *Emotions on wet roads on autumn nights;*
> *All pleasures and all pains, remembering*

> *The bough of summer and the winter branch.*
> *These are the measures destined for her soul.*

Evidently it was no great hardship for Stevens at the end of "Sunday Morning" to give up religion for the truth that

> *We live in an old chaos of the sun,*
> *Or old dependency of day and night,*
> *Or island solitude, unsponsored, free,*
> *Of that wide water, inescapable.*

"Sunday Morning" is not a religious poem; it is an early poem of pleasure, giving up an abstract heaven for this wonderful earth. In the "isolation of the sky"

> *At evening, casual flocks of pigeons make*
> *Ambiguous undulations as they sink,*
> *Downward to darkness, on extended wings.*

And *our* pleasure (our "island solitude, unsponsored, free," is so much in the American grain) is in the words. "Poetry" has won over religion, and now occupies the sacred place religion once occupied. One fiction has replaced another. Poetry is all, as religion once was all. Of course this was not the whole story: Stevens wrote remarkable poems, crushing poems, to satisfy his basic conviction that one poem differs from another as one perspective differs from another, one individual from another. But he always kept above the battle. As perhaps there was no battle. His sense of his own creativity dimmed everything else for him.

Replacing religion with literature, Stevens was laboring within his inheritance of religion. Like many celebrities of the 1920s and early 1930s, he could not forget the fathers he was leaving behind. The mockery of the old-time religion in H. L. Mencken, Sinclair Lewis, Eugene O'Neill, Thorstein Veblen, Upton Sinclair, James Branch Cabell, Theodore Dreiser, Dorothy Parker, Ring Lardner, Edna Millay, Carl Sandburg, Edmund Wilson, Ezra Pound, not to forget *The New Yorker* ("not for the old lady from Dubuque"), suggested a second American Enlightenment. But such a star of the period as Ernest Hemingway was not on the comfy bandwagon of all-out sophistication. At the end of

The Sun Also Rises (1926) Jake Barnes (impotent, a war wound) goes down to Madrid to rescue his true love Lady Brett Ashley from still another of her disastrous crushes—this time a bullfighter is her victim. Jake is the principal one. They drink, they drink, then drink some more. Suddenly Brett has an insight.

"You know it makes one feel rather good deciding not to be a bitch." "Yes." "It's sort of what we have instead of God." Jake: "Some people have God. Quite a lot."

The romantic pathos and the avowal (through clenched teeth) belong to a period condemned during the depression as self-deluding. The music never stopped, so they wouldn't hear that the greatest little old period in American history was about to fizzle. In "A Clean, Well-Lighted Place," from Hemingway's third book of stories, *Winner Take Nothing* (1933), an old man, drunk, cannot bear to leave the café even when the younger waiter wants to close it and go home. The older waiter understands the old man all too well and fruitlessly explains to the younger, "This is a clean and pleasant café. It is well lighted." When he finally turns off the electric light, he continues the conversation with himself.

> What did he fear? It was not fear or dread. It was a nothing that he knew too well. It was all a nothing and a man was nothing too. It was only that and light was all it needed and a certain cleanness and order. Some lived in it and never felt it but he knew it all was nada y pues nada y nada y pues nada. Our nada who art in nada, nada be thy name thy kingdom nada thy will be nada in nada as it is in nada.

Hemingway was a superb and original artist who, like the older waiter in the story, "never had confidence." It was all very well for Freud in *The Future of an Illusion* to explain belief in God as a substitution for dependency on one's parents. Hemingway really believed—from time to time. In Spain as a correspondent during the civil war, he remembered that he was nominally a Catholic and went from church to church (those that were still intact) praying for a Loyalist victory. He was not a great and good man, but he said wonderful things. In "The Snows of Kilimanjaro" (1936) a writer is dying of gangrene in sight of Africa's highest mountain, Kilimanjaro. He can no longer explain himself to the mistress hopelessly trying to keep him alive. He is trapped in his memories of a falsely heroic life. "It was not so much that he lied as that there was no truth to tell."

In an abrasively skeptical period, Hart Crane, another escapee to New York from a conventional Midwest upbringing, was not afraid to replay Whitman's easy spiritualizing of brute matter in "Crossing Brooklyn Ferry." *The Bridge* (1930) was to be *the* modern epic of an America on its way back to the old idealism. It was to express a twentieth-century poet's need to make a myth for the future out of the iron and grit of daily living beside Brooklyn Bridge. So Whitman in the 1850s had transcended the ruins of the old religion in a myth of joining Brooklyn and Manhattan, island and island, earth and water. But of course New York for Crane was no longer the neighborhood it had been for Whitman. Even Columbia Heights facing the harbor, where he slunk home after looking for sailors, who often beat him up, was no neighborhood for him. He seemed to have little confidence in his power to receive love. But how he loved John Roebling's bridge as the great Other, and what passing originality he gave to celebrating it! His words were tortured, ornate, but catch us up in an overwhelming tide of feeling:

> *O harp and altar, of the fury fused,*
> *(How could mere toil align thy choiring strings!)*
> *Terrific threshold of the prophet's pledge,*
> *Prayer of pariah, and the lover's cry,—*
>
> . . . .
>
> *O sleepless as the river under thee,*
> *Vaulting the sea, the prairies' dreaming sod,*
> *Unto us lowliest sometime sweep, descend*
> *And of the curveship lend a myth to God.*

It was wonderful, it was pitiful, all too much yet perhaps not enough. God needed to be lent a myth so we could say "God" without being ashamed of the cliché. But Crane was practically the last of the true believers, even if he was worshiping a symbol. He was *involved*, he was right in there, open-mouthedly suffering the bridge he adored in a language often desperate to say it right—and not always succeeding.

Crane was the last—or nearly the last—writer to love and praise God as if he knew what he was getting at. Even one of the few practicing Christians in Nazi Germany, the Lutheran pastor Dietrich Bonhoeffer, wrote his fiancée before being hanged by Hitler in 1944: "God him-self commands us not to believe in him." What does it mean, now, in an America where the great majority go to church, synagogue, and mosque, where many confess to believe in the Devil, where fundamen-talists have captured the Republican party South and West, where every attempt is being made to brook no separation between church and state? It means that a politicized, intolerant, and paranoic religion, always crowing of its popularity, is too public and aims to coerce the rest of us.

Melville to Hawthorne, 1851: "The Godhead is broken up like the bread at the Supper, and . . . we are the pieces." More than ever, the sig-nificant American writers resist being on the side of the mob. "Religion is what man does with his solitariness," said Alfred North Whitehead.

Thomas Pynchon in *Vineland* (1990): "We are digits in God's com-puter. . . . And the only thing we're good for, to be dead or living, is the only thing He sees. What we contend for, in our world of toil and blood, it all lies beneath the notice of the hacker we call God." John Ashbery, as executive editor of *ARTnews*, "saluted the gambler's instinct that ex-perimental art seems to require" and drew an analogy to religion. "Most reckless things are beautiful in some way, and recklessness is what makes experimental art beautiful. Because of the strong possibility that they are founded on nothing. We would all believe in God if we knew He existed, but would this be much fun?" Richard Ford in the story "Great Falls" in the collection *Rock Springs* (1987): "But I have never known the answer to these questions, have never asked anyone their an-swers. Though possibly it—the answer—is simple: it is just low-life, some coldness in us all, some helplessness that causes us to misunder-stand life when it is pure and plain, makes our existence seem like a bor-der between two nothings, and makes us no more or less than animals who meet on the road—watchful, unforgiving, without patience or de-sire."

"Do you think God cares?" the American priest in Robert Stone's *Flag for Sunrise* rebuts the chief of police in a Central American coun-try who demands absolution after murdering a Canadian girl scout hik-ing in his country. That is not the question a Catholic writer used to ask. The indomitable Flannery O'Connor, the greatest American Catholic writer, was informed by Mary McCarthy, a lapsed Catholic, that *she* thought of the Host as a symbol, "and implied that it was a pretty good one." O'Connor describes the incident in a letter of December 16, 1955: "I then said in a very shaky voice, 'Well, if it's a symbol, to hell with it.' That was all the defense I was capable of, but I realize now that this is all I will ever be able to say about it outside of a story, except that it is the center of existence for me; all the rest of life is expendable."

The Israeli novelist Amos Oz complains of American Jews: "You don't see the stars in their writing." Apparently an honest belief in God still, even in our time, includes the covenant. Not many American novelists today can say what Saul Bellow in *Mr. Sammler's Planet* has an old man (he escaped from Nazis shooting Jews by crawling through the bodies piled on top of him) say in prayer to God about his dead nephew: "He was aware that he must meet, and he did meet—through all the confusion and degrading clowning of this life through which we are speeding—he did meet the terms of his contract. The terms which, in his inmost heart, each man knows. As I know mine. As all know. For that is the truth of it—that we all know, God, that we know, that we know, we know, we know."

ALFRED KAZIN
October 3, 1996

1

Hawthorne and His Puritans

Just art thou in these thy judgments, thou who art and wast, O Holy One. For men have shed the blood of saints and prophets. And thou has given them blood to drink! It is their due!

REVELATION 16:5–6

Let us thank God for having given us such ancestors; and let each successive generation thank him not less fervently for being one step further from them in the march of ages.

HAWTHORNE, *"Main Street"*

A BEAUTIFUL WOMAN condemned for adultery—she wears the scarlet letter A on her breast—stands on a scaffold in front of old Boston's prison door holding a three-month-old baby in her arms. Just released from prison, she must now for three hours expose her shame to the full view of the crowd while the governor and magistrates in their office above look down on her and spiteful old women in the crowd standing below her demand that she be physically punished, even mutilated.

There are already thousands of emigrants in Massachusetts, but she is the main object in view, the focus of all attention, publicly denounced as a sinner while clergymen belabor her demanding the name of her lover. Nothing else seems to be happening in Boston except the revelation of this woman's crime and the spectacle of her punishment. Nothing could be more dramatic than the sight of her standing *above* the crowd. The moral ferocity directed against her on this glowing June day in old Boston—the only sight in town—becomes keener, more intense, more merciless as Hawthorne sets up the gloomy piety of the people, the heaviness and meanness surrounding the woman on the scaffold.

This is an ecclesiastical state. These are God's people.

"A throng of bearded men, in sad-colored garments and gray, steeple-crowned hats, intermixed with women, some wearing hoods, and others bareheaded, was assembled in front of a wooden edifice, the door of which was heavily timbered with oak, and studded with iron spikes." Although the settlement is only some fifteen or twenty years old, "the wooden jail was already marked with weather-stains and other indications of age, which gave a yet darker aspect to its beetle-browed and gloomy front. The rust on the ponderous iron-work of its oaken door looked more antique than any thing else in the new world." To a "new world" these Puritans have transferred less of what they enjoyed in their native England than everything rigid in their religion concerning the human person.

Or so Hawthorne seems to be saying about his Puritans as he opens the book by setting the stage (literally) with a beautiful woman on a scaffold in front of the town prison.

> Before this ugly edifice, and between it and the wheel-track of the street, was a grass-plot, much overgrown with burdock, pig-weed, apple-peru, and such unsightly vegetation, which evidently found something congenial in the soil that had so early borne the black flower of civilized society, a prison.

To complete the ferocious contrast, perhaps intended to win a measure of sympathy as well as our full attention, the young woman is tall, beautiful, "with a figure of perfect elegance," and has "dark and abundant hair, so glossy that it threw off the sunshine with a gleam," and "deep black eyes." Her face,

> besides being beautiful from regularity of feature and richness of complexion, had the impressiveness belonging to a marked brow and deep black eyes. . . . Those who had before known her, and had expected to behold her dimmed and obscured by a disastrous cloud, were astonished, and even startled, to perceive how her beauty shone out, and made a halo of the misfortune and ignominy in which she was enveloped.

> On the breast of her gown, in fine red cloth, surrounded with an elaborate embroidery and fantastic flourishes of gold thread, appeared the letter A. It was so artistically done, and with so much fertility and gorgeous luxuriance of fancy, that it had all the effect of a last and fitting decoration to the apparel which she wore.

Wonderful. As the novel proceeds to show us her solitude in an abandoned hut on the shore with her maddeningly candid child, Pearl, and her tender goodness to townspeople who despise her, Hester seems altogether heroic, admirable. But Hawthorne does not allow his evident feeling for her to take over the book. His subject is not just Hester but New England early in the seventeenth century, a world dominated by a sense of sin that, far from vanishing for him, has become all wonder, story, and drama to Hawthorne in 1850. It is because Hester *is* a sinner in her own eyes that we know where we are with her—the seventeenth century. And it is because Hawthorne two centuries later is struggling with himself over the moral drama Hester presents that the book is at once so stark as fact and psychologically rich. Hawthorne the descendant of Puritans was mesmerized by what he feared and hated in their sense of justice.

As Hester stands on the scaffold castigated for her sin, she is horrified to see in the crowd Roger Chillingworth, her shriveled, twisted-looking old husband. This is a novel as overwhelming in named guideposts to character as Hawthorne's beloved *Pilgrim's Progress*. As if Chillingworth's name were not sign and token enough of his frigid nature, he is a morbid scholar long absorbed in libraries and laboratories removed from human concerns. How he persuaded young and shining Hester to marry him in their "old Europe"—she never pretended to love him—is never made clear. One can only guess that, like so many mad scientists in Hawthorne's work—"The Birthmark," "Rappaccini's Daughter"— Chillingworth has magnetic powers over young women. His left shoulder is higher than his right, typical of his "low, dark, misshapen" nature. With his unlimited curiosity, he journeyed beyond the first white settlement, was kidnapped by Indians, and is in the crowd staring at his wife's public disgrace because an Indian has delivered him back to Boston seeking ransom for him. Nothing further is heard of ransom, but Hawthorne has established his point. Chillingworth is like no one else. He is so removed from "the magnetic chain of humanity" that even when this "fiend" moves himself into Arthur Dimmesdale's house to "study" his wife's lover, we cannot be sure that he is not as genuinely eager to dissect Dimmesdale psychologically as he is to destroy him. To Hawthorne pure "scientific" intelligence was the same as heartlessness, and where the "heart" is not, there is nothing and no one to be trusted.

At the most critical stage of the story, when Hester pleads with Chillingworth to let Dimmesdale off, the villain turns out to be more deeply (and sadly) versed in the central Puritan dogma of original sin than the clergyman Dimmesdale.

"Peace, Hester, peace!" replied the old man, with gloomy sternness. "It is not granted me to pardon. I have no such power as thou tellest me of. My old faith, long forgotten, comes back to me, and explains all that we do, and all we suffer. By thy first step awry, thou didst plant the germ of evil; but, since that moment, it has all been a dark necessity. . . . It is our fate. Let the black flower blossom as it may!"

By contrast, Dimmesdale is indeed "dim," lost in his heavy folios and black-letter books of theology. Hawthorne was ro great admirer of theologians, either in the seventeenth century or in his own time, when he satirized his Concord neighbor Emerson as "this prophet" whose "master word" was eagerly besought by "such a variety of queer, strangely dressed, oddly behaved mortals, most of whom took upon themselves to be important agents of the world's destiny." In his early story "Dr. Bullivant" Hawthorne said of the gloom and chill prevailing in Puritan times: "Every vain jest and unprofitable word was deemed an item in the account of criminality. . . . The specimens of humour and satire, preserved in the sermons and controversial tracts of those days, are occasionally the apt expressions of pungent thoughts; but oftener they are cruel torturings and twistings of trite ideas, disgusting by the wearisome ingenuity which constitutes their only merit."

Hawthorne, so taciturn by nature that Emerson said "in his conversation, . . . you feel there is some bitter fairy, which is biting him all the time, and which he is unable to conceal," has his fun with Dimmesdale's public eloquence. This is lofty enough to arouse "the young virgins in their white bosoms," who dream that he will come down to earth long enough to notice them. Of course, Dimmesdale soars in public because he tortures himself in private over his sin. He bears his own scarlet letter far within. Exhausted by his fruitless efforts to find in religious tomes relief from his self-torture, he studies himself in the mirror to find a clue to his own enigma. This is a stock device in Hawthorne's work, born of the ten solitary years after Bowdoin College he spent in his room learning his craft. He often studied himself in the mirror for sheer company. (He also ran out to see every fire.) His psychology was a watered-down version of the Puritan belief in some ultimately detachable, aboriginal human nature. This afflicted him along with the judicial crimes of the first Hawthornes in Salem. Man all by himself, man all within himself as he "really is"—Hawthorne for literary purposes believed in man's unchanging, unchangeable nature. Since narrative depends on development, Dimmesdale, for the greatest part of the novel a helpless victim because a sinner in his theology, tries to find his way out through more theology. But Hawthorne's contempt for theology is ambiguous.

Melville's widow was astonished to find how little she could get for his library of theology. Hawthorne, after living in Ezra Ripley's Old Manse, still filled (as it is to this day) with piles of old sermons, derided "books of religion" in his preface to *Mosses from an Old Manse*. "Such books so seldom really touch upon their ostensible subject, and have therefore so little business to be written at all. So long as an unfettered soul can attain to saving grace, there would seem to be no deadly error in holding theological libraries to be accumulations of, for the most part, stupendous impertinence."

Impertinent, yes, because "religion" claimed to hold an explanation of—and even a solution to—eternal wrongdoing before God. Hawthorne in his own person does not seem to have been much interested in "God." Like any good nineteenth-century New Englander, he was sure his moral sentiments were as good as any, and he was romantic (like Emerson and Thoreau) in interpreting the vicissitudes of nature— the very turns of the weather itself!—as speaking for the human heart. But Puritan theology, for all the darkness it cast upon the miseries of a believer like the Reverend Arthur Dimmesdale (there were so many like him), was deep like sleep—the secrets betrayed in sleep. In "The Haunted Mind" Hawthorne stipulated that "in the depths of every heart, there is a tomb and a dungeon, though the lights, the music, and revelry may cause us to forget their existence, and the buried ones, or prisoners whom they hide. . . . Pass, wretched band! Well for the wakeful one, if, riotously miserable, a fiercer tribe do not surround him, the devils of a guilty heart, that holds its hell within itself."

In "The Custom-House," the surly preface he wrote to *The Scarlet*

Letter, Hawthorne imagined his ancestors condemning him as a mere "writer of story-books" (a sore point with him, who could hardly make a living at it) and by contrast with their lives in faith, deriding him as a "degenerate fellow" whose business in life was no "mode of glorifying God." No, his work did not "glorify" God. The "crooked timber of humanity" did not receive from Nathaniel Hawthorne anything like the grace that the Puritans saw descending on human beings whether (in most cases) they expected it or not. What had descended on Hawthorne was the sense of "something wrong about us as we presently stand" that William James was to portray in his *Varieties of Religious Experience*. But this without the belief in salvation through the extraordinary, complex, and ultimately inexplicable will of God that kept the Puritans snug and safe (despite predestination) in this world. God was their ultimate home, something Hawthorne couldn't bring himself to believe.

In some respects he was harsher than the Puritans, and left out of his work the love and fellowship that the leaders of Puritan society invoked for their own members. *They* had a covenant with God. "Thus stands the cause between God and us," John Winthrop confidently assured his flock on the *Arbella*, "we are entered into covenant with him for this worke, wee haue taen out a Commission, the Lord hath guen us leaue to draw our own Articles wee haue professed to enterprise these Accioins upon these and these ends . . . if the Lord shall please to hear us, and bring us in peace to the place wee desire, then hath hee ratified this Covenant and sealed our Commission." The first settlement itself Winthrop described as "a household of faith . . . our selves knitt together by this band of loue in the exercise of it." Members of "Christ's visible kingdom," sure above all things of God's sovereignty, they *knew* that because the world was *made*, the Creator had purposes for it—well entrusted to His elect.

Grace for all our corruption would not finally be denied us, and, glory be to God, was by His special Providence, an imparting of His spirit.

Hawthorne never felt he belonged to any such community of love and belief. Only four when his father, Daniel, reputed to be the harshest ship's captain out of Salem, died of yellow fever in Surinam, Hawthorne certainly had forefathers. His mother, always in black, retired to her room. Hawthorne was pretty much left to her family in

Maine, the Mannings, and it was on frozen Sebago Lake that the young Hawthorne liked to skate alone in blackest night. He would never have said, like the self-pleasing bachelor Thoreau, "Cold and solitude are friends of mine." But as a writer of fiction Hawthorne was alone learning his art, and then was commercially helpless in the hands of the publisher Samuel G. Goodrich, who paid Hawthorne less than a dollar a page for his stories when he paid at all. Goodrich published them anonymously on the grounds that "As they are anonymous, no objection arises from having so many pages by one author, particularly as they are as good, if not better, than anything else I get."

From first to last—in his last years he came apart professionally—Hawthorne felt that to be a "mere storyteller" in conventionally moral New England, and this about *Puritan* New England, demanded more of his imaginative will, more in personal dread, than was asked of writers who did not care for fiction and were not so beset by the past. His neighbor Emerson in Concord said Hawthorne's fiction was "good for nothing" (Emerson could not read any fiction). On Hawthorne's death in 1864, Emerson could only say, "I thought there was a tragic element in the event, that might be more fully rendered—in the painful solitude of the man, which, I suppose, could no longer be endured, and he died of it."

Emerson probably never read Hawthorne's "Main Street," where Hawthorne called up "the multiform and many-colored" story of their town in a puppet show attended by a few skeptical and hostile neighbors. He did not flatter the place.

> There stands the meeting-house. . . . [A] meaner temple was never consecrated to the worship of the Deity. . . .

> And there a woman,—it is Ann Coleman,—naked from the waist upward, and bound to the tail of a cart, is dragged through the Main-street at the pace of a brisk walk, while the constable follows with a whip of knotted cords. . . . He puts his heart into every stroke, zealous to fulfill the injunction of Major Hawthorne's warrant, in the spirit and in the letter. There came down a stroke that has drawn blood! Ten such stripes are to be given in Salem, ten in Boston, and ten in Dedham; and with those thirty stripes of blood upon her, she is to be driven into the forest.

In imagination, Hawthorne felt he was there with Ann Coleman, as he was with the old women his ancestor in Salem had hanged—and with Hester Prynne. When his college friend Franklin Pierce left the White House and Hawthorne lost his job at the Custom House, he was free to write *The Scarlet Letter*. Suddenly Hawthorne knew he was putting the whole Puritan story together at last, doing it right, because the petty provincial stage to which his characters are confined becomes the key image. The extraordinary narrowness (meaning pious self-approval) that obsessed Hawthorne about Puritans (*his* Puritans) is concentrated between the wilderness and the ocean. Theatrically, all the action is constricted—first Hawthorne describes so much of the "interior heart," then not more than two of the four main characters usually meet at all. Hester's only companion is her daughter, Pearl, who stands out in this somber place as "made up of new elements." Pearl—supposedly an emblem of the "lawlessness" in her mother's suppressed nature—is a trying example of Hawthorne's unrestrained use of character as explicit symbol. Only Hester escapes being tagged like "fiend-like" Chillingworth, who has moved in on Dimmesdale to "study," and eventually to expose, the man he has spotted as his wife's lover—who meanwhile is deteriorating under the inability to confess his guilt.

What with Hester unable to control her flamboyant daughter, Roger secretly preying on Arthur, Arthur helplessly trying to resist his supposed benefactor and terrible enemy, the concentration of repressed thought and feeling on the part of Hester and Arthur gets more and more pent-up, and breaks out in the grand denouement, the most theatrical imaginable. The formal procession of the townspeople in celebration of Arthur's overcharged Election Day sermon ends with his public confession on the scaffold. The idea of building his book on all that can be held back in such a society induced Hawthorne to create a consistency of tone that startled him. He described the novel "as positively a hell-fired story, into which I found it impossible to throw any cheering light." He recalled years later "my emotions when I read the last scene of the Scarlet Letter to my wife just after writing it—tried to read it, rather, for my voice swelled and heaved, as if I were tossed up and down on an ocean, as it subsides after a storm."

Why was he emotionally bound to this book and more disturbed by it than by anything else he ever wrote? Because putting it all together, as he could not in any one of his greatest stories, he indeed created a formally proper conclusion to Hester Prynne's long struggle within herself. She restores the scarlet letter of her own accord in acceptance of the law the Puritan "iron men" set down for sinners like her. That is *her* religious solution. It is not necessarily Hawthorne's. Only in a work of art, of the intensest emotions, did there surface his own long struggle with his ancestors. Hawthorne is all over his book, loving Hester and chastising her, hating Chillingworth and despising Dimmesdale, using little Pearl to say the commonplaces of freedom that no one else dared say—and all the while affirming and subverting the standards of an age he profoundly distrusted. There was no rejecting the past; it was truly "biting" him. There was no great comfort for him in writing this "hell-fired" book. As Chillingworth said, "It has all been a dark necessity." The only relief this bitter man gave himself was in creating Woman. The only admirable character in the book is Hester. Quite apart from her "elegant figure" and hair so glossy dark and abundant the sun gleams on it, Hester is the only character big enough to sustain doubts about Puritan justice equal to Hawthorne's own. In a book without heroes, Hester is a heroine. She has to carry her love story all by herself.

The Scarlet Letter was recognized on its publication in 1850 as the masterpiece a young and self-conscious culture was waiting for. It was assimilable in a way that works by two feisty New Yorkers, Melville's *Moby-Dick* (1851) and Whitman's *Leaves of Grass* (1855), were not. New England still seemed the head and fount of an American civilization founded on Puritan respectability. It is impossible to imagine Melville and Whitman being accepted as Hawthorne was—for the moment. They were engaged as true American originals in creating a vernacular, the prodigious language experiment necessary to their "primitive" confrontation with life as they knew it—meaning life at the bottom.

Hawthorne was a true son of institutional New England in his formal and even stately style. It had great tonality of sound and enormous suggestiveness—irony was one of Hawthorne's favorite maneuvers in telling a story. The dark and solemn music of Hawthorne's unrelenting commentary on the story he is presenting—intervening at one point to tell us that Hester all alone was intuiting a "freedom of speculation" inconceivable to the rest of Boston—carries the emotional background and reinforces it at crucial points. *The Scarlet Letter* is an elaborately stylized and patterned performance. It never bursts out from the depths of our hidden animal nature, as the productions of Melville and Whitman do. Just as the structure of the novel climaxes in a sermon, so the Puritan tradition of reading sermons *to an audience that always knew what to expect* lies behind Hawthorne's method. The moralist in him is always beckoning to the reader to join him in regretting "the dark necessity" of the story he feels he *has* to tell. There is a kind of literary domesticity in Hawthorne's many appeals to the reader that is very New England, based on the sermon—and the congregation to hear it—which is the chief medium of the Protestant message. *We are all of one culture*—still.

In *The Scarlet Letter*, for once in his anxious literary career, Hawthorne and his immediate New England audience weren't always at home with each other. An aggressive religious conservative soon to turn Catholic, Orestes Brownson, thought the book grossly immoral. "There is an unsound state of public morals," he complained, "when the novelist is permitted, without a scorching rebuke, to select such crimes, and to invest them with all the fascination of genius, and all the charms of a highly polished style." An article in the *Church Review* asked: "Is the French era actually begun in our literature?" This rear guard saw the erotic in the book as its admirers did not. Hawthorne was a deeply sexual man. Hester was the creation of someone who loved Woman, who saw Hester not as the heretic she never is but as emotionally sacred in a diminished world.

In revisiting the old Puritan tyranny, Hawthorne was lucky, for once, in his chance to write about love. *The Scarlet Letter* was his great literary success in a peculiarly hard and solitary career as a writer. He was forty-five when he set out to write the book. He scorned the uplift philosophy of the Transcendentalists in Concord. Emerson, a prig for all his genius, was hostile. Hawthorne was always alone in the literary New England of his day—a grimly honest storyteller fascinated by the perversity in human affairs central to his hereditary Calvinism.

There was a lot of hackwork behind him, and like so many American authors in the nineteenth century, Hawthorne needed political appointments. He was a solid adherent of the Democratic party, which as the party of Andrew Jackson officially represented the masses but so dominated the South that it rejected criticism of slavery. This suited Hawthorne's indifference to slavery. New England was "as large a lump of earth as [his] heart [could] hold." He was lucky in having as a close friend Franklin Pierce, who in 1853 became the fourteenth president of the United States. In 1846 Hawthorne's party friends secured him an appointment as surveyor of Salem, his native town. He needed to show himself in the Custom House only a few morning hours before getting back to his writing. In 1848, alas, the Mexican-American War hero Zachary Taylor, running as a Whig, was elected president, and Hawthorne lost his place.

This was devastating. Friends like Longfellow and Lowell opened a subscription for his support. Hawthorne took his dismissal as a summons to begin *The Scarlet Letter*, long in his mind. The situation Hawthorne claimed to have discovered at the Salem Custom House in a file of old papers forgotten at the outbreak of the American Revolution by loyalists fleeing to Nova Scotia. Hawthorne pictured himself brooding over the ancient story in the office where he had to associate with fossilized political hacks.

Hawthorne even claimed to have found a "rag of scarlet letter" with still visible traces of the letter A. The cruelty of the story possessed him, as did every record and relic of the Puritan period in which one Hawthorne had a woman hanged and another had a Quaker woman flogged. Hawthorne abominated the best-selling "damned mob of scribbling women," but he was certainly drawn to women as patient sufferers. (Sophia, his wife, had been such when they met.) Everything about the old Puritan world was central to Hawthorne's interior life. In some way that was an ordeal but also his opportunity as a writer, Hawthorne was bonded to the past. He associated shame over his terrible ancestors with the guilty excitement he felt in taking up the story. But as with his attraction to the long-forgotten woman who had to wear the letter A, he now pursued the woman and her story to the depths of his own erotic imagination. "The past is not even past," said William Faulkner, another hereditary Calvinist obsessed by the past of his homeland.

In "The Custom-House" preface Hawthorne imagined his terrible judicial ancestors now sitting in judgment on *him*:

No aim, that I have ever cherished, would they recognize as laudable; no success of mine—if my life, beyond its domestic scope, had ever been brightened by success—would they deem otherwise than worthless, if not positively disgraceful. "What is he?" murmurs one gray shadow of my forefathers to the other. "A writer of story-books! What kind of a business in life,—what mode of glorifying God, or being serviceable to mankind in his day and generation,—may that be? Why, the degenerate fellow might as well have been a fiddler!" Such are the compliments bandied between my great-grandsires and myself, across the gulf of time! And yet, let them scorn me as they will, strong traits of their nature have intertwined themselves with mine.

That "intertwining" was subtle and, for all of Hawthorne's raillery in "The Custom-House," painful to discover in himself. That old world always in Hawthorne's mind was grimly devoted to the identification of evil at the center of human affairs. For all his conservatism in party politics, Hawthorne, born only four years after the eighteenth century ended, was a beneficiary of the American Revolution and a product of *its* new world. (At one point in *The Scarlet Letter*, Hester in her own thought veers toward "the freedom of speculation" identified with the revolutionary eighteenth century.) The terrifying John Calvin may not have had as much influence on the Puritans as their old divines in England, but they certainly understood him when he identified original sin with sex alone. In *Institutes of the Christian Religion* (Book 11, Chapter 1) he roundly declared:

> Original sin is seen to be an hereditary depravity and corruption of our nature, diffused into all parts of the soul. . . . Those who have defined original sin as the lack of the original righteousness with which we should have been endowed . . . have not fully expressed the positive energy of this sin. For our nature is not merely bereft of good, but is so productive of every kind of evil that it cannot be inactive. Whatever is in man, from intellect to will, from the soul to the flesh, is all defiled and crammed with concupiscence; or, to sum it up briefly, the whole man is in himself nothing but concupiscence.

It is startling to realize that of all the American masters in this period, Hawthorne was the only one capable of acknowledging full heterosexual love in his work. Thoreau? Emerson? Poe? Melville? Whitman? Hawthorne and Sophia were so avidly married that Sophia was sure "nobody but we ever knew what it was to be married." Certainly no other writer's wife in this period was capable of saying of sexual intercourse that "the truly married alone can know what a wondrous instrument it is for the purposes of the heart." Until premature middle age overtook him and he grew a heavy mustache, Hawthorne was astonishingly handsome. (His sisters loved to play with his long eyelashes.) D. H. Lawrence, not fooled by the "hellfires" waiting for New England, saw the virtuous Hawthorne as "the blue-eyed Nathaniel."

In the stage picture of Hester on the scaffold with which the story opens, Hawthorne made a point of the "fertility and gorgeous luxuriance of fancy" with which she had defiantly decked out the badge of her official shame. It even pleases Hawthorne in his excitement over the picture Hester presents to imagine a Papist worshiping her as "an image of the Divine Maternity." As for the overdecorated A, it was "of a splendor in accordance with the taste of the age, but greatly beyond what was allowed by the sumptuary regulations of the colony."

The "taste" of the age refers to the England Hester had left—not the New England in which the prison was built along with the meeting-house—an England that had not shed its Elizabethan vitality. When Hester alone on the scaffold dreams back to her youth in England, it is of a sensuous world. The splendid attire and armorial trappings enveloping Governor Bellingham when he doubts that Hester is worthy of bringing up her child are vanities not permitted to women. So Hester must parody her badge of shame by turning it into such a startling thing of beauty that it captivates some of the younger women. Her skill at the needle makes her indispensable to the town and helps to dissipate her stigma. Nevertheless, she remains a figure of mystery, the strangest of living legends.

What no one knows but Hester is the extraordinary inner freedom she has attained in her excluded state. Her sexuality is still her life, just as it made her at the pillory superior to her withered husband and afflicted lover. She rises above both in the rejection of her aged, twisted, fiendish husband and in the strength of her passion for Dimmesdale.

After seven years in her hut by the shore, she contrives to meet him in the forest so that she can at last disclose that Chillingworth is her husband. Begging him to forgive her for the long silence Chillingworth had forced on her, she is overcome by her feelings. The "black man" who tempts poor beings to sin, and whose only home could be this forest, is for once forgotten. The forest now exists for love. In a story full of relentless silent brooding over sex, punishable but not mentionable, the god of guilt gives way to Hester's gift of love.

> With sudden and desperate tenderness, she threw her arms around him, and pressed his head against her bosom; little caring though his cheek rested on the scarlet letter. He would have released himself, but strove in vain to do so. Hester would not set him free, lest he should look her sternly in the face. All the world had frowned on her,—for seven long years had it frowned upon this lonely woman,—and still she bore it all, nor ever once turned away her firm, sad eyes. Heaven, likewise, had frowned upon her, and she had not died. But the frown of this pale, weak, sinful, and sorrow-stricken man was what Hester could not bear, and live!

When he does abjectly "forgive" her for waiting so long to confess her marriage to Chillingworth, he agrees that "that old man's revenge has been blacker than my sin. He has violated, in cold blood, the sanctity of a human heart. Thou and I, Hester, never did so!" Triumphantly, she whispers back, "Never, never! . . . What we did had a consecration of its own! We felt it so! We said so to each other! Hast thou forgotten it?"

This has to be set against the scene in which Hester begs her husband to pardon Dimmesdale as he has just indifferently "pardoned" her. "It is not granted me to pardon. . . . Let the black flower blossom as it may." In the opening scene of the novel Hawthorne called the prison the "black flower" of Puritan civilization. For Chillingworth the "black flower" remains the iron law of necessity that will operate against Hester's perilous inner freedom as woman and thinker. Her development was so prodigious that it seemed "the scarlet letter had not done its office."

But it has—it will. In the beautiful forest scene, "A Flood of Sunshine," that marks the loving reconciliation of Hester and Arthur, she frees herself of the letter, unpins her hair, and finally persuades him to leave the settlement with her. But he is dying under the torment of his long-sustained guilt. In the final scene he can finally come clean, hand in hand with Hester and Pearl on the scaffold where Hester suffered alone. Then he dies there, the only way he can be reconciled with himself.

The "iron men" who rule Boston, and whom Hester bitterly names to Arthur as the tyranny they can escape (she has for once forgotten Chillingworth), are only the legatees of the Old World's tyranny. But, as yet, the New World is bound to it—and to them. Puritanism held the faithful by picturing the human race entirely under God's sovereignty. Hence a home for the spirit, no matter how uncertain the chance of salvation. So at the very end Hester returns to Boston from England, where she has left Pearl, and resumes wearing the scarlet letter. With a free heart, she takes up again the penitence long ago imposed on her. She may be transfigured by her beauty, intelligence, personal nobility, but in her conscience she *is* an "adulteress." She is back in the endless chain of guilt that is her religious history.

So Puritanism, tradition, moralism, the "world's law" that once was "no law for her mind," all triumph in the end. The "dark necessity" in all human affairs is the inheritance from his forefathers Hawthorne did not quite know what to do with. He was a storyteller, and never wished or pretended to be anything else. No orthodoxy, ever, permits the irony, skepticism, personal despair—above all the sense of contradiction and unreality in human affairs that makes up the true storyteller. Hawthorne would have agreed with William Blake:

> *Do what you will, this life's a fiction*
> *And is made up of contradiction.*

But if life's a fiction, nothing in it is ever quite novel. The Puritan habit of finding correspondences and symbols in everything so worked itself into Hawthorne's inkstand that his moral reflections in the story, intervening at every point, threaten to sugarcoat a tragedy inextricably what it is—the first American tragedy in the novel. Yet the symbol-driving in Hawthorne that for Henry James amounted to "importunity" can also be seen as an attempt on Hawthorne's part to keep his distance from his "hell-fired" story. Even Hawthorne's habit of wrapping everything in his always solemn and formal style can be seen as a way of standing aside. The absolutism of seventeenth-century dogma could be too much for a nineteenth-century American democrat. He was so afraid of his material that his publisher had to talk him out of wanting to include other "tales" with *The Scarlet Letter*. "Keeping so close to its point as the tale does," he wrote James Fields, "and diversified no otherwise than by turning different sides of the same, it will weary many people and disgust some. Is it safe, then, to stake the fate of the book entirely on this one chance?"

He could not read his manuscript aloud without trembling.

2

Emerson and the Moral Sentiment:
We Are as Gods

Since religion is dead, religion is everywhere. Religion was once an affair of the church; it is now in the streets, in each man's heart. Once there were priests; now every man's a priest.

RICHARD WRIGHT, *The Outsider* (1953)

Emerson's quality, his meaning, has the quality of the light of day, which startles nobody. You cannot put your finger upon it, yet there is nothing more palpable, nothing more wonderful, nothing more vital and refreshing. There are some things in the expression of this philosoph, this poet, that are full mates of the best, the perennial masters, and will so stand in fame and the centuries. America in the future, in her long train of poets and writers, while knowing more vehement and luxuriant ones, will, I think, acknowledge nothing nearer [than] this man, the actual beginner of the whole procession.

WALT WHITMAN TO HORACE TRAUBEL (1883)

THERE WERE six students (some accompanied by family) in the senior class of Harvard's Divinity School when Emerson addressed them on Sunday evening, July 15, 1838. The lecturer was not only an ex-minister, he had left the Church, which makes one suspect that the students more than the faculty were interested in hearing him. But as he opened up on the beauty of "this refulgent summer, it has been a luxury to draw the breath of life," he was certainly far from arguing with anybody about anything. He was positively radiant himself, glorying in the eternal wonder of what nature regularly bestows on man. "The corn and the wine have been freely dealt to all creatures, and the never-broken silence with which the old bounty goes forward, has not yielded yet one word of explanation. One is constrained to respect the perfection of this world, in which our senses converse."

He is enchanted, and so will enchant others. As a man sees, so he is. This is a wondrous world, perfect to man's soul. Even its manifold surface is full of wonders. (The ex-minister, when he first had to earn his living as a lecturer, gave in the same enthusiastic vein talks on popular science.) Now he passes beyond all external signs. The world is really a spiritual phenomenon. As soon as man begins to think, his mind opens itself to "the laws which traverse the universe, and make things what they are." "Then shrinks the great world at once into a mere illustration and fable of this mind."

Pure idealists in philosophy had analyzed the relationship between subject and object to demonstrate that perception so dominates its object that (for someone like Bishop Berkeley) mind can be said to supplant it. But Emerson was too caught up in his rapture to think he had to analyze anything. The enchanter chanted that the mind, by understanding the world, actively contains it. He then went on to say that to understand by way of affirmation from the heart was an example of virtue. Man is virtuous because the world is open to him. "He learns that his being is without bound; that, to the good, to the perfect, he is born, low as he now lies in evil and weakness."

> That which he venerates is still his own, though he has not realized it yet. *He ought.* He knows the sense of that grand word, though his analysis fails entirely to render account of it. When in innocency, or when by intellectual perception, he attains to say,—"I love the Right; Truth is beautiful within and without, forevermore. Virtue, I am thine: save me: use me: thee will I serve, day and night, in great, in small, that I may be not virtuous, but virtue";— then is the end of the creation answered, and God is well pleased.

In a flash Emerson has taken us so quickly from perception of the world to the virtuousness of the mind, then to the adoration of "Virtue" itself, that we land with a jolt in the lap of God, who is well pleased that virtue is the final, the absolute. And so is "the end of the creation answered." Virtue is all this because the world is made irreducibly moral by our bearing the moral law, the moral sentiment, in our hearts.

How does Emerson know all this? It is because he knows nothing else, and so brings a passion to the subject that is irresistible to people brought up on the language of religion. He is by nature *and* clerical tradition (eight Emerson forefathers in the pulpit before him) such a religious, naturally devout creature. God has long been within him. He has been so thoroughly formed to do right and be right in the eyes of Heaven that he can now joyously throw aside orthodox Christianity's complex version of human nature to affirm goodness, virtue, in and of itself. The moral sentiment is "the essence of all religion." To know that by intuition is to become aware that the "laws of the soul" are perfect.

> These laws execute themselves. They are out of time, out of space, and not subject to circumstance. Thus; in the soul of man there is a justice whose retributions are instant and entire. He who does a good deed, is instantly ennobled. He who does a mean deed, is by the action itself contracted. He who puts off impurity, thereby puts on purity. If a man is at heart just, then in so far is he God; the safety of God, the immortality of God, the majesty of God do enter into that man with justice.

Since a lecture by such an original in the full radiance of inspiration is not always easy to grasp at the moment, it is doubtful that Emerson's six earnest senior students in divinity were with him at this point. Emerson was not delivering an academic lecture, he was rhapsodizing out of his heart and soul, communing with himself in order to address his audience. In 1838 New England had not heard that God was dead; Emerson's religious self-confidence was familiar enough at the Divinity School of which he was a graduate. But when Emerson's more senior detractors, like Andrews Norton, put down the Divinity School Address as "the latest form of infidelity," they overlooked the rapture, the heedlessness, the overflow of passionate conviction with which Emerson pronounced, "If a man is at heart just, then in so far is he God."

When Emerson rhapsodized that man bore the "moral sentiment" within him, that the human creature was inescapably moral, he did not admit that conscience was all that was left to him of his *Christian* faith. Emerson's God did not make this world or provide salvation in the next. He did not lay down commandments, reward the righteous, or condemn sinners. He was another side of oneself, the ideal, the ultimate—to be reached in the perfection of one's consciousness. Father, Son, and Holy Ghost were now just beautiful figures of speech. Theology was a touching reminder that the supernatural was once actually believed in. An inescapable sense of divinity remained an ever-present fact in New England, and in his now refreshing perfection a person could *accomplish* divinity. Later generations would find the purely ethical the residue of the old-time religion. Emerson at the Divinity School *begins* with the purely ethical—man attesting to everything from the soundness of his own nature. The person did it all by his inborn righteousness.

What was new in Emerson was not the "moral sentiment" but his exaltation of it—in and for itself—as the one human attribute that keeps religion alive. There was a certain Yankee smugness in Emerson's celebration of the virtue surrounding him which was familiar enough in New England. The Protestant, in declaring faith as his path to salvation rather than the Catholic insistence on works, proudly interpreted his overworked conscience as a sign of his righteousness. Calvin in his commentary on Saint Paul's Epistle to the Romans affirmed that God has set in all men's minds a knowledge of Himself—"his eternity, power, goodness, truth, righteousness and mercy." In *Institutes of the Christian Religion* Calvin referred to that "interior law . . . imprinted upon the heart of everyone, which in some sense conveys the teaching of the Commandments. The inner monitor that expresses this is conscience." And since Calvin condemned man not only for inheriting original sin but for being unable to avoid committing sin in his sexual depravity ("concupiscence" being his essential nature), conscience for Calvin was not moral superiority of itself (as it now appeared to Emerson) but had constantly to struggle against man's inherent corruption.

The Enlightenment shrugged all this off. Kant, in his *Critique of Practical Reason*, concluded, "Two things fill the mind with ever new and increasing wonder and awe, the more often and the more seriously reflection concentrates upon them: the starry heaven above me and the moral law within us." His famous categorical imperative: A duty or an order conceived as a good in itself became categorical when issued from a will conforming to reason.

The lofty absolutism of such ethics, distinguished from doing good for a purpose, is certainly strenuous when compared with Emerson's belief that everyone, anyone, the merest child, knows "*he ought*." "He knows the sense of that grand word, though his analysis fails entirely to render account of it." It is entirely natural, primitive, unconscious, to do right—the moral sentiment is just part of us.

With this preamble to his central and more unexpected message, Emerson is off and running.

> See how this rapid intrinsic energy worketh everywhere, righting wrongs, correcting appearances, and bringing up facts to a harmony with thoughts. Its operation in life, though slow to the senses, is, at last, as sure as in the soul. By it, a man is made the Providence to himself, dispensing good to his goodness, and evil to his sin. Character is always known. Thefts never enrich; alms never impoverish; murder will speak out of stone walls. The least admixture of a lie,— for example, the taint of vanity, the least attempt to make a good impression, a favorable appearance,—will instantly vitiate the effect. . . . Speak the truth, . . . and the very roots of the grass underground there, do seem to stir and move to bear you witness. See again the perfection of the Law as it . . . becomes the law of society.

Of course we do not "see" anything of the sort. Is it possible that even at Harvard in 1838 one could hear or read that "character is always known"—"thefts never enrich"—"murder will speak out of stone walls"—without laughing? Sermons notoriously do not descend to plain facts, and in passages like these the ex-minister seems never to have descended from his pulpit. The brilliant critic John Jay Chapman, who deeply admired Emerson's belief in the individual ("If a soul be taken and crushed by democracy till it utter a cry, that cry will be Emerson"), nevertheless found "something false" in the theory of the self-sufficiency of each individual, men and women alike.

> If an inhabitant of another planet should visit the earth, he would receive, on the whole, a truer notion of human life by attending an Italian opera than he would by reading Emerson's volumes. He would learn from the Italian opera that there were two sexes; and this, after all, is probably the fact with which the education of such a stranger ought to begin.

Yet Emerson calls "facts" his declaration that "the good, by affinity, seek the good; the vile, by affinity, the vile. Thus of their own volition, souls proceed into heaven, into hell." What has the powerful second sentence to do with the banality of the sentence preceding it? There is no argument—one sentence does not necessarily connect with another. But they are links in a chain, metaphors, illustrations of the

> sublime creed, that the world is not the product of manifold power, but of one will, of one mind; and that one mind is everywhere active . . . ; and whatever opposes that will, is everywhere balked and baffled, because things are made so, and not otherwise. Good is positive. Evil is merely privative, not absolute: it is like cold, which is the privation of heat. All evil is so much death and nonentity.

By this time it is useless to ask how we got from the moral law in each of us to the one will or mind that runs the world in the same moral spirit. And for Emerson "moral" is all benevolence, "absolute and real." Good is alone positive. Obviously this is not a description of the world as even Emerson knew it, of the human history recorded in his Bible. It is an immensely private view of the creation, such as only great men— and madmen—insist on in face of convention.

Emerson is not mad, he has just turned his absolute ethic into a law for the universe. "The perception of this law of laws awakens in the mind a sentiment which we call the religious sentiment, and which makes our highest happiness." This may not be my "religious sentiment," but it is certainly Emerson's. And having worked it out of a "law of laws" known to him, he is in ecstasy, in "highest happiness." And communicates this with the literary power that generation after generation has enabled some Americans to thank Emerson for making the world new again, giving us our own republic of the soul, our inner American Revolution and Declaration of Independence:

> Wonderful is its power to charm and to command. It is a mountain air. It is the embalmer of the world. It is myrrh and storax, and chlorine and rosemary. It makes the sky and the hills sublime, and the silent song of the stars is in it. By it, is the universe made safe and habitable, not by science or power. Thought may work cold and intransitive in things, and find no end or unity; but the dawn of the sentiment of virtue on the heart, gives and is the assurance that Law is sovereign over all natures; and the worlds, time, space, eternity, do seem to break out into joy.

Perhaps Emerson's six students were embarrassed by what D. H. Lawrence called the "inrushes" Emerson got from his "wild and genuine belief." As usual with this great man, his passion has stalled us in our commonsense limits. We cannot help acknowledging the truth of Emerson's saying that by the religious sentiment "is the universe made safe and habitable, not by science or power." A century after Emerson, the French biologist Jacques Monod remarked, "Religion conceived the world so we could love it." Freud was to call religion the "illusion" that makes the world safe—for believers. Illusion or not, religion does that.

Austere Freud was above consolation, and mocked mere religious "sentiment." But Emerson in his "inrush" says that the sentiment "is divine and deifying." Without the slightest attempt to prove that there is a God, it is enough for Emerson to say that the "sentiment" is "the beatitude of man. It makes him illimitable." Here is the crux of the Emerson religion, which is not God but man's excited sense of what the "religious sentiment" does for him. Always the sentiment and never the Godhead! Melville wrote to Hawthorne that "the Godhead is broken up like the bread at the Supper, and . . . we are the pieces." This transposition from God to man is the real American creed for both the natural believer Emerson and the tormented agnostic Melville. Both have magnetized writers to this day. In any event, by "man" Emerson means ME, ME separated from all teachers but ME, ME ENTIRELY ON MY OWN.

> Meantime, whilst the doors of the temple stand open, night and
> day, before every man, and the oracles of this truth cease never, it is
> guarded by one condition; this, namely; it is an intuition. It cannot
> be received at second hand. Truly speaking, it is not instruction,
> but provocation, that I can receive from another soul.

It is easy to say that the times were ripe for a prophet like this. There were many other such "prophets" then and now—not least among minorities and the oppressed. The loose American religion made it possible for a self-appointed leader to build on *himself* to infinity! But what did Emerson understand of his role when he told Divinity School students to abjure all they were being taught? In his journal entry for April 1, 1838, months before the Divinity School Address of that summer, he notes that

the Divinity School youths wished to talk with me concerning theism. I went rather heavy hearted for I always find that my views
chill or shock people at the first opening. But the conversation
went well & I came away cheered. I told them that the preacher
should be a prophet smit with love of the harmonies of moral nature; and yet look at the Unitarian Association & see if its aspect is
poetic. They all smiled No. A minister nowadays is plainest prose,
the prose of prose. He is a Warming-pan, a Night-chair at sick
beds & rheumatic souls; and the fire of the minstrel's eye & the vi-
vacity of his word is exchanged for intense grumbling enunciation
of the Cambridge sort, & for scripture phraseology.

What this comes to—your minister nowadays is not a writer like
Emerson. Imagine the usual Unitarian minister likening himself to an
artist with God as his fellow artist! "The maker of a sentence, like the
other artist," Emerson wrote in 1834, "launches out into the infinite and
builds a road into Chaos and Old Night, and is followed by those who
hear him with something of wild, creative delight." Only Emerson
would have felt that crossing a bare common, he was "glad to the brink
of fear." In his journal: "I dreamed that I floated at will in the great
Ether, and I saw this world floating also not far off, but diminished to
the size of an apple. Then an angel took it in his hand and brought it to
me and said, 'This thou must eat.' And I ate the world."

The egotism of this is as fervid as Scripture. Emerson could never
have said, with Saint John, "In the beginning was the Word." For him,
as for the Creator, all was silence, emptiness, the void, until he filled it
with *his* word. He exemplifies the traditional role of the founder of new
religions by providing his audience, his necessary disciples, with a set
of sayings that give names to spiritual things—and so, whether they
are "real" or not, make them *present* to us. Such sayings lay down a line
of stepping-stones for us to cross what would otherwise be the terror
of an utterly unfamiliar world. Without man, there is utter silence; a
true sentence cuts into this silence and gives man a home in the
universe.

Emerson was a poet in the old universal sense—an artist, a great
artist, coming out of a tradition fundamentally religious. He taught the
divinity students, in effect, that they had to be equally fervid in uphold-

ing the spirit. He did not *say* he was an example to them, but he became one by writing in letters of fire:

> Jesus Christ belonged to the true race of prophets. He saw with open eye the mystery of the soul. Drawn by its severe harmony, ravished with its beauty, he lived in it, and had his being there. Alone in all history, he estimated the greatness of man. One man was true to what is in you and me. He saw that God incarnates himself in man, and evermore goes forth anew to take possession of his world. He said, in this jubilee of sublime emotion, "I am divine. Through me, God acts; through me, speaks. Would you see God, see me; or, see thee, when thou also thinkest as I now think." But what a distortion did his doctrine and memory suffer in the same, in the next, and in the following ages! There is no doctrine of the Reason which will bear to be taught by the Understanding. The understanding caught this high chant from the poet's lips, and said, in the next age, "This was Jehovah come down out of heaven. I will kill you, if you say he was a man."

This is the high flame, the matchless *sursum corda*, the lifting of the heart, that Emerson has been leading up to in correction of the existing Church. Jesus was a "poet" in the beauty of his style, but "the idioms of his language, and the figures of his rhetoric, have usurped the place of his truth; and churches are not built on his principles, but on his tropes." But these principles, according to Emerson, show a scant respect for religious tradition—for Moses and the prophets. The miracle is life itself and at all times, never more so than now, "the eternal revelation in the heart. Thus was he [Jesus] a true man."

There are so many conflicting images and interpretations of Jesus (starting within the Gospels) that Emerson is free to transform the Jesus established by historical Christianity into an orphic genius like himself. All Jesus taught, Emerson insists, was the doctrine of the soul, but official religion "has dwelt, it dwells, with noxious exaggeration about the *person* of Jesus. The soul knows no persons. It invites every man to expand to the full circle of the universe, and will have no preferences but those of spontaneous love."

In short, any of us can be as commanding a force as Jesus. Any of us, expanding to the full circle of the universe, may yet enjoy the jubilee of sublime emotion that Jesus knew in recognizing God in Himself. God dwells in us, too. No need to restrict ourselves to the narrowness of a Christianity that instructs us to *imitate* Jesus. "That is always best which gives me to myself. Obey thyself. That which shows God in me, fortifies me."

At this point, Emerson seems to have done with Jesus. The perfect man has become a figure of speech. As Emerson now goes after the Church, ridiculing its pretensions to authority, Jesus as its glorified figurehead becomes as dispensable as everything else about the Church. *Man no longer needs the Church.* "Commanded" by the moral sentiment, man is himself commanding. He, too, like the true preacher Emerson dreamed of, "deals out to the people his life,—life passed through the fire of thought."

We do not know what Emerson's general audience thought in response to all this. In a lifetime of lecturing all over the country, once all the way to California, he probably never exchanged views with his audience. In his first period as a lecturer he seemed to expect everything of the individual American, but he was too private a man to "entertain" questions and disagreements. Apparently it was the usual habit of the lecture committee to wait on him with a basket of apples and pronounce that he had "given satisfaction." In San Francisco the local newspaper reported that on the platform he was a lofty, impressive figure and that he had spoken impressive, undeniable wisdom about the First Cause. After Emerson became an American icon, William Dean Howells said, "It would be hard to persuade people now that Emerson once represented to the popular mind all that was most hopelessly impossible, and that in a certain sort he was a national joke, the type of the incomprehensible, the byword of the poor paragrapher. . . . Twenty years before his death he was the most misunderstood man in America."

The private Emerson in his journals was skeptical, shrewd, and acidly objective, not a victim of the "sky-blue" idealism his friend Carlyle saw in his early lectures. For a man so easily given to transports, he was a great critic and mercilessly intelligent. If some of his lecture audiences seemed numb, Emerson certainly returned the compliment. Melville, who thought Transcendentalism just moonshine, was overjoyed to learn that for Emerson "the calamity is the masses." His appeal was to the individual, but only if he was as reflective and open to the universe as Emerson himself—Thoreau, Whitman, Nietzsche, Matthew Arnold, Justice Holmes. In the Divinity School he mocked the local ministers for being prose, while he—like Jesus—was a "poet."

When did Emerson come to full consciousness of himself as a great man? The evidence for his thinking himself not just "free" but superior is implicit in the Divinity School Address. But there he is also appealing to everyone, anyone within the sound of his voice to recognize that the "moral sentiment" has given him godlike powers. The address is his most evangelical.

In "Self-Reliance" the self-confidence comes down to earth, and applies equally to Yankee ingenuity. "A sturdy lad from New Hampshire or Vermont, who in turn tries all the professions, who *teams it, farms it, peddles*, keeps a school, preaches, edits a newspaper, goes to Congress, buys a township, and so forth, in successive years, and always, like a cat, falls on his feet, is worth a hundred of these city dolls. . . . [H]e does not postpone his life, but lives already." Emerson, though of course he did not share his friend Carlyle's savage idolatry of mere authority, did come to believe that the superior individual is our only resource. "Accept the place the divine Providence has found for you. . . . Great men have always done so. . . . But . . . when the unintelligent brute force that lies at the bottom of society is made to growl and mow . . . treat it godlike as a trifle of no concernment."

Emerson was never that superior before. The world is no longer as fresh and new as it was to the young man who in his twenties left the ministry, and in the first awareness of his genius wrote *Nature*, which ends in a positive sense of transfiguration.

> Know then, that the world exists for you. For you is the phenomenon perfect. What we are, that only can we see. All that Adam had, all that Caesar could, you have and can do. . . . Yet line for line and point for point, your dominion is as great as theirs, though without fine names. Build, therefore, your own world. As fast as you conform your life to the pure idea in your mind, that will unfold its great proportions. A correspondent revolution in things will attend the influx of the spirit.

Alas, that "correspondent revolution in things" never happened. Emerson is well on his way to *Representative Men*, where "it is natural to believe in great men." He hymns Napoleon as the truly great *modern* man, the very symbol of the active new middle class.

> Such a man was wanted, and such a man was born; a man of stone and iron, capable of sitting on horseback sixteen or seventeen hours, of going many days together without rest or food, except by snatches, and with the speed and spring of a tiger in action; a man not embarrassed by any scruples; compact, instant, selfish, prudent, and of a perception which did not suffer itself to be baulked or misled by any pretences of others, or any superstition, or any heat or haste of his own.

Napoleon as a man of war fascinates Emerson by his total competence, which entails freedom from mere scruples. Napoleon is *history*. Nothing is now said of the moral sentiment *in* history, for the great man decides everything by ignoring purely moral issues. In *War and Peace* Prince Andrey Bolkonsky, wounded on the field of Austerlitz, experiences a shock more painful than his physical wounds when he overhears *his* hero, Napoleon, calmly surveying the mass of dead bodies, obscenely announce, "All those bodies can be replaced in a single night." Like Tolstoy, Prince Andrey knew war, where Emerson in his Concord study just had lofty thoughts about it. In the reflections on history that conclude *War and Peace*, Tolstoy argued, in the face of his own wishes, that the course of human events never had a single meaning, that it could never be portrayed as a seamless web. The truth was in an often bewildering variety of material causes.

Emerson never found a great man—or thought to find one—in the America around him. He was above the battle—not that he ever thought there *was* one until the Civil War, when he condescended to Lincoln as he did to everyone else in power. In his own person Emerson summed up in his self-sufficient religion all the innocence left in New England's high regard for its virtuousness. On that plane it was easy "to believe in great men." But of course Emerson never saw around him a man greater than himself.

Emerson to Carlyle soon after the Civil War: "My countrymen do not content me, but they are susceptible of inspirations." No doubt "inspirations" signified the realization of American unity through the terrible Civil War. The word was so lofty as to be patronizing. Emerson would not admit that the religious revolution he had so eloquently personified had not reached and changed the American people but had been mostly confined to himself. As he required of the ideal minister, Emerson had passed out his life to the people in the hope of gathering them into his passion. As the Reformation turned every man into a priest, Emerson hoped to turn every American into a genius. But Thoreau was the only other literary-religious genius in the vicinity for whom religion was the seeking of perfection, not a set of opinions. In his preface to *Mosses from an Old Manse* Hawthorne in Concord derided Emerson's adoring disciples, especially young Transcendentalists, as

> hobgoblins of flesh and blood . . . attracted thither by the wide-spreading influence of a great original Thinker, who had his earthly abode at the opposite extremity of our village. His mind acted upon other minds, of a certain constitution, with wonderful magnetism, and drew many men upon long pilgrimages, to speak with him face to face. Young visionaries—to whom just so much of insight had been imparted as to make life all a labyrinth around them—came to seek the clue that should guide them out of their self-involved bewilderment. Uncertain, troubled, earnest wanderers, through the midnight of a moral world, beheld his intellectual fire, as a beacon burning on a hill-top. . . . The light revealed objects unseen before—mountains, gleaming lakes, glimpses of a creation among the chaos—but also, as was unavoidable, it attracted bats and owls. . . .
>
> . . . For myself, there had been epochs of my life, when I, too, might have asked of this prophet the master-word . . . but now, being happy, I felt as if there were no question to be put, . . . and therefore sought nothing from him as a philosopher.

This could have been devastating to everyone except Emerson, who once he had found God in himself was always "happy," confident of his wisdom about everything that came to his attention. The "infinitude of the private mind"—the essence of Emerson's message—would bring no great "awakening" in America. He became a prophet not of God in every American heart but of rugged individualism. Any American can become just about anything he liked. Yes! Alexis de Tocqueville warned that this unprecedented faith in the individual could make a man forget his ancestors and trap him "within the solitude of his own heart."

In Concord, Emerson's sometime handyman and baby-sitter, Henry David Thoreau, had reason to resent Emerson's public recognition, Olympian serenity, and detachment. No one else in town was so alone as Thoreau. But he certainly had a bond to Emerson. He told a friend that in Emerson he had found "a world where truths existed with the same perfection as the objects he studied in external nature, his ideals real and exact." He differed from Emerson in one great respect. He tried to *live* these truths, perfect as the objects he studied in external nature, as if he wished for nothing else. He tried to live them with a wholeness of heart to which his writing and his writing alone would be testimony. There is no perfection to be found in the world without someone appealing in the right words for recognition of it and gratitude for it. The perfection Thoreau found in a day, in an hour, even of a moment spent in the rapt stillness of Walden Pond called to him for the most exact and intense recall of it in his daily journal.

This was not just a book, it was life lived as an ideal, the only way this man described by his boating companion Hawthorne as "ugly as sin, long-nosed, queer-mouthed, . . . inclined to live a sort of Indian life among civilized men" wanted to live. Or could.

> I learned this, at least, by my experiment; that if one advances confidently in the direction of his dreams, and endeavors to live the life which he has imagined, he will meet with a success unexpected in common hours. He will put some things behind, will pass an invisible boundary; new, universal, and more liberal laws will begin to establish themselves around and within him; or the old laws be expanded, and interpreted in his favor in a more liberal sense, and he will live with the license of a higher order of beings.

This was very grand. But how to prove it, first to himself, then to the neighbors he regarded as spiritually mediocre, except in language solid as the creation? Emerson was a naturally lyric, orphic writer who took his gift for granted. He, too, kept a journal, but it was his "savings bank," his memoranda, into which he put anything that crossed his mind. Thoreau intently put his life into his journal because there was no other place to put it. He did not just write his journal, he practiced it first in field notes drawn from his studied observations, then rewrote them in his journal, and rewrote them still again for the publishable book. All this in order to show in one gleamingly exact sentence after another that he was entirely at home with nature, God, and himself. No problems! None whatever! He was totally free in all things. He had made it—the ideal American—now at the summit of a pastoral village in reclusive New England.

> I do not propose to write an ode to dejection, but to brag as lustily as chanticleer in the morning, standing on his roost, if only to wake my neighbors up.

> I am freer than any planet; no complaint reaches around the world. I can move away from public opinion, from government, from religion, from education, from society. . . . Shall I raise corn and potatoes in Massachusetts, or figs and olives in Asia minor? sit out the day in my office in State Street, or ride it out on the steppes of Tartary.

> These are but few of my chances, and how many more things may I do with which there are none to be compared!

> Cold and solitude are friends of mine. . . . I come to my solitary woodland walk as the homesick go home. This stillness, solitude, wildness of nature is a kind of thoroughwort or boneset, to my intellect. This is what I go out to seek. It is as if I always met in these places some grand, serene, immortal, infinitely encouraging, though invisible companion, and walked with him.

Some critic (Kenneth Burke?) ruefully noted that "we have been sentenced to the sentence." For Thoreau the perfectly accomplished sentence had to be the quotient of his living—maxim, aphorism, sensation all in one. It was at the farthest remove from any writer's routine self-correction. It had to reflect Thoreau's overwhelming moral urgency, the call for a new life, the true life. It was not the process of life that aroused him but taxonomy, listing one detail after another. No observer of nature could have been less the Darwinian. And all this was born of the perfect romance with the life in nature, which proved what an almighty purpose was instilled in every particle of creation. He described Walden Pond as if he had baptized himself in its waters. Where man is so entirely alone, God is felt to be near. Of course Thoreau spoke not of a personal God but of a world made holy again. With which he was intimately living. It was all so perfectly endearing, so enchanting, that he could not understand why people were always busy with business and did not live as he did. In the perfect stillness at Walden Pond he describes himself banging his oar against the side of his canoe to hear the echo, to surmise something other.

It came with a rush and a bang louder than anything he knew. On October 16, 1859, John Brown, with sons and followers, attacked the government arsenal at Harpers Ferry with the intention of arming slaves. It was a debacle. Brown suffered great losses, and was captured and sentenced to hang. He had so alarmed the South with the threat of slave uprisings that war was inevitable. In Concord, Brown's attack on government property clearly roused in Thoreau a powerful sense of identification. After all, he had spent a night in jail for not paying the tax for which his father was responsible. And had written a glowing memoir of his incarceration, "Civil Disobedience," to show that as an individualist in the loftiest sense, *he* was not to be intimidated by any government.

Two weeks after Brown made his attack, Thoreau defended him in "A Plea for Captain John Brown," delivered in the Concord Town Hall. Emerson's son Edward said Thoreau read the speech as if it "burned" him.

> We aspire to be something more than stupid and timid chattels, pretending to read history and our Bibles, but desecrating every house and every day we breathe in. . . . [A]t least a million of the free inhabitants of the United States would have rejoiced if his [last attack] had succeeded. . . . Though we wear no crape, the thought of that man's position and probable fate is spoiling many a man's day here at the North for other thinking. If any one who has seen him here can pursue successfully any other train of thought, I do not know what he is made of. If there is any such who gets his usual allowance of sleep, I will warrant him to fatten easily under any circumstances which do not touch his body or purse.

As for himself, Thoreau added, "I put a piece of paper and a pencil under my pillow, and when I could not sleep, I wrote in the dark." Writing was what he had lived for, lived by, lived in. The word was the light, the word was the church, and the word was now Thoreau's only deed. He said of the organized Church that it "can never have done with excommunicating Christ while it exists." He said, "I am here to plead his cause with you. I plead not for his life, but for his character—his immortal life; and so it becomes your cause wholly, and is not his in the least. Some eighteen hundred years ago Christ was crucified; this morning, perchance, Captain Brown was hung. These are the two ends of a chain which is not without its links."

For Emerson, Brown "had made the gallows as beautiful as the cross."

Thoreau the quietist and pacifist was not vexed by Brown's favorite maxim: "Without the shedding of blood there is no remission of sins." Except for slavery, Thoreau did not much believe in "sins." It was easy for any man to see the light! But Brown (originally from New England) was clearly a believer in absolutes. On this familiar ground Thoreau was aroused to equal in biblical passion the Brown who had said to the court that condemned him:

> Had I so interfered in behalf of the rich, the powerful, the intelligent, the so-called great . . . it would have been all right. . . . I am yet too young to understand that God is any respecter of persons. I believe that to have interfered as I have done—as I have freely admitted I have done—in defense of His despised poor was not wrong but right.

Actually, Thoreau was concerned not with God's poor but with righteousness. Except for their holy narrowness, he and Brown could not have been more different. Brown was a true revolutionary—he expected to liberate all slaves by force, no matter what it cost him, his sons, and anyone who got in his way. In "bloody Kansas" he and a few sons grabbed men *rumored* to be proslavery and cut their throats. Thoreau had long before this thrown away his gun and no longer ate meat. He just wanted to be eternally right with himself, the only saint in the neighborhood. He lived just long enough into the Civil War to disapprove of it. An "angel of light," he instructed his disciple Parker Pillsbury (a man who tried to live without money) that he should have absolutely nothing to do with the war.

3

Christians and Their Slaves
(Harriet Beecher Stowe and Others)

I did not write it. God wrote it. I merely did His dictation.
HARRIET BEECHER STOWE

THOMAS JEFFERSON'S earliest memory was of being carried on a silk pillow by a slave. On the death of his father-in-law, John Wayles, in 1773, Jefferson inherited 11,000 acres of land and 135 slaves. He sold half of the land, and eventually liberated only two of his slaves—one of whom bought his own freedom. Slave labor worked Jefferson's vast estate, under his direction built magnificent Monticello and Jefferson's exquisite summer retreat at Poplar Forest, staffed his household wherever he lived, and eventually built the coffin in which he was buried.

Jefferson published one book during his lifetime, *Notes on the State of Virginia*, which was written in response to queries put to him by a French diplomat in Washington. Having lived all his life as master of a slave society, Jefferson, who said he disapproved of slavery, made it clear in his response to "Query XIV" that he thought little of the blacks as a race.

> To our reproach it must be said, that though for a century and a half we have had under our eyes the races of black and of red men, they have never yet been viewed by us as subjects of natural history. I advance it therefore as a suspicion only, that the blacks, whether originally a distinct race, or made distinct by time and circumstances, are inferior to the whites in endowments both of body and mind.

In his response to "Query XVIII" Jefferson must have astonished himself—as he does the contemporary reader—by breaking out against the unhappy influence on the manners of our people produced by the existence of slavery among us. The whole commerce between master and slave is a perpetual exercise of the most boisterous passions, the most unremitting despotism on the one part, and degrading submissions on the other. Our children see this and learn to imitate it. . . . The parent storms, the child looks on, catches the lineaments of wrath, puts on the same airs in the circle of smaller slaves . . . , and thus nursed, educated and daily exercised in tyranny, cannot but be stamped by it with odious peculiarities.

No abolitionist before the Civil War condemned slavery as fiercely as Jefferson did in 1781. But unlike the abolitionist, Jefferson was more concerned with the degradation of his fellow slave owners, and saw no stop to it. The master's children picked up his worst habits and tyrannized over the smaller slaves. One half of the citizens were given absolute rights to trample on the other half. With the morals of the people went the destruction of their industry. In a warm climate no man will labor for himself who can make another man labor for him. Very few slave owners are ever seen to labor themselves. Jefferson the Deist finally broke through his principles to cry, "Can the liberties of a nation be thought secure when we have removed their only firm basis, a conviction in the minds of the people that these liberties are of the gift of God? That they are not to be violated but with his wrath? Indeed I tremble for my country when I reflect that God is just: that his justice cannot sleep forever: that considering numbers, nature and natural means only, a revolution of the wheel of fortune, an exchange of situation, is among possible events: that it may become probable by supernatural interference!"

Jefferson at the last thought a better spirit was coming in with the American Revolution. "The spirit of the master is abating, that of the slave rising from the dust, his condition mollifying, the way I hope preparing, under the auspices of heaven, for a total emancipation." Needless to say, Jefferson hoped this would happen "with the consent of the masters, rather than by their extirpation."

As president, Jefferson in 1806 rejoiced that under Article I, section 9 of the Constitution, the importation of slaves from abroad would be prohibited after 1808. In his sixth annual message, he wrote, "I congratulate you, fellow citizens, on the approach of the period at which you may interpose your authority constitutionally to withdraw the citizens of the United States from all further participation in those violations of human rights which have been so long continued on the unoffending inhabitants of Africa."

> *When a man strikes his slave, male or female, with a rod, and he dies under his hand, he must be avenged. But if he survives a day or two, he is not to be avenged, since he is the other's property.*
>
> EXODUS 21:20

New England believed it supplied the moral force propelling antislavery "agitation." As early as 1783 the chief justice of the Commonwealth proclaimed the end of slavery in Massachusetts:

> The doctrine of slavery and the right of Christians to hold Africans in perpetual servitude, and sell and treat them as we do our horses and cattle has been countenanced by the Province laws formerly, but nowhere is it expressly enacted or established. It has been a usage . . . which took its origin from the practice of some of the European nations, and the regulations of the British government respecting the then colonies, for the benefit of trade and wealth. But whatsoever sentiments have slid in . . . upon us by the example of others, a different idea has taken place with the people of America, more favorable to the natural rights of mankind, and to that natural, innate desire of Liberty, which with Heaven (without regard to color, complexion, or shape of noses) has inspired all the human race.

A remarkable Connecticut Yankee Frederick Law Olmsted (after the Civil War he was among the first to build our public parks) described in letters to *The New York Times* his travels through the Southeast and Texas and his journey from New Orleans to Richmond. These went into his classic surveys—*A Journey in the Seabord Slave States* (1856), *A Journey Through Texas* (1857), and *A Journey in the Back Country* (1860), all condensed in *The Cotton Kingdom* (1861). Eric Homberger, in

Scenes from the Life of a City, reports Olmsted asking an overseer how he felt about punishing slaves and receiving the casual reply, "It's my business, and I think nothing of it. Why, sir, I wouldn't mind killing a nigger more than I would a dog."

Olmsted hoped his books would intensify British support for the North. More concerned than abolitionists were about the poverty of the South itself, Olmsted said of the primitive hospitality he encountered in "aristocratic" Virginia, "No lyceum or public libraries, no public gardens, no galleries of art, no public resorts of healthful and refining amusement; no place better than a filthy, tobacco-impregnated barroom or a licentious dance cellar." Staying in many homes, "I found no garden, no flowers, no fruit, no tea, no cream, no sugar, no bread . . . no curtains, no lifting windows, no couch. . . . For all that, the house swarmed with vermin. There was no hay, no straw, no oats, . . . no discretion, no care, no honesty." Slaves were so strongly disciplined that Olmsted could report:

> I repeatedly rose through the lines at a canter, with other horsemen, often coming upon them suddenly, without producing the smallest change or interrupted action in the dogged action of the labourers, or causing one of them, so far as I could see, to lift an eye from the ground. A very tall and powerful negro walked to and fro in the rear of the line, frequently cracking his whip, and calling out, in the surliest manner, to one and another, "Shove your hoe, there! Shove your hoe." But I never saw him strike any one with a whip.

The scholar of world slavery David Brion Davis reports that the British Society for the Propagation of the Gospel not only owned slaves but branded them "Society." At an exhibition of the famous Gilman Collection of historic photographs at the Metropolitan Museum of Art in New York, I was devastated to see, in a photograph of a group of slaves, "Wilson Chinn, black, branded on forehead with hot iron by owner Volsey B. Marmillion, sugar planter 45 miles above New Orleans. He made it a practice to brand his Negroes."

In founding *The Liberator* in 1831, William Lloyd Garrison said that after trying to "excite the minds of the people by a series of discourses on the subject of slavery," but "palsied by public indifference," he had determined "that a greater revolution in public sentiment was to be effected in the free states—*and particularly in New England*—than at the South." This was typical of Garrison, who soon demanded immediate and complete emancipation, denounced slavery and slave owners violently, and on July 4, 1854, alarmed many supporters by publicly burning the Constitution, explaining, "So perish all compromises with tyranny."

Garrison is not a hero to the Lincoln expert David Herbert Donald, who, less moved by slavery, sees the abolitionists not as perturbed consciences but as spokesmen for the industrial North. Robert Fogel called his book *Time on the Cross*, but put down abolitionists as "mystics" who transcended reason and trusted in *their* access to divine inspiration. For them slavery was not just a sin but an extraordinary sin, a sin so "corrupting" as to create "an insurmountable barrier to both personal and national salvation." Since slavery was "always, everywhere, and only a sin," the remedy was to stop sinning. At once. Garrison: "No plan was needed to stop sinning."

The hidden strength of Garrison the disunionist was that the North and democratic Europe were on the side of freedom. The abolitionist movement, despite the most violent opposition, had a moral influence beyond earnest, peaceful appeals to Southern and Northern conscience alike. Tolstoy (he read English and greatly admired *Uncle Tom's Cabin*) was more impressed by Garrison's pacifism than by the end of American slavery—the only one of some twenty slave societies unable to find a peaceful way to emancipation. In *The Kingdom of God and Peace Essays*, Tolstoy wrote in 1904 that in reading a short biography of Garrison, "I recalled the spring of my awakening to true life. Garrison's speeches and articles vividly bring back to me the spiritual joy I experienced twenty years ago when I learnt that the law of nonresistance had been recognized and proclaimed by him even as far back as the eighteen-forties . . . and that he had made it the basis of his practical activity for the emancipation of the slaves. I myself had been inevitably brought to the law of non-resistance by recognizing the full meaning of the Christian teaching, which disclosed to me the great and joyful idea to be realized in Christian life." Tolstoy:

Garrison understood what the most advanced of the other fighters against slavery did not understand: that the only irrefutable argument against slavery is a denial of any man's right over the liberty of another under any conditions whatsoever.

For the purpose of combating slavery he advanced the principle of a struggle against all the evil of the world.

This principle put forward by Garrison was irrefutable, but it affected and even overthrew all the foundations of established social order, and so those who valued their position in that existing order were frightened at its announcement and still more at its practical application to life. . . . The result of this evasion of the recognition of the unlawfulness of coercion was the fratricidal war, which externally solving the slavery question, introduced into the life of the American people the new and perhaps even greater evil of that corruption which accompanies every war.

To this absolutism of principle (one Garrison aspired to in apocalyptic language) there is of course no answer, since it has nothing to do with the violence with which the South sustained and defended its system. Tolstoy, excommunicated by the Holy Russian Synod, was overcome by the contrast between his splendid life, talent, and wealth and the rigidity of the system ignoring the misery everywhere around it. He opted for a kind of sainthood. He could afford it. He understood perfectly well that other people did not feel, think, and live at their own behest as he did. So John Brown insisted on the eve of his execution that "religion pure and undefiled" had led him to sacrifice his sons and to bring the maddened South nearer to war. He did not end slavery. Neither did William Lloyd Garrison, who sent Tolstoy the photograph of himself that still hangs in Tolstoy's old study at Yasnaya Polyana. The inscription reads LIBERTY FOR ALL, FOR EACH, FOREVER!

Nathaniel Hawthorne was not a moral absolutist and did not approve of those, like Emerson's hangers-on in Concord, who had vague aspirations in that regard. New England was not all saintly territory. Hawthorne's college friend Franklin Pierce from New Hampshire was a wily political operator who in the Mexican war managed to attain the rank of brigadier general without participating in a single battle. The

Democrats in 1852 nominated him for the presidency when they could not agree on anybody else. Pierce, who was indifferent to slavery and a conciliator of the South, of course accepted the Compromise of 1850 that included the Fugitive Slave Act, which mandated the capture of fugitives and particularly outraged antislavery opinion. Emerson, whose disapproval of slavery was usually cool and theoretical, was infuriated enough to write in his journal, "This filthy enactment was made in the 19th century, by people who can read & write. I will not obey it, by God."

This was hardly the tone taken by Franklin Pierce's campaign biographer, Nathaniel Hawthorne. Hawthorne was closer to an old college friend like Pierce than to the religious idealists who surrounded him in Concord; the biography, apart from the preposterous idealization of a presidential candidate expected in 1852, is astounding in its personal views of slavery and the struggle between North and South that disturbed Hawthorne more than slavery ever did.

Hawthorne's loyalty to Pierce was particularly to anger antislavery opinion in New England in 1863 when he dedicated his impressions of England, "Our Old Home," to the discredited ex-president Pierce, now viewed as a bungler whose futile attempts to conciliate the South had helped to bring on the Civil War. Hawthorne belligerently defended himself, saying his first obligation was to friendship. He did not mind separating himself, in the midst of the Civil War, from the now general disapproval of Pierce, and in 1852 he advanced views on slavery that went beyond anything the always cautious politician Pierce could possibly have expressed on the subject.

New Hampshire in 1852 was so faithful to the Puritan past that certain state offices could be held only by Protestants. Hawthorne thought it necessary to defend Catholics as loyal to their "adopted country." Were they all immigrants? He had said, "New England is as large a lump of earth as my heart can hold." He praised Pierce's friendliness to the South as a noble attempt to keep the Union together. This glossed over the fact that Pierce was a party Democrat, as was Hawthorne himself when he was collector at the Salem Custom House under a Democratic administration. Up to the Civil War the Democrats were the nation's majority power and usually favored the South. There were "conscience Whigs" unhappy with slavery. There were no "conscience Democrats."

Pierce personally was just as indifferent to slavery as Hawthorne himself. The South was just too distant, "exotic," and troublesome for New England even to *think* of slavery. Hawthorne was to say on the outbreak of the Civil War that he had never really believed the South was truly part of the Union and that he was not unhappy to see it secede.

In 1852, while reverting to the stock rhetoric of the time about the sacredness of the Union in order to praise Pierce as patriot, Hawthorne betrayed his own disdain for antislavery agitators and his contempt for the slaves themselves. The antislavery movement was "evil" because it could only lead to "the aggravated injury of those whose condition it aimed to ameliorate, and terminating, in its possible triumph—if such possibility there were,—with the ruin of two races which now dwelt together in greater peace and affection, it is not too much to say, than had ever elsewhere existed between the taskmaster and the serf."

Hawthorne compared the "theorist" and the "philanthropist" in their opposition to slavery with "the statesman of practical sagacity—who loves his country as it is, and evolves good from things as they exist. . . . Such a man . . . must not narrow himself to adopt the cause of one section of his native country against another. He will stand up, as he always stood, among the patriots of the whole land. And if the work of antislavery agitation, which it is undeniable leaves most men who earnestly engage in it with only half a country in their affections,—if this work must be done, let others do it."

Hawthorne scorned "those Northern men . . . who deem the great cause of human welfare as represented and involved in this present hostility against Southern institutions." He sneered that they "conceive that the world stands still except in so far as that goes forward." Very well, such would not vote for Pierce. But there is another view of slavery, and probably just as "wise" a one.

It looks upon slavery as one of those evils which divine Providence does not leave to be remedied by human contrivances, but which, in its own good time, by some means impossible to be anticipated, but of the simplest and easiest operation, when all its uses shall have been fulfilled, it causes to vanish like a dream. There is no instance, in all history, of the human will and intellect having perfected any great moral reform by methods which it adapted to that end; but the progress of the world, at every step, leaves some evil or wrong on the path behind it, which the wisest of mankind, of their own set purpose, could never have found the way to rectify.

In the light of future history, this is so maladroit and insensitive that one wonders what this extraordinary man could have been thinking of when he wrote that slavery would end "when all its uses shall have been fulfilled." Hawthorne was descended from Puritans who had made the Reformation solid, who had left their country to settle in a near wilderness because they believed, as Keats put it in a letter of 1818, that "the Reformation produced such immediate and great benefits, that Protestantism was considered under the immediate eye of Heaven. . . . It proves there is really a grand march of intellect,—it proves that a mighty providence subdues the mightiest minds to the service of the time being, whether it be in human knowledge or religion."

Hawthorne was born in the lap of the American Revolution and was a proud citizen of the only country then able to describe itself as one it had itself newly created. It was officially secular. How was it possible for him to call slavery "one of those evils which divine Providence does not leave to be remedied by human contrivances"? Obviously he did not believe in "divine Providence." He was a pessimist and fatalist to the core. Religious intensity was so little to his taste that when the Civil War finally broke out, he wondered how God could handle so many opposing prayers from both North and South. To an English friend he wrote in 1863, "I have been publicly accused of treasonable sympathies,— whereas I sympathize with nobody and approve of nothing; and if I have any wishes on the subject, it is that New England might be a nation by itself."

Until war broke out and religious enthusiasm for the war pervaded many Northern soldiers as they marched to the "Battle Hymn of the Republic" (published in 1862), Northern churches left the "agitation" over slavery to troublemakers like William Lloyd Garrison, head of the American Anti-Slavery Society. By and large popular opinion was inert, when it was not hostile. The abolitionist editor Elijah Lovejoy began his fight against slavery in St. Louis as editor of a Presbyterian weekly. When he moved to Alton in Illinois to edit the abolitionist *Observer*, his printing press was destroyed several times and he was shot dead defending another press. Until the fugitive slave Anthony Burns was arrested in Boston and to the city's general fury led through the streets to be returned to his master in Virginia, slavery did not much trouble the elite conscience even in Boston. Henry Adams remembered that

> nothing quieted doubt so completely as the mental calm of the Unitarian clergy. . . . Doubts were waste of thought; nothing exacted solution. . . .
>
> Of all the conditions of his youth which afterwards puzzled the grown up man, this disappearance of religion puzzled him most. . . . He went through all the forms; but neither to him nor to his brothers was religion real. . . . The religious instinct had vanished, and could not be revived, although one made in later life many efforts to recover it. That the most powerful emotion of man, next to the sexual, should disappear, might be a personal defect of his own; but that the most intelligent society, led by the most intelligent clergy, in the most moral conditions he ever knew, should have solved all the problems of the universe so thoroughly as to have quite ceased making itself anxious about past or future, and should have persuaded itself that all the problems which had convulsed human thought from earliest recorded time, were not worth discussion, seemed to him the most curious social phenomenon he had to account for in a long life.

Emerson was the most famous, the most public literary figure in New England, but before the issue heated up in the fifties, what he thought of slavery and the Negro he confided to his private journal. And his God, unlike Thoreau's, was not on the slave's side. He first considered as "a declaration of heaven" the necessary subservience of the Negro. In 1822, at nineteen, he pronounced:

> I believe that nobody now regards the maxim "that all men are born equal," as any thing more than a convenient hypothesis or an extravagant declamation. . . . This inequality is an indication of the design of Providence that some should lead, and some should serve. . . . [T]he same pleasure and confidence which the dog and horse feel when they rely upon the superior intelligence of man is felt by the lower parts of our own species. . . .

I saw ten, twenty, a hundred large lipped, lowbrowed black men in the streets who, except in the mere matter of language, did not exceed the sagacity of the elephant. . . . Are not they an upper order of inferior animals . . . ?

If we pursue a revolting subject to its greatest lengths we should find . . . the advantage which they derive from our care; for the slaveholders violently assert, that their slaves are happier than the freedmen of their class; and the slaves refuse oftentimes the offer of their freedom.

By 1835 he was trying to bring his religious views to bear on the subject. "Let Christianity speak ever for the poor & low." His approach was theoretical. "If by opposing slavery I go to undermine institutions, I confess I do not wish to live in a nation where slavery exists. The life of this world has but a limited worth in my eyes & really is not worth such a price as the toleration of slavery." Two years later he made fun of his inaction when the temperance crusaders called. "Then a friend of the slave shows me the horrors of Southern slavery—I cry guilty guilty!" In 1841 "I told Garrison that I thought he must be a very young man or his time hang heavy on his hands to think much & talk much about the foibles of his neighbors, or *denounce* and play 'the son of thunder' as he called it. I am one who believe all times to be pretty much alike and yet I sympathize so keenly with this."

In this entry for October 1841 the keen sympathy with Garrison vanishes into his usual irritation with reformers. "We wish to take the gas which allows us to break through your wearisome proprieties, to plant the foot, to set the teeth, to fling abroad the arms, & dance and sing." To be antislavery was a duty, but Emerson was as removed from slavery and detached from its horrors as most of New England. The actual powerlessness of the Negro slave was lost in Emerson's usual pursuit of his self-liberation. One shudders at the thought of the following being read to a slave and even to a slave owner:

Nobody can oppress me but myself. Once more, the degradation of that black race, though now lost in the starless spaces of the past, did not come without sin. The condition is inevitable to the men they are, & nobody can redeem them but themselves. An infusion from God of new thought & grace can retrieve their loss, but nothing less. The exertions of the abolitionist are nugatory except for themselves.

It was typical of the times that Emerson as antislavery lecturer had in 1845 to refuse lecturing at the New Bedford Lyceum, which excluded Negroes. His cool stance is shown in his unexpected recognition of 1846 that slavery came down to private property. (A late twentieth-century conservative apologist for the South's sacred order, M. E. Bradford of Dallas, would argue that Lincoln violated the rights of private property in the Emancipation Proclamation.) Emerson was perfectly true to himself in all respects when he opposed slavery from his usual lofty perch. He just didn't know anything about it. But he certainly came to life when the fugitive law came in under the Compromise of 1850.

The South constantly accused the North of meddling in other people's affairs. Emerson in his journal:

> We are glad at last to get a clear case, one on which no shadow of doubt can hang. This is not meddling with other people's affairs—this is other people meddling with us. This is not going crusading after slaves who it is alleged are very happy & comfortable where they are: all that amiable argument falls to the ground, but defending a human being who has taken the risks of being shot or burned alive, or cast into the sea, or starved to death or suffocated in a wooden box—taken all this risk to get away from his driver & recover the rights of man. And this man the Statue says, you men of Massachusetts shall kidnap & send back again a thousand miles across the sea to the dog-hutch he fled from. And this filthy enactment was made in the 19th century, by people who could read & write.
>
> I will not obey it, by God.

The indifference and worse of the churches aroused him more than slavery ever did:

> I fear there is no reliance to be put on any kind of covenant, no, not on sacred forms, none on churches, none on bibles. For one would have said that a Christian would not keep slaves;—but the Christians keep slaves. . . . They quote the Bible, quote Paul, quote Christ, to justify slavery. If slavery is good, then so is lying, theft,

arson, homicide, each and all good, and to be maintained by the Union societies. . . .

Whenever a man has come to this mind, there is no Church for him but his believing prayer; no Constitution but his dealing well and justly with his neighbor.

Emerson once described himself as an abolitionist "of the most absolute abolition," but the "absolute" passion against slavery that was lived by Thoreau, Harriet Beecher Stowe, Garrison, Wendell Phillips, Theodore Weld, was never really to his taste. More of a realist on the subject than the others, he called Lincoln's election in 1860 "sublime" and recognized in the Civil War—as the impatient abolitionists urging immediate total emancipation without regard to political realities never did—the one tragic solution to the problem. Thoreau out of pacifism and Hawthorne out of indifference to the South's remaining in the Union were repelled by the war. In Emerson's enthusiasm for it— "gunpowder smells good"—one recognizes, along with his acceptance of the inevitable and necessary—the relief of the intellectual liberated from his books and papers.

By 1862, of course, he complained, "I find this Civil War abominably in my way, and, if peace comes again, I can still find blackbears enough in bad neighbors, failing resources, & ah & alas! the pathos of the house." Who but Emerson among American writers would have complained of "this Civil War" that it was "abominably in my way"? As always, his relation to God was strictly personal. But unlike the lesser Transcendentalists, who saw the war entirely in terms of sin and salvation, Emerson was a realist, and appreciated the liberating strength of the state he had once disparaged as a poor weak beast whose throat he could willingly cut. He regarded Lincoln most favorably when they met in 1862. He would have appreciated Lincoln's rejoinder to the New England clergymen who told him that God had ordered *them* to obtain immediate emancipation. Lincoln: "Don't you think, gentlemen, He might have spoken first to *me*?"

Only Thoreau among New England writers identified his life, and his looming early death, so wholly with the sacred liberation of the slaves as John Brown did. Of course Brown became Thoreau's saint, his idea of perfect holiness in action. Each in his religious arrogance impaled himself on a single idea, an exclusive view of life, that permitted no compromise with what the rest of the world might think. Each regarded himself beyond a shadow of doubt as infallible, the very image of God. Whitman in old age was still struck by Thoreau's "superciliousness." "He couldn't put his life into any other life—realize why one man was so and another man was not so. It was rather a surprise to me to meet in Thoreau such a very aggravated case of superciliousness."

Not among slaveholders defending slavery by quotations from Leviticus, not among abolitionists relying on the moral purity of their outrage, were there two men so driven to see the world confirm the promise of God's word. And Brown was an extreme Calvinist, certain that since everything was ordained and foretold, as "captain" of the "colony" he had established on the Osawatomie River in Kansas, he was there to carry out God's will.

Brown's last speech, November 2, 1859. Of course he began by lying and probably believed his lie. He was his own ideal persona. "I never did intend murder, or treason, or the destruction of property, or incite slaves to rebellion, or to make insurrection." The attack on the federal arsenal at Harpers Ferry was to be the first step in establishing a stronghold from which to advance the forcible liberty of slaves.

In Kansas, 1855, Brown, with four of his sons and two accomplices, murdered five reputedly proslavery settlers who lived along Pottawotamie Creek in order to cause a "restraining fear."

Brown gripped the imagination, then and now, because he interpreted his every act of violence as a righteous one. On Sunday night, October 16, 1859, at the head of twenty-one men (three were left as a rear guard in charge of arms and supplies), Brown had led the attack on the federal arsenal at Harpers Ferry. After initial success he soon lost the initiative, and by noon on Monday he and his men were surrounded by Virginia militia. On Tuesday morning U.S. marines, under the command of Colonel Robert E. Lee, battered down the doors of the engine-house in the armory yard and the fight was over.

Of Brown's original army of twenty-two men, ten were killed outright, seven (including Brown) were hanged, and five escaped. In jail, when asked, "Mr. Brown, who sent you here?" he replied, "No man sent me here; it was my own prompting and that of my Maker, or that of the Devil,—whichever you please to ascribe it to. I acknowledge no master in human form."

Brown, after being sentenced to death:

Now if it is deemed necessary that I should forfeit my life for the furtherance of the ends of justice and mingle my blood further with the blood of my children and with the blood of millions in this slave country whose rights are disregarded by wicked, cruel, and unjust enactments,—I submit so let it be done!

On the morning of his execution, December 2, 1859, Brown handed a guard the following statement: "I John Brown am now quite *certain* that the crimes of this *guilty* land *will* never be purged *away* but with Blood. I had *as I now think* vainly flattered myself that without *very* much bloodshed it might be done."

As Brown dropped, Colonel Robert E. Lee is supposed to have declared, "Thus perish all enemies of the human race!"

Hawthorne: Brown had "preposterously miscalculated the possibilities." Emerson, in a lecture entitled "Courage" in Boston, on November 8, 1859, had predicted that Brown's martyrdom "will make the gallows as glorious as the cross." In Salem, on January 6, 1860, he pronounced Brown

a fair specimen of the best stock of New England, having that force of thought and that sense of right which are the warp and woof of greatness.

Thus was formed a romantic character absolutely without any vulgar traits; living to ideal ends . . . abstemious, refusing luxuries . . . quiet and gentle as a child in the house. And as happens usually to men of romantic character, his fortunes were romantic.

Whitman, a New Yorker never particularly impassioned against slavery, was welcomed in Boston by the abolitionist Franklin Benjamin Sanborn when Longfellow, Lowell, and Holmes declined to meet him. Sanborn was New England agent for John Brown, and was arrested in April 1860 for refusing to testify before the U.S. Senate on Brown's intentions. Whitman, out of friendship to Sanborn, sat in the courtroom in his workman's outfit.

Melville, another New Yorker fairly aloof about slavery ("Who ain't a slave, tell me that!" Ishmael laughs in *Moby-Dick*), saw Brown not as a "martyr" but as "the meteor of the war." Among the poems, "imparted by the fall of Richmond," that went into *Battle-Pieces and Aspects of the War* (1866) was "The Portent" on the hanging of John Brown:

> *Hidden in the cap*
> *Is the anguish none can draw;*
> *So your future veils its face,*
> *Shenandoah!*
> *But the streaming beard is shown*
> *(Weird John Brown),*
> *The meteor of the war*

A civic leader in New York, George Templeton Strong, as prominent in the city as Melville emphatically was not after such failures as *Moby-Dick* (1851) and *Pierre* (1852), was oddly impressed by John Brown, though he believed Brown "justly hanged." In his now famous diary portraying the upper-class New York of his time, he said Brown's "simplicity and consistency, the absence of fuss, parade and bravado, the strength and clearness of his letters all indicate a depth of conviction that one did not expect in an Abolitionist (who is apt to be a mere talker and sophist). . . . Slavery has received no such blow in my time as his strangulation."

This was the worldly, the entirely secular view of a gentleman much respected in fashionable society. In Concord the self-exiled Thoreau, of whom it was rumored that he "lived in a swamp," was driven by John Brown's death to the horror and exaltation that can still attend thought of the cross.

Thoreau first met Brown in March 1857 when Brown visited Sanborn in Concord and took lunch with Thoreau at his home. After hearing Brown's farewell address in the Concord Town Hall before he departed for Virginia—Thoreau even made a small monetary contribution—he praised Brown: He "had the courage to face his country herself when she was in the wrong."

On hearing the news of Brown's arrest, Thoreau read "A Plea for Captain John Brown" in the Concord Town Hall on October 30. Emerson's son Edward, who heard him, said Thoreau delivered his speech as if it burned him. One can well believe it. As God finally disappears from the Bible, so Thoreau's kind of holy rage—God's day had come with John Brown, "an angel of light!"—disappeared with the end of slavery:

> Our foes are in our midst and all about us. There is hardly a house but is divided against itself, for our foe is the all but universal woodenness of both head and heart, the want of vitality in man, which is the effect of our vice; . . . We are mere figure-heads upon a hulk with livers in the place of hearts.

> A church that can never have done with excommunicating Christ while it exists!

> This most hypocritical and diabolical government looks up from its sea on the gasping four millions, and inquires with an assumption of innocence: "What do you assault me for? Am I not an honest man? Cease agitation on this subject, or I will make a slave of you, too, or else hang you."

> I am here to plead his cause with you. I plead not for his life, but for his character—his immortal life; and so it becomes your cause wholly, and is not his in the least. Some eighteen hundred years ago Christ was crucified; this morning, perchance, Captain Brown was hung. These are the two ends of a chain which is not without its links. He is not Old Brown any longer; he is an angel of light.

Thoreau as an opponent of slavery had only his ethic to offer. He knew no Negroes and had never experienced the slightest oppression. The idea that Walden was "a secret station for the underground railroad" was ludicrous; the pond was the worst place for a station in the town. Thoreau was a radical individualist as free as air. Up to the Fugitive Slave Act his only social antagonist was the disapproval, mockery, or indifference of his Concord neighbors. He never knew what the struggle of modern politics can mean for people who identify and associate with one another. He was a pure idealist living on principle, a man who in *Walden* proposed to teach others to be as free of society, sex, love, and marriage as himself.

"Civil Disobedience" is refreshing, and can still stir us by the urgency of its love of freedom. But it was the American state that finally, at the cost of almost a million lives, brought slavery to an end. It was not the kind of individual that Thoreau depended on to counter what he called "slavery in Massachusetts." He of all people could not grant that property is the greatest passion and the greatest cause of social conflict and wars. Yet he insisted "that if one thousand, if one hundred, if ten men whom I could name,—if ten *honest* men only,—aye, if *one* HONEST man, in this State of Massachusetts, *ceasing to hold slaves*, were actually to withdraw from this copartnership, and be locked up in the county jail therefor, it would be the abolition of slavery in America." This could have been said in the Gospels. It is "religion pure and undefiled," as John Brown liked to say; to which only he could have added, "Without the shedding of blood there is no remission of sins." Thoreau was so much against killing that he hoped his "prospective reader ignores Fort Sumter, and 'Old Abe' and all that, for that is just the most fatal, and indeed, the only fatal weapon you can direct against evil ever; for, as long as you *know of it*, you participate in the crime. What business have you, if you are an 'angel of light,' to be pondering over the deeds of darkness, reading the *New York Herald* and the like?"

Yes, he had deteriorated badly by then from lung disease, and in a year would be dead at forty-five. What is missing in his opposition to slavery, as in Brown's, is the presence of an actual, living, breathing slave. Harriet Beecher Stowe was to supply one in *Uncle Tom's Cabin*, and this, she claimed, not without the assistance of God.

She said that the book first came to her, as she was sitting in church, in a vision of Uncle Tom's violent death. This was also her protest against the Church, which in the North and South failed to condemn slavery as Christians should. In her "concluding remarks" to the novel (it was that kind of novel) she compared the courage of so many blacks in undertaking lives of their own with the failure of the Church to support them. "If this persecuted race, with every discouragement and disadvantage, have done thus much, how much more they might do, if the Christian church would act towards them in the spirit of her Lord!"

But she and the Church started from different premises. "This is an age of the world," she wrote confidently, "when nations are trembling and convulsed. A mighty influence is abroad, surging and heaving the world, as with an earthquake. And is America safe? Every nation that carries in its bosom great and unredressed justice has in it the elements of this last convulsion.

"For what is this mighty influence thus rousing in all nations and languages those groanings that cannot be uttered, for man's freedom and equality?

"O, Church of Christ, read the signs of the times! Is not this power the spirit of HIM whose kingdom is yet to come, and whose will to be done on earth as it is in Heaven?"

"The signs of the times" for Mrs. Stowe were humane and rhapsodically democratic, but for the Church it was business as usual, especially since there was so much business with the South. It recognized no "convulsion," no mighty stirring for a new equality between men, between the races, between men and women. "Agitation" over slavery threatened the evangelical movement. Even abolitionists among the Northern clergy like Mrs. Stowe's father, Lyman Beecher, became less interested in the slave as the "manifest destiny" of an entire continent to be settled heated up enthusiasm for bringing the word to the frontier.

Uncle Tom's Cabin, the biggest best-seller of the nineteenth century after the Bible, became a central event in American history by showing the slave as a human being in a family where everyone was frantically devoted to everyone else. As Toni Morrison pointed out in an interview, in *Conversations with American Writers*, the slave depended on love among his own, and could not survive without it.

It was the love things that were psychically very important. Nobody could have endured that life in constant rage. They would have all gone mad, and done what other cultures have done when they could not deal with the enemy. . . .

Some aspects of Christianity are very exclusive . . . tells you who can or can't be in, and what you have to do in order to be in. But the openness of being saved was one part of it—you were constantly being redeemed and reborn, and you couldn't fall too far, and couldn't ever fall completely and be totally thrown out. . . . Which is why the New Testament is so pertinent to black literature—the lamb, the victim, the vulnerable one who does die but nevertheless lives.

But in order to victimize the slave to the uttermost, the slaveholder had to deny the slave his humanity, just as the Nazis justified their slaughter of Jews by labeling them "subhuman." Emerson had said that the purpose of slavery was to turn the slave into a "monkey." Dr. Josiah C. Nott of Mobile was the leader of a small group who carried racism to the extreme position of denying that Negroes and whites belonged to the same species. While the Northern section of the Presbyterian Church admitted slavery was an evil that ought to be abolished, it added that slavery was not a sin to be punished by exclusion from communion of the saints. James Henley Thornwell from South Carolina, the leading provider of Christian sanctions for slavery, sternly told Northern Presbyterians "to get entirely quit of the subject." "The Presbyterian Church . . . [is] enabled by divine grace . . . to pursue a thoroughly scriptural policy in relation to this delicate question. It has planted itself upon the word of God and utterly refused to make slaveholding a sin or nonslaveholding a term of communion."

By concentrating on and fully dramatizing the routine breakup of black families under slavery—this beyond the usual abstract condemnation of slavery in itself—Harriet Stowe elevated the slaves in the minds of people who had despised them as supposed brutes or who were just indifferent to their fate. "Uncle Tom" was to be derided by later generations precisely because he was *real* in all his humility and helplessness as no black in American fiction had been before him. He was a great and loving character crucified for refusing to beat his fellow slaves. The book was so much *his* that it aroused the most passionate indignation throughout the world against the unrelenting cruelty of American slavery, the worst in the world. It became the first book written in English to be translated into such remote languages as Illyrian and Wallachian. The heartbreak of families casually separated by slave traders and owners under economic pressure inflamed the universal audience for the book, especially among women whose prime belief was the Christian sacredness of the family.

With one book, Mrs. Stowe became the conscience of her time for millions of Americans who had abominated other antislavery writers for disturbing the country to the point of civil war. Which she certainly was. As Lincoln said when she visited the White House, "This is the little lady who brought about the great big war." Appealing directly to the reader to share her tumultuous feelings of pity and outrage, writing as if in a trance (or so she claimed when in later life she testified, "I did not write it. God wrote it. I merely did His dictation"), the book solidified antislavery opinion in the ambivalent North and maddened the South.

The leading Southern apologists for slavery were so deeply embedded in the system (and proud of its economic advantages even when they did not share them) that attacks on slavery left them incredulous and reduced to angry bluster when they retaliated. But some reflective Southerners understood that Harriet Stowe in her religious radicalism was threatening not only slavery but the very idea of institutions. In the *Southern Literary Messenger* the writer George Frederick Holmes claimed that the book was not so much untrue as unreal. A "tissue of moral absolutes that if taken as a political philosophy could only lead to anarchy," for Mrs. Stowe seemed to believe that institutions marred by any imperfection whatever should be destroyed.

> It would demonstrate that all order, law, government, society was a flagrant and unjustifiable violation and mockery of the rights of man and ought to be abated as a public nuisance. . . . The fundamental position, then, of these dangerous and dirty little volumes is a deadly blow to all the interests and duties of humanity, and is utterly impotent to show any inherent vice in the institution of slavery which does not also appertain to all other existing institutions.

This of course was Edmund Burke's protest against the French Revolution, which by way of eliminating long-standing abuses destroyed the very fabric of a society that had tolerated revolutionary criticism and had kept revolutionaries from devouring one another. Though Holmes's attack on *Uncle Tom's Cabin* did not admit slavery involved any abuses, and was equally dishonest in supposing that slavery was an institution like any other (which may have been true in the antebellum South!), he understood that the book was not just an appeal to conscience but a celebration of the slave as a human being who longed for brotherhood. To avoid this as well as to grind him as labor was one reason why the South resisted emancipation at the cost of a civil war. To avoid this was equally important to the North, then and now. "I have a dream," said Martin Luther King, Jr., who dreamed of equal citizenship under the law and of official obedience to the law. The dream will never cease and never be fulfilled, for it contains the idea of that true equality in human relationships which for five centuries, ever since the first black slaves were deposited in Virginia in 1619, has been approached only through violence.

Still, this was Harriet Stowe's Christianity, which became clamorous as strictly her own, but was born of her involvement in her family and in the Christian consciousness of family. Born in 1811 in Connecticut, she was the seventh child and fourth daughter of Lyman Beecher, New England's most vociferous evangelical clergyman. All her brothers (the best remembered was the flamboyant Henry Ward Beecher) were clergymen; her sisters married clergymen; and she herself married an ordained minister, seminary professor, and polymath, Calvin Stowe, and was to bear six children. Harriet Stowe felt she needed to soften Lyman Beecher's hard-bottomed theology, while retaining the enthusiasm with which he propagated his gospel. His fellow Presbyterians in the North tolerated slavery in the South, while Presbyterians in the South defended it with gritted teeth. But the influence of a father who spoke in the voice of ancestral Calvinism which could still terrify a descendant of the first Puritans in New England was hard to shake off. She believed most intensely in a personal savior. The death by drowning in 1857 of her oldest son, Henry, was to cause Harriet terrible anxiety about the uncertain state of his soul before death.

Uncle Tom's Cabin is founded on a "religion of the heart": natural to what Alfred North Whitehead was to call "the century of hope"—hope because every day seemed to bring still another invention that would advance mankind by freeing it from deadening manual labor. Harriet Stowe was consumed by a personal, achingly assured emotional Christianity that might also be called a nineteenth-century invention: it was so particularly and immediately addressed to the healing, redeeming power that she felt, as a Christian woman, directly in touch with God. She believed that women generally were the more "feeling," more emotionally sensitive and generous half of the human race. *Uncle Tom's Cabin* owed its particular success in England to women who turned the book into a cause and eventually welcomed Harriet to England as their heroine.

Stowe's religion softened Calvinism's insistence on human depravity into an appeal not just to the goodness lurking under the harshness of society but to the great new message of the century: the awakened solidarity of the human race. There was no question in her mind that God heard this message. It was to be brought home by a novel, the most open and expansive literary form developed in the nineteenth century for alerting readers to the issues of the day.

So it did not matter to readers of *Uncle Tom's Cabin* any more than it would matter to readers of *Les Misérables*, *Oliver Twist*, and Dostoevsky's *Poor People* that Stowe's novel was diffuse in its organization and charged with intensity over slavery to the point of hysteria. Human liberation was in the air, spread by European writers from the most advanced literary cultures—Heine, Victor Hugo, Dickens, Tolstoy—who like millions of readers were aroused by this impassioned tract-novel from missionary America.

When Lyman Beecher in 1832 moved his tribe to Lane Theological Seminary in Cincinnati, he was more concerned with converting the frontier than with the slave system visible across the Ohio River in Kentucky. But getting this close to slavery moved his daughter away from belief in the self-declared uniqueness of Calvinism's Old Testament Father (who so much resembled bossy, excitable Lyman Beecher) and toward an exclamatory, flaming commitment to the Son as the suffering standard of her wholly personal religion. No one in history had ever suffered as Jesus had suffered for trying to restore moral order to tyrannized, forgotten people. So the black slave, suffering right under our indifferent and even hostile eyes, could never concede—must not be allowed to concede—that his suffering was of no account. While he had no rights that the government need respect and he was always under the feet of overseers who could kill him as easily as look at him, he had no one to appeal to but Jesus. And Jesus was nearer and closer than the Father-God; one could believe in Jesus and love Jesus as someone who had also lived on earth in peril of His life. But Jesus had transcended peril and fear through His overwhelming gift of love. So Stowe's Uncle Tom, the least of men in this society, loved Jesus back, loved and impersonated Him that, robbed of his wife and children, fated to be beaten to death for refusing to become "hard" toward Simon Legree's five other slaves, he became a figure of absolute good and left a message through his death. Like Jesus.

The full title is *Uncle Tom's Cabin; or, Life Among the Lowly*. The subject of the novel is not Négritude but what Latin Americans in the era of liberation theology called the religion of the oppressed. In "the century of hope" Heine, though scornful of the power of the majority in America, believed in "the liberation war of humanity." In both her preface and her "concluding remarks" Stowe emphasized the connection between slaves and the "lowly" of every race and condition. This was aimed at the Southern apologists for slavery, who claimed that slaves fortunate enough to be part of Christian society were "raised" from their initial barbarism; they rationalized the exploitation of the slaves on the grounds that, unlike "free" labor in the North, slaves were paternally cared for.

The "lowly" for Stowe represented the victims of economic masters everywhere, human beings so generally disregarded when they were not at work that they were invisible. Living in darkness not always their own, they became "black," like slaves in America. Color became the distinguishing mark of those who were simply not seen. Tolstoy called those he stumbled on in the worst slums of Moscow the "dark people."

This was the tone Mrs. Stowe brought to her book. The cause was not political but entirely religious; it did not admit the toleration of slavery in the South by which "Free-Soilers" like Lincoln, before he became president, thought to confine slavery and keep it from spreading to the West. By transforming public opinion so that many Americans eventually, no matter how unwillingly, came to accept emancipation as "righteous" and "just," *Uncle Tom's Cabin* showed the power of religious sentiment as no other American work of literature had done. Such feeling as there was for blacks among the elite (it did not survive the Civil War) was charged up by the zeal still strong in American Protestantism. For Stowe it was all the more charged up because of her faith in the coming democracy of the age, in Americans solidly brought up on the maxims of Christianity. She condemned the Church itself as a vain, self-enhancing institution that had forgotten the "heart."

The intensity of Stowe's argument for a broad people's Christianity, with the martyrdom of a black slave at its center which had first come to her sitting in church, was of course challenged, hated, and denied. Stowe's masterpiece has been so continuously mocked, travestied, and lampooned that in our day it is still difficult, especially among those who mistake Uncle Tom's religion for submission to slavery, to recognize the book's wild literary power.

Uncle Tom's Cabin was a sensation: on publication day in 1852 it sold three thousand; within the year there were 120 editions; over one and a half million copies were circulated in Great Britain and the colonies. It was quickly and crudely dramatized. There were eventually eight different theatrical versions, six of them produced even before the Civil War. Soon people who had never read the book routinely spoke of someone being an "Uncle Tom," or a "Simon Legree," snickered at the death of "Little Eva," laughed at Topsy as a minstrel-show "darkey."

The mature Henry James found the book too coarse, as one would expect. But in *A Small Boy and Others*, reminiscences of his early life in New York, he described with relish how

> one lived and moved at that time, with great intensity, in Mrs. Stowe's novel. . . . There was, however, for that triumphant work, no classified condition. . . . [I]t knew the large felicity fathering alike the small and the simple and the big and the wise, and had above all the extraordinary fortune of finding itself, for an immense number of people, much less a book than a state of vision, of feeling and consciousness, in which they didn't sit and read and appraise and pass the time, but walked and talked and laughed and cried. . . . Nothing in the guise of a written book, therefore a book printed, published, sold, bought and "noticed," probably ever reached its mark, the mark of exciting interest, without having at least groped for that goal as a book.

James as an old man in England was still amused by the play he had seen as a child. "The small boy could hear less the audible creak of carpentry as Eliza jumped from one floe to another" than "the sound of the water being pumped by a Mr. Crummles." And when Eva falls into the Mississippi and is rescued by Tom, both emerge "perfectly dry!" With such memories of the ridiculous play, no wonder that James in his 1874 essay on Turgenev made a point of saying that while *A Sportsman's Sketches* may have helped free the serfs (a dubious assertion), it was "much less a passionate *pièce de circonstance*" than a "disinterested work of art." "Turgenev did not produce an agitation, he presented the case with an art too insidious for instant recognition, an art that stirred the depths more than the surface."

This was a crack at *Uncle Tom's Cabin*, and in a sense set the tone (even for people who would never read Turgenev) when the book fell into disfavor and became something of a joke. The war was over, and many slaves had opted for freedom with their feet as the Confederacy fell apart. Post-1865 American realism, except for a novel as deep into race as *Huckleberry Finn* (and this by a former Confederate volunteer from a slaveholding family), was cool and careful on a subject that now required the most careful handling rather than moral outrage. There had been nothing like *Uncle Tom's Cabin*; her book, like Stowe herself, was an idiosyncrasy. Never again would one hear in a novel such pulsations as when Stowe put her desperate characters to the ultimate test of their virtue, courage, cruelty, and terror as husbands were torn from their wives, children from their parents. Under Reconstruction and after the founding of the Ku Klux Klan, when so many blacks were free only to be tenant farmers and when lynchings (when they were even reported) ran into the hundreds a year, what happened to the confidence Mrs. Stowe had expressed in her preface?

> Another and better day is dawning, every influence of literature, of poetry and of art, in our times, is becoming more and more in unison with the great master chord of Christianity, "good will to man."
>
> The hand of benevolence is everywhere stretched out, searching into abuses, righting wrongs, alleviating distresses, and bringing to the knowledge and sympathies of the world the lowly, the oppressed, and the forgotten.

The moment that Mrs. Stowe seized had passed and she could not go on with the same apostolic power to the next. Slavery had possessed her, and religion, in her frenetic, all-redeeming kind of Christianity, had provided the reason for condemning slavery absolutely. Whatever her differences with Garrison, she agreed that slavery was the ultimate sin. From sin followed every conceivable inhumanity. But as the Gospels had shown generation after generation, there is no drama like that of the suffering servant, the good and pure man *things are done to*, who is beaten to death like Uncle Tom. He is "Uncle," the custodial father figure who throws into relief the unjust world around him, which everyday sinners tolerate, join, and exploit.

The familiar objection to the novel is that Uncle Tom is too good, too simple, just as the slave traders are too beastly, Simon Legree too awful, Eva too saintly, Topsy too cute. It can be maintained that the only complex character in the book is Augustine St. Clare, who disdains the slave system that enables him to live with so much beauty and in supreme comfort. Married to an entirely selfish woman whom he despises, St. Clare has wearily learned to tolerate the conditions of his existence.

St. Clare, surviving by irony, is a character who can interest the modern reader, but his irony and complexity are not what matters in the book. When he is stabbed to death trying to break up a barroom fight, this is for the sake of the plot: Tom will now be sold Deep South and finished off. The importance of the supreme good in *Uncle Tom's Cabin* is that this is a novel not about character, not in any sense psychological, like most modern novels, but an impassioned narrative wrapped entirely around slavery as the ultimate evil—meaning total domination, victimization, and demonization practiced on human beings.

What is peculiar to slavery, and distinguishes it from free servitude, is evil, and only evil, and that continually. . . . The great object of the author in writing has been to bring this subject of slavery, as a moral and religious question, before the minds of all those who profess to be followers of Christ, in this country.

Alexis de Tocqueville, visiting America thirty years before the Civil War erupted—he had feared that the political hatreds created by slavery would culminate in war—was astonished by the equanimity, indifference, and moral carelessness with which Americans everywhere managed to live with slavery. How could these people not see the lie slavery gave to their professed democracy and that the violation threatened them as it brutalized the slave?

Oppression has, at one stroke, deprived the descendants of the Africans of almost all the privileges of humanity. The Negro of the United States has lost even the remembrance of his country; the language which his forefathers spoke is never heard around him; he abjured their religion and forgot their customs when he ceased to belong to Africa, without acquiring any claim to European privileges. But he remains halfway between the two communities, isolated between two races; sold by the one, repulsed by the other, finding not a spot in the universe to call by the name of country, except the faint image of a home which the shelter of his master's roof affords.

Of course Tocqueville, speaking too generally from his distant vantage point as a European Catholic aristocrat, was wrong to assume that "the Negro, plunged in this abyss of evils, scarcely feels his own calamitous situation. Violence made him a slave, and the habit of servitude gives him the thoughts and desires of a slave; he admires his tyrants more than he hates them, and finds his joy in the servile imitation of those who oppress him." This was for its time as doubtful as the claims for slave militancy made by leftist historians and then by the black nationalists who in the 1960s vehemently attacked William Styron's *Confessions of Nat Turner* because Styron's character was too complex to fit the political slogans of the moment.

Nevertheless, Tocqueville was right to fear the deep effects of slavery on its victims, and to predict that the freed slaves would be too weakened to overcome the racial fear and hatred that would become ever more virulent after emancipation in whatever form it came. Slavery would never leave the American mind. Slavery demanded total domination. And as twentieth-century totalitarianism even in defeat has shown, the experience of total domination can seem irrevocable to its victims. Nor does oppression elevate and purify the character. What baffles us and can provoke us now, when we encounter Mrs. Stowe's optimism at the end of her book about the emancipation that had to come, is her faith in a continuing Christianity all her own.

A day of grace is yet held out to us. Both North and South have been guilty before God; and the *Christian church* has a heavy account to answer. Not by combining together, to protect injustice and cruelty, and making a common capital of sin, is this Union to be saved,—but by repentance, justice and mercy, for, not surer is the eternal law by which the millstone sinks in the ocean, than that stronger law, by which injustice and cruelty shall bring on nations the wrath of Almighty God!

The question of God's possible wrath over slavery was raised in public by the rationalist and religious skeptic Abraham Lincoln. He had once declared, "I hate . . . the monstrous injustice of slavery . . . because it deprives our republican example of its just influence in the world." On his second inauguration as president, March 4, 1865, he went further and uttered a great public cry of willingness to accept a different vision:

> Fondly do we hope, fervently do we pray, that this mighty scourge of war may speedily pass away. Yet if God wills that it continue until all the wealth piled by the bondman's two hundred and fifty years of unrequited toil shall be sunk, and until every drop of blood drawn by the lash shall be paid by another drawn by the sword, as was said three thousand years ago, so still it must be said, "The judgments of the Lord are true and righteous altogether."

Still, Lincoln cautiously asked "*if* God wills"—a condemnation of slavery that would finally bring an end to it. Harriet Beecher Stowe had no possible doubts as to God's will. Her book claimed entire communion with His will and "wrath." No wonder she was able to convince millions that her book had the truth of Scripture. *Uncle Tom's Cabin* was New England's last holiness.

4

Melville in the Holy Land

Can you draw out Leviathan with a fishhook,
Or press down his tongue with a chord?
Can you put a rope in his nose,
Or pierce his jaw with a hook?
Will he make many supplications to you?
Will he speak to you soft words?
Will he make a covenant with you to take him for your servant for ever?
                                                              JOB 41:1–4

The divine darkness which is unveiled in the book of Job . . . the shat-
tering emotion which the unvarnished spectacle of divine savagery and
ruthlessness produces in me.

                                        CARL GUSTAV JUNG, *Answer to Job*

How can the prisoner reach outside except by thrusting through the wall?
                                                                    AHAB

O N   N O V E M B E R 20, 1856, the American consul in Liverpool, who
happened to be Nathaniel Hawthorne, noted in his journal that the
week before, Herman Melville had come to see him at the consulate and
that Melville "was looking much as he used to do (a little paler and perhaps a little sadder), in a rough outside coat, and with his characteristic
gravity and reserve of manner."

Describing Melville's visit he admitted:

I felt rather awkward at first; because this is the first time I have
met him since my ineffectual attempt to get him a consulate appointment from General Pierce. However, I failed only from real
lack of power to serve him; so there was no real reason to be
ashamed, and we soon found ourselves on pretty much our former
terms of sociability and confidence. Melville has not been well of
late; he has been affected with neuralgic complaints in his head and
limbs, and no doubt has suffered from his too constant literary oc-

cupation, pursued without much success, latterly; and his writings, for a long time past, have indicated a morbid state of mind. So he left his place at Pittsfield, and has established his wife and family, I believe, with his father-in-law in Boston, and is thus far on his way to Constantinople. I do not wonder that he found it necessary to take an airing through the world, after so many years of toilsome pen-labor and domestic life, following upon so wild and adventurous a youth as his was. I invited him to come and stay with us at Southport, as long as he might remain in this vicinity.

Hawthorne noted in wonder that Melville left his trunk at the consulate and departed for the East with barely one shirt. He was planning to end his tour in Palestine.

In 1883 Hawthorne's son Julian, who was writing a biography of his father, called on Melville "in a quiet side-street in New York, where he was living almost alone." Melville was "looking pale, somber, nervous, but little touched by age. . . . He conceived the highest admiration for my father's genius, and a deep affection for him personally." But "with a melancholy gesture, implying that the less said or preserved, the better," Melville admitted he had long since destroyed the letters Hawthorne had written in reply to the exultant letters to Hawthorne on the flood tide of *Moby-Dick*.

Melville's talk "was not in the improvisatorial style of the red-cottage days. . . . [H]e seemed depressed and aimless." Julian was referring to the high point of Melville's life, 1850–51, when Melville, signing himself "a Virginian spending July in Vermont," had written an ecstatic personal tribute to Hawthorne's *Mosses from an Old Manse*. He finally met his hero at a picnic near Pittsfield. Melville was living at "Arrowhead," a farmhouse down the road from Pittsfield, and beginning an adventure story about whaling he hoped would bring back the many readers who had relished *Typee* and *Omoo* at the beginning of his career.

The Hawthornes occupied a red cottage at Tanglewood, six miles down the road from Melville. Melville was so carried away by his meetings with Hawthorne that he let slip his descent from Scottish nobles; he was so mesmerizing in his talk that on one occasion, after Melville had departed, Sophia Hawthorne kept searching for a walking stick Melville had described. There was no walking stick.

Melville was transformed by reading, and then meeting, Hawthorne, whom he recognized as the only genius in the neighborhood. Hawthorne's very presence (along with Melville's astonished reading of Shakespeare) went far to transform *Moby-Dick* from the commercial whaling story he first took on. The book written "just to buy a little tobacco with," as he said of preceding works essentially autobiographical, *Redburn* and *White-Jacket*, turned into the world-storming, totally defiant, and prophetic masterpiece whose unconscious depth and wild humor obsess many of us in the twentieth century like no other American book.

Melville dedicated the book to Hawthorne "In Token of My Admiration for His Genius." We do not know what Hawthorne replied, but Hawthorne told others how deeply he admired the book and regretted the reviews. Writing his giant book in the vast room that looked out on Mount Greylock, Melville felt he was writing for another giant, Nathaniel Hawthorne. In the rapturous letters he was sending down to Tanglewood from Arrowhead, Melville was positively intoxicated by what in his essay "Hawthorne and His Mosses" he had earlier hailed as the "shock of recognition." "For genius, all over the world, stands hand in hand with genius, and one shock of recognition runs the whole circle round."

In these exuberant letters—the most intense I have ever encountered from one American writer to another—we see Melville at thirty-one and thirty-two trembling with love, gratitude, and sudden pride indistinguishable from one another. Hawthorne's uniqueness has led Melville positively to float on his own power. And this in a still provincial literary situation where the few significant writers seemed hardly aware of one another, allowing Melville to call Hawthorne and himself "God's posts around the world." Melville's letters to Hawthorne are all the more poignant in their overflow of emotions proud and beseeching because we know nothing of how Hawthorne (fifteen years older and of another temperament) responded to the younger man's excitement in discovering he had the genius to write *Moby-Dick*.

Melville surely destroyed Hawthorne's letters out of disappointment at their formality. Melville's own letters reach such a peak of ominously self-driven elation that it is clear why, in knowing Hawthorne and imagining a new *Moby-Dick*, Melville could not retain the same transcendence. The rest of his life, ending in the literary anonymity that led him defiantly to hide *Billy Budd* where it would not be found until the twentieth century, was anticlimax. The two great experiences of 1850–51 melted into one. This was the pattern of Melville's life, as had set in after the vogue of *Typee*—a peak to which there was no returning. The end was already in sight.

> July 1851—I am like one of those seeds taken out of the Egyptian Pyramids which, after being three thousand years a seed and nothing but a seed, being planted in English soil, it developed itself, grew to greenness, and then fell to mould. So I. Until I was twenty-five, I had no development at all. Three weeks have scarcely passed, at any time between then and now, that I have not unfolded within myself. But I feel that I am now come to the inmost leaf of the bulb, and that shortly the flower must fall to the mould.

You can see why Hawthorne—like Melville's own family—came to think of him as "morbid." After being derided for *Moby-Dick* ("so much trash belonging to the worst school of Bedlam literature"), insulted over *Pierre*, and after failing to interest his old public in *Israel Potter* and *The Piazza Tales*, Melville returned with family in 1866 to his birthplace, to earn his living as a deputy inspector of customs at the port of New York. His son Malcolm kept a pistol under his pillow and (perhaps accidentally) killed himself. His son Stanwix escaped to the West as an itinerant dentist. Members of the family thought Melville "crazy." His wife Elizabeth secretly arranged to leave Melville but remained with him out of compassion. His great-grandson Paul Metcalf, who of course never knew him, wrote, "This going mad of a friend or acquaintance comes straight home to everyman who feels his soul in him,—which but few men do." But "most personally, because of my relation to him, Melville was the monkey on my back . . . and I could never come to terms with myself until relieved of him." This in a book bitingly called *Genoa*, after another discoverer of new worlds who ended badly.

When Hawthorne praised *Moby-Dick*, Melville was uplifted as he would never in life be again.

Pittsfield, November 17(?), 1851:

A sense of unspeakable security is in me this moment, on account of your having understood the book. I have written a wicked book, and feel spotless as the lamb. . . . It is a strange feeling—no hopefulness is in it, no despair. Content—that is it; and irresponsibility; but without licentious inclination. I speak now of my profoundest sense of being, not of an incidental feeling.

Whence come you, Hawthorne? By what right do you drink from my flagon of life? And when I put it to my lips,—lo, they are yours & not mine. I feel that the Godhead is broken up like the bread at the Supper, and that we are the pieces. Hence this infinite fraternity of feeling.

A very different Melville sought out Hawthorne in Liverpool. Between 1853 and 1856 he had published fourteen tales and sketches in *Putnam's Monthly Magazine* and *Harper's Monthly Magazine*. Five of the tales were to come out in *The Piazza Tales*, containing the masterpieces "Benito Cereno," "Bartleby the Scrivener," and "The Encantadas, or Enchanted Isles." In 1855 he had expanded and reimagined the true story of a Revolutionary War soldier, Israel Potter, taken prisoner by the British and unable to get home. But when Melville turned up at the American consulate in 1856, he informed Hawthorne that he had "pretty much made up his mind to be annihilated." Hawthorne's journal for November 12, 1856, recounts a walk the two men took along the shore of the Irish Sea at Southport in Lancashire. This explains why Melville included the Holy Land on his itinerary of a trip to Greece and the Middle East financed by his father-in-law, Lemuel Shaw, chief justice of Massachusetts. Its purpose was to rest this much troubled man and restore his "mental balance."

Melville, as he always does, began to reason of Providence and futurity, and of everything that lies beyond human ken, and informed me that he had "pretty much made up his mind to be annihilated." But still he does not rest in that anticipation; and, I think, will never rest unless he gets hold of a definite belief. It is strange how he persists—and has persisted ever since I knew him, and probably long before—in wandering to and fro over these deserts, as dismal and monotonous as the sandhills amid which we were sitting. He can neither believe or be comfortable in his unbelief; and he is too honest and courageous not to try to do one or the other. If he were a religious man, he would be one of the most truly religious and reverential; he has a very high and noble nature, and better worth immortality than most of us.

And so to the Holy Land, for his "mental health." Why the Holy Land at this particular point, why the rotted Palestine run by derisive Turks just because his genius had outrun the literary market? Of course he was a famous voyager, in life as in books, and he was going to stop in Greece and Egypt, and in Italy on his way back. To ask the question is to overlook the spell of the Bible on a writer so studiously brought up in New York's Dutch Reformed Church that in the great book of his life he gave his characters Old Testament names and attributes, and filled it with over a thousand references to Scripture. God might be "dead"—a proposition that only a German minister's madly agnostic son would raise (laughing that the masses had not yet heard the news)—but for Melville the Bible was like his parents, and even replaced the father who had died when Melville was thirteen.

"Call me Ishmael" indeed. He was not the son of the promise, like Isaac to his father Abraham. He was the son of the bondwoman Hagar, sent out by Abraham's jealous wife Sarah into the wilderness. Where legend relates Ishmael became the founder of the black, the pariah people. And an archer, which is close enough to the wielder of harpoons. Hawthorne was fated to disappoint a Melville always the outcast in his genius and temperament—the eternal orphan, "Isolato" (a term he invented), castaway, desperado, wanderer, and ill-starred pilgrim. Out of nowhere Ishmael in *Moby-Dick* utters the cry that drove Melville to the Holy Land. "Where is the foundling's father hidden?"

The name Yishmael—"God listens, God hearkens."

He retained faith even if he did not always know what and where and whom to believe. An agony in the nineteenth century, wistful confession in the twentieth. The most haunting expression of this in *Moby-Dick* comes, appropriately enough, in the storm scene that brings the first lowering to capture a whale (Chapter 48) to near disaster:

> The rising sea forbade all attempts to bale out the boat. The oars were useless as propellers, performing now the office of life-preservers. So, cutting the lashing of the waterproof match-keg, after many failures Starbuck contrived to ignite the lamp in the lantern; then stretching it on a waif pole, handed it to Queequeg as the standard-bearer of this forlorn hope. There, then, he sat, holding up that imbecile candle in the heart of that almighty forlornness. There, then, he sat, the sign and symbol of a man without faith, hopelessly holding up hope in the midst of despair.

The man who wrote that—was he looking to the *landscape* of the Bible to bring out, to bring back, indomitable *words* in the Bible he had from childhood stored in his heart? Melville was not alone in his pilgrimage. Christians oddly energized by doubt—Gogol, Lamartine—went to Jerusalem, like so many English Protestants, to see, even to touch, what remained of the sacred places. And of course there were natural skeptics before Mark Twain, who looked at relics only to laugh at their supposed authenticity in *The Innocents Abroad* (1869). The future novelist of the Civil War John W. De Forest, visiting Palestine the year Melville did, noted in *Oriental Acquaintance; or, Letters from Syria* (1856) that the revered localities and traditions held "such an air of absurdity" that they excited "unbelief and irreverence rather than faith and devotion." The eruption of fisticuffs among the rival sects claiming authority over the Church of the Holy Sepulcher "was enough to encourage a Turk to remain a Turk."

There were already Christian Zionists in Palestine eager for the Jews to return. There, at last, they could be converted en masse. Melville was usually ironic about Jews, deplored the Jehovah Christians shared with Jews, and in Palestine could not overlook Christians too much interested in Jews. And if it had suddenly become necessary for Herman Melville to visit the Holy Land for the sake of his morale, his journals show that he was more than usually wrought up on the voyage.

After dutiful sightseeing in England, he sailed from Liverpool for Constantinople. He was not enraptured by his first sight of the isles of Greece. Feeling himself trapped in Constantinople's maze of streets, he showed signs of his old terror of being hemmed in that had been behind his old invocation of the sea and wide-ranging space. As Ahab says in his great harangue to the crew on the need to capture the white whale, "How can the prisoner reach outside except by thrusting through the wall?" So Bartleby the Scrivener reaches his low point by working before "high blank walls," in front of a screen, by tunneling himself within his employer's office. So Pierre Glendinning, thinking to escape in New York the shame of his father's sin clouding his country estate, barricades himself in a New York garret in order to write the masterpiece that will save him and his entourage. There Melville parodied his own self-enclosure, when he left Pittsfield to complete *Moby-Dick* in New York. He distrusted his native city, and associated it with his father's death, which ended his expected chances in life. New York represented a class from which he had been expelled. In "The Two Temples" he described the sexton who once chased him out of the newly built Grace Church on lower Broadway fit only for the respectable.

This habitual fear of confinement could become threatening in the Near East. Here the God who escaped you everywhere else suddenly closed in on you. Like another great beast, "the greatest animated mass since the Flood," with the terrible divinity born of nothing but his greater power. No wonder you wanted to be attached to him, if only to kill him out of awe. Melville's hurried stream-of-consciousness travel journals anticipate Leopold Bloom's reverie in *Ulysses* over the ancient land the Jews departed. In a pork butcher's shop he picks up a flyer urging the purchase of land in Palestine. Printed—another sly touch—in Bleibtreustrasse, Berlin. A planter's company is selling shares with which to buy sandy tracts from the Turkish government and plant eucalyptus trees. "Excellent for shade, fuel and construction. Orange groves and immense melon fields north of Jaffa. You pay eight marks and they plant a dunam of land for you with olives, almonds or citrons. . . . [E]very year you get a sending of the crop."

Leopold, "gravely" reading the flyer, pictures to himself "a barren land, bare waste. Volcanic lake, the dead: no fish, weedless, sunk deep in the earth. No wind would lift those waves, grey metal, poisonous foggy waters. Brimstone they called it raining down: the cities of the plain, Sodom, Gomorrah, Edom. All dead names. A dead sea in a dead land, grey and old. Old now."

And with similar images here is Melville in Egypt, January 1, 1857, as on his way to Palestine he dazedly gets down his impressions of the Pyramids—some of them frightening.

> Pyramids from distance purple like mountains. Seem high and pointed, but flatten & depress as you approach. Vapors below summits. Kites sweeping & soaring around, hovering right over apex. At angles, like broken cliffs. . . . Precipice on precipice, cliff on cliff. Nothing in nature gives such an idea of vastness. . . . Old man with the spirits of youth—long looked for this chance—tried the ascent . . . too much for him; oppressed by the massiveness and mystery of the pyramids. I myself too. A feeling of awe & terror came over me. Dread of the Arabs. Offering to lead me into a side-hole. The Dust. Long arched way,—then down as in a coal shaft. At one moment seeming in the Mammoth Cave. Subterranean gorges, &c. Then as in mines, under the sea. The stooping & doubling. It was in these pyramids that was conceived the idea of Jehovah. Terrible mixture of the cunning and awful. Moses learned in all the lore of the Egyptians. The idea of Jehovah born here.

If Melville's journal astonishingly resembles Leopold Bloom's journey into his innermost consciousness, Melville's own deepest impressions and convictions, while those of another perennial outsider, are not affable. Only five years separate the awestruck visitor to the Pyramids from the sailor who alone on the *Pequod* recognized in the "whiteness of the whale" that "though in many of its aspects this visible world seems formed in love, the invisible spheres were formed in fright." That is Melville, all right, the all-freezing nihilist behind the frantic seeker of the God he lost. "Love" is for Melville never the point. His contemporaries made nothing of the "Whiteness of the Whale" chapter. But that is Melville at his deepest, his most intrepid, as he faces his central fear—the meaninglessness of it all. Just reading Hawthorne's *Mosses*, he pounced on the "blackness" in them, celebrated this because it was really his own. "For spite of all the Indian-summer sunlight on the hither side of Hawthorne's soul, the other side—like the dark half of the physical sphere—is shrouded in blackness, ten times black."

Even at thirty, writing "The Whiteness of the Whale," Melville saw the universe in uniform color. What was "blackness" in Hawthorne became frightening "whiteness" everywhere, starting with the whale. It was the unyielding uniformity that counted, not the color. In its meaning, which was the lack of meaning, the world was solid, all the same. Melville's favorite thesis—*appearances* are the great lie. "Yet for all these accumulated associations, with whatever is sweet, and honorable, and sublime, there yet lurks an elusive something in the innermost idea of this hue, which strikes more of panic to the soul than that redness which affrights in blood."

There is a jaunty, defiantly lower-class humor as *Moby-Dick* opens that verges onto farce at the expense of Quaker whalers bloodying all the world's seas in their pursuit and butchering of whales. But the farce also consists in the sheer incongruity of the battle scenes between man and the sea, man and the whale, the crew of the *Pequod* and torrentially "mad" Captain Ahab. Nothing could be more farcical than the solemnity with which the earthlings pursue and hack away at the whale while Ahab, obviously owing more to Shakespeare's "bold and nervous lofty language" than to his employers, noisily hammers the quarterdeck on his wooden leg keeping the fo'c'sle from sleep.

Farce is catastrophe without a context and without a solution. *Moby-Dick* so often trembles on the verge of farce—that multicultural crew, the Parsee and fellow zombies, suddenly appearing on deck just to make sure that Ahab hid them for a reason—that one understands why Conrad thought there was "not a sincere line" in the book. Actually, the book is all too "sincere," expressing as it does Melville's epic contradictions as artist and believer and Ishmael's affecting eloquence. This situation is primitive, the language that of the noblest epic. In the heartrending scene of "The Castaway" (Chapter 93), Pip, the poor little Negro cabin boy, repeatedly jumps out of the boat, forcing Stubb, the second mate, finally to leave him adrift. The style is now sharpest in its despair, taking us where no one wants to go.

> The intense concentration of self in the middle of such a heartless immensity, my God! who can tell it? . . . By the merest chance the ship itself at last rescued him; but from that hour the little negro went about the deck an idiot; such, at least, they said he was. The sea had jeeringly kept his finite body up, but drowned the infinite of his soul. Not drowned entirely, though. Rather carried down

alive to wondrous depths, where strange shapes of the unwarped primal world glided to and fro before his passive eyes; and the miser-merman, Wisdom, revealed his hoarded heaps . . . among the joyous, heartless, ever-juvenile eternities.

Melville said of his book to the Hawthornes, "It is not a piece of fine feminine Spitalfields silk—but it is of the horrible texture of a fabric that should be woven of ships' cables & hawsers. A Poland wind blows through it, & birds of prey hover over it." In the struggle between man's effort to find meaning in nature, against the indifference of nature itself, which always eludes him—and this in a world suddenly emptied of God, one where an "intangible malignity" has reigned from the beginning—Melville's ultimate strangeness is to portray the struggle from the side of nature itself. In the ultimate scenes of "the chase" he sees the whale's views of things far more than he does Ahab's. Moby-Dick's milk-white head, the tail feathers of the seabirds streaming from his back like pennons, are described with a rapture that is the adoration of a god. Even in the terrible scene of the shark massacre, where the sharks bend around like bows to bite at their own entrails, or in the ceaseless motion of "my dear Pacific," "the Potters fields of all four continents," I feel that Melville is transported by the naked reality of things, the great unending flow of the creation itself, where the great shroud of the sea rolls over the doomed *Pequod* "as it rolled five thousand years ago."

The American who imagined all that was not one of the diligent Victorian tourists who kept an item-by-item list of their pious itinerary. They had their reward, as the Bible says; no doubt had reassuring news to bring home. Not so Melville, who always wrote in a hurry, never more so than when he was pursuing his own hit-and-miss travel plans in the Holy Land. With his bad eyesight, his handwriting was often near illegible. (The first complete and accurate version of his journal, edited by Howard C. Horsford with Lynn Horth, Northwestern University Press, was published in 1989.) There were sudden panics and a sense of homelessness as he remembered, in sight of the barrenness that everywhere surrounded him, his literary and domestic failures back home. Beginning with the section on Constantinople, where Melville describes his entanglement in the maze of streets, and going on to his bitterness at

the desolation of Jerusalem in 1856–57, he found the road to the Dead
Sea, and other scriptural places contributed nothing of the spiritual uplift he may have hoped for.

We see Melville the consummate artist of travel brilliantly searching
the depths of negation. No American writer had put so much of the
world into novels of personal experience. Charles Olson saw him "riding on space." Now he is in the land his religious training has pursued
since childhood. But he is there at the lowest point of his career—and
seeking something he no longer knows how to ask for. He writes in sour
bursts, often in extreme personal chagrin, discharging his clotted impressions in a fever of travel excitement. The disappointment is as
much with himself as with the fabled land itself.

Melville's mind naturally dwelt in contraries; he approached everything as a stranger, Ishmael wandering in from another mental world
expecting to oppose what he saw. Now the holiest of holy places for
Christian and Jew—to which he brought his own lovelessness—seems
as abandoned as he himself. Jerusalem once seemed the center and
"navel" of the world. Now it is another of those end-of-the-world
places Melville knew from rounding Cape Horn in a storm, Tierra del
Fuego, the Galápagos, the "starry isles" he described in the "Pacific"
chapter of *Moby-Dick* as "Asiatic lands older than Abraham."

The Holy Land is just old, horribly old. Remembering every name
and place, Melville cannot confess his terror of the Pyramids—"Pyramids still loom before me—something vast, indefinite, incomprehensible, and awful"—without adding, "These the steps Jacob lay at."

> Line of desert & verdure. Plains as line between good and evil. An
> instant collision of the two elements. A long billow of desert for-
> ever hovers as in an act of breaking, upon the verdure of Egypt.
> Grass near the pyramids, but will not touch them—as if in fear or
> awe of them. Desert more fearful to look at than the ocean.

The man is haunted. In the presence of the desert, "more fearful to
look at than the ocean," he experiences what Kierkegaard, justifying
God's command to Abraham to kill his beloved son Isaac, called "fear
and trembling." No sales pitch here for your friendly house of worship.
We cry with Job, "Have pity upon me! Have pity upon me! O ye my
friends, for the hand of God hath touched me." And in a way as re-

moved from Jehovah's personal declamation of the Law to the Israelites as it is from Jesus praying to His Father to do His will on earth as He does in Heaven, Melville seems to feel *nothing* but the residual power of the ancient Deity. (This was the man who saw divinity in the terrible mass of the white whale.) He is fascinated and appalled by this, and recoils from the ability of the Jews to leave so many traces of *their* divinity in a desert whose barrenness still evokes Jehovah.

A hundred impressions hit Melville at once. And he is alone with it all, complaining, on January 22, 1857, "I am the only traveller sojourning in Joppa. I am emphatically alone, & begin to feel like Jonah." Laughs at a Mr. and Mrs. Saunders, American missionaries outside the walls. "Might as well to convert bricks into bride-cake as the Orientals into Christians. It is against the will of God that the East should be Christianized."

Then his most inflamed entry, recounting the passage from Jerusalem to the Dead Sea. Everything exhausted and sterile he sees en route brings home his sense of failure and abandonment.

> Where Kedron opens into plain of Jericho looks like Gate of Hell. . . . Thunder in mountains of Moab—Lightning—cry of jackal and wolf—Broke up camp—Rain—rode out on mouldy plain—nought grows but wiry, prickly bush.

> Ride over mouldy plain to Dead Sea—Mountains on other side—Lake George—all but verdure—foam on beach & pebbles like slaver of mad dog—smarting bitter of the water—carried the bitter in my mouth all day—bitterness of life—thought of all bitter things—Bitter is it to be poor & bitter, to be reviled & Oh bitter are these waters of death, thought I—Rainbow over the Dead Sea—heaven, after all, has no malice against it—Old boughs tossed up by water—relics of pick-nick—nought to eat but bitumen & ashes with desert [*sic*] of Sodom apples washed down with water of Dead Sea. Must bring your own provisions, as well, too, for mind as body—for all is barren. Drank of brook but brackish—Ascended among the mountains again—barren.

Melville goes on, under the heading "Barrenness of Judea," to put together as its dominant elements "the whitish bleached mildew pervading whole traces of landscape, leprosy, encrustation of curses—old cheese—bones of rocks, crushed, knawled & mumbled—mere refuse and rubbish of creation like that laying outside of Jaffa Gate—all Judea seems to have been encrustations of this rubbish."

The significant phrase, playing on the unleavened bread the Israelites hurriedly took to their Exodus: "the unleavened bread of desolation." As he goes on and on in an ecstasy of disgust—plains with snails, "tracks of slime, all over, shut in by ashy hills"—you feel that Melville has indeed made up his mind "to be annihilated." And things don't get brighter when he notes, "pressing forward to save the rain," that seeing Jerusalem from a distance, "unless knew it, could not have recognized it—looked exactly like arid rocks."

"Jerusalem January 1857—a Village of Lepers, their houses facing the wall, their park a dung-heap. They sit by the gates asking alms —their whine—avoidance of them & horror." Even the old names— Jehoshaphat (supposedly the very spot where the dead would arise!) or Hinnom—seem to him "ghostly." He complains of wandering among tombs "till I begin to think myself one of the possessed with devels [*sic*]. The Church of the Holy Sepulcher amounts to broken dome, dingy, queer smell."

He bursts out: "The mind can not but be sadly & suggestively affected with the indifference of Nature & Man to all that makes the spot sacred to the Christian. Weeds grow upon Mount Zion; side by side in impartial equality appear the shadows of church & mosque, and on Olivet every morning the sun indifferently ascends over the Chapel of the Ascension."

"Indifference" was a quality in nature—it distinguished the gods— that stuck in his throat. "Oh! Ahab," cried Starbuck, "not too late is it, even now, the third day, to desist. See! Moby Dick seeks thee not. It is thou, thou that madly seekest him!"

Here and there were strange personages all too easy to meet in the emptiness of the Holy Land. Some were to go into the long dramatic poem *Clarel* he worked up from his journal. "Warder Crisson of Philadelphia—an American turned Jew—divorced from his former wife— married a Jewess here. Sad." An old Connecticut man wandering about with tracts: "knew not the language—hopelessness of it—his lonely batchelor [*sic*] rooms—he maintained that the expression Oh Jerusalem!, was an argument proving that Jerusalem, was a bye-word, etc."

Melville says "Jew" contemptuously. He is terrified of Jewish theology, which he ascribes to the "diabolical landscapes" of a great part of Judea. He is stunned by the Valley of Jehoshaphat, but even in his revulsion describes it with his old genius. "Jew graves lie as if indiscriminately flung abroad by a blast in a quarry. So thick, a warren of the dead—so old, the Hebrew inscriptions can hardly be distinguished from the wrinkles formed by Time." Half-mockingly, he wonders why the Jews cling to their ancient shrines: "Is the desolation of the land the result of the fatal embrace of the Deity? Hapless are the favorites of heaven." Then crushingly (Melville and the Deity had yet to "embrace" each other): "In the emptiness of the lifelong antiquity of Jerusalem the emigrant Jews are like flies that have taken up their abode in a skull."

The Holy Sepulcher fares no better:

terraces of mouldy grottos, tomb, & shrines. Smells like a deadhouse, dingy light.—At the entrance, in a sort of grotto in the wall a divan for Turkish policemen, where they sit crosslegged & smoking, scornfully observing the continuous troops of pilgrims entering & prostrating themselves before the anointing-stone of Christ, which veined with streaks of a mouldy red looks like a butcher's slab. Nearby is a blind stair of worn marble, ascending to the reputed Calvary where among other things the showman points you by the smoky light of old pawnbrokers lamps of dirty gold, the hole in which the cross was fixed and through a narrow grating as over a cole-cellar [*sic*], point out the rent in the rock!

So he acidly goes on. "The color of the whole city is grey & looks at you like a cold grey eye in a cold old man. The city is besieged by an army of the dead." But you see from his growing interest in pilgrims, tourists, and wayfarers that he is leaving behind his personal travail in the Holy Land and coming to think of other people there as characters like himself, ultimately seeking the meaning of their lives in *the* place, like no other.

Melville's *Clarel*, "A Poem and Pilgrimage in the Holy Land," was privately published (at his uncle Peter Gansevoort's expense) twenty years after he left Palestine. In those twenty years he had come to live with his worldly failure as an author, to think of the catastrophe that ends *Moby-Dick* as second nature. "He certainly is much overshadowed since I saw him last," Hawthorne had observed of Melville in Liverpool. In his unloved New York and with his family often dubious about his sanity, he was now earning $1,500 a year as a United States customs inspector of cargoes at Hudson River piers. In the "nerve-shredded evenings" at East Twenty-sixth Street after his day's work he was writing *Clarel.* "Go mad I can not: I maintain / The perilous outpost of the sane." Elizabeth Melville wrote to her mother, "Pray do not mention to *any one* that Herman has taken to writing poetry—you know how such things spread."

Melville had often introduced poetry into his prose. *Mardi* is full of irregular rhapsodies. Whenever Ishmael is alone with his own thoughts, *Moby-Dick* rises to lyric heights. *Billy Budd* concludes with a wonderful poem, "Billy in the Darbies," which presents Billy the night before his hanging serenely meditating on his end in the lightest, most affable tone. In 1866 Melville had published poems on the war "impelled by the fall of Richmond," *Battle-Pieces and Aspects of the War.*

Melville did not write poetry so much as he practiced it. For *Clarel* he had chosen a crabbed iambic tetrameter in varying rhymes and a diction distinctly archaic. After writing without thought of publication his 1856–57 journal, a tormented stream-of-consciousness monologue presenting his solitary struggle with the land of faith, he now, in a poem of 150 cantos, longer than most long poems, benevolently relapsed into a Victorian poet intellectually beset by the ever-sacred land and trying to get over the crisis produced by Darwinism and modern science. An archaic form and diction for a contemporary dilemma!

Somehow it works, by fits and starts, thanks to Melville's skill at enveloping us in constant dialogue as he sets the stage for each person's inquiry of the other. In the journal the traditional fixtures of Christianity looked dead or dying. In *Clarel,* working around the young pilgrim with characters some of whom are monomaniacs in their zealous certainty, Melville revived for a fictional journey of ten days *The Canterbury Tales* in nineteenth-century Palestine. Minus the freshness, ribaldry, and gusto that came with medieval certainty. *Clarel* vocalizes in dialectic all the residual certainties and uncertainties possible to men making their way past sacred surroundings.

Clarel could have been written only by a pilgrim who, though a "truly religious man," as Hawthorne described him, "can neither believe nor disbelieve." He was now trying to reason out his conflict by assigning the different sides to characters who exist only to debate one another. With them thought is truly caged not only by the metric but by the message available to each. Each has come to the Holy Land alone; each is a particular text revealing the divergence of his thought. Since they are such authorities to themselves, in character as in conviction, Clarel the confused young theology student turns to each of them in turn. Even his love for the young "Jewish" Ruth is a seeking of her authenticity, and when he returns from his journey to the Wilderness, the monastery at Mar Saba and Bethlehem, to come upon her interment, her death confirms that he is truly alone without a settled position to rest on, but can accept the Cross as the pain everyone finally lives with.

We first see Clarel brooding alone "in chamber low and scored by time / . . . Much like a tomb new cut in stone." He pauses from pacing up and down to ask,

> *Other cheer*
> *Than that anticipated here,*
> *By me the learner, now I find.*
> *Theology, art thou so blind?*
> *What means this naturalistic knell*
> *In lieu of Shiloh's oracle*
> *Which here should murmur? Snatched from grace*
> *And waylaid in the holy place!*

Clarel is open to everyone he meets, even his landlord, "the Black Jew," Abdon the hostel owner, who represents the Jew returned to Palestine, after long, strange exile. "From Ind to Zion have I come." By moonlight Clarel sees Olivet, the Mount of Olives, and typically tries to convince himself that Jesus did, yes, trod "the ideal upland."

The Sepulcher inspires distrust.

> *But little here moves hearts of some;*
> *Rather repugnance grave, or scorn*
> *Or cynicism, to mark the dome*
> *Beset in court or yard forlorn*

> *By pedlars versed*
> *in wonted trick*
> *Venders of charm or crucifix.*

Unlike Clarel, many in the courtyard "are unvexed by Europe's doubt." Which asks, "And can the Father be?" But Clarel, who is emotionally sensitive to the Gospel story that has entangled him in doubt, before the Sepulcher imagines the three Marys returning from Golgotha: "O empty room, / O leaden heaviness of doom." He encounters Nehemiah, a converted Jew from Rhode Island turned missionary and forever passing out tracts, who for forty years, like the Israelites in the desert, has worn the same garment. The Roman hunchback Celio wears "Absalom's locks but Esop's hump."

> *This world clean fails me; still I yearn.*
> *Me then it surely does concern*
> *Some other world to find. But where?*
> *In creed? I do not find it there.*

Amid "demoniacs in view," Celio broods on the Arch of Titus in Rome, which portrays the imperial legions after the fall of Jerusalem carrying off the menorah and other religious objects sacred to the Jews.

> *He is beset by the past.*
> *The Past is half of time,*
> *The proven half.—Thou Pantheon old*
> *Two thousand years have round thee rolled*

(virtually the imagery Melville used for the drowning of the *Pequod*).

There are hesitations and crudities in the verse line which at intervals make *Clarel* as baffling as a cathedral explored by flashlight. But when it comes to his more temperamental characters, Melville rises to the occasion. Celio is by turns impatient, enraptured, furious at the delayed—unfulfilled?—promise incarnate in Christ.

> *Nature and thee in vain we search;*
> *Well urged the Jews within the porch—"How long wilt make us*
>   *still to doubt?"*
> *How long?—Tis eighteen cycles now—*

> *Enigma and evasion grow;*
> *And shall we never find Thee out?*

This could be the Grand Inquisitor in *The Brothers Karamazov* berating Christ when He suddenly appears at an auto-da-fé. But these are minor characters beside Melville's self-portrait as Rolfe and his portrait of Hawthorne as Vine. Derwent the complacent Anglican cleric, Margoth the Jewish geologist in whom Melville locates the current heresy of scientific materialism, Mortmain the Swede who served as revolutionary leader in Paris—these pale beside the "geniuses" Rolfe and Vine and the still militant Confederate veteran Ungar, scornful of the tyrannical future.

Vine: Melville's obsession with the Hawthorne who, admiring as he was, was too private, somehow always eluded Melville's passion! Vine is "the Recluse," "a fountain sealed."

> *Ere yet they win that verge and line,*
> *Reveal the stranger. Name him—Vine.*
> *His home to tell—kin, tribe, estate—*
> *Would naught avail . . . No trace*
> *Of passion's soil or lucre's stain,*
> *Though life was now half-ferried o'er*
> *. . . A charm of subtle virtue shed*
> *A personal influence coveted,*
> *Whose source is difficult to tell . . .*
> *A saint do we here unfold? Nay, . . . Flesh, but scarce pride,*
> *Was curbed . . .*
> *But less indeed by moral sway*
> *Than doubt if happiness through clay*
> *Be reachable.*

And what is he doing in the Holy Land? As in life, to be the supreme observer—who here, among so many crazies, can be benevolent, though, as Melville would have said, for reasons incommunicable. Rolfe, to whom Melville has given so many of his experiences as a sea-wanderer, is paired with Vine as "Peers, peers—yes, needs that these must pair." That is Clarel speaking, who soon learns that Vine is not for the asking.

> *So pure, so virginal in shrine*
> *Of true unworldliness looked Vine.*
> *Ah, clear sweet ether of the soul*
> *(Mused Clarel), holding him in view.*
> *Prior advances unreturned*
> *Not here he recked of, while he yearned—*
> *O, now but for communion true*
> *And close; let go each alien theme;*
> *Give me thyself!*

What I carry away most from *Clarel*, for all the wonderful travel atmosphere, is that even among so many appeals to "love" and "faith," there is no "communion true" and no fulfillment for those "seeking" it here. Those who already had faith may always have it. The past holiness of the land does nothing for those who bring nothing but their uncertainty. There is no magic in relics. Melville by the end affirms nothing but the Cross as the pain we must carry. Not even America's vaunted democracy escapes his sense of original sin as Ungar scorns the future:

> *Hypothesize:*
> *If be a people which began*
> *Without impediment, or let*
> *From any ruling which foreran;*
> *Even striving all things to forget*
> *But his—the excellence of man*
> *Left to himself, his natural bent,*
> *His own devices and intent;*
> *And if, in satire of the heaven,*
> *A world, a new world have been given*
> *For stage whereon to deploy the event;*
> *If such a people be—well, well,*
> *One hears the kettle-drums of hell!*

What is clearest in *Clarel*, as in all reports from the Holy Land through the ages, is the monomania that often attaches itself to religious sites. Israeli psychiatrists report case after case of tourists who suddenly believe that they are, among many others, John the Baptist or Mary Magdalene. Zealots on both sides of the Arab-Israeli conflict "know" that *they* are "the people of God." The great Victorian traveller and Arabist Charles M. Doughty likened Semites to people "sitting in a cloaca up to their eyes but with their brows touching Heaven." T. E. Lawrence said of his experience in the desert, "The Semite can be stretched on an idea as on a chord."

5

Walt Whitman: I Am the Man

You have waited, you always wait, you dumb, beautiful ministers,
We receive you with free sense at last, and are insatiate henceforward.
WHITMAN, *"Crossing Brooklyn Ferry"*

The priest departs, the divine literatus comes.
WHITMAN, *Democratic Vistas*

WHEN WALT WHITMAN, age thirty-six, a former "jour-printer," delivered himself of "Song of Myself" (1855)—of course no other date would do for this but the Fourth of July—only he knew that American individualism, American strut and brag, American egocentricity, American triumphalism in all departments, had just found in him their most extreme and shameless expression.

Although there was no author's name on the cover, deep in the poem the author described himself as "Walt Whitman, an American, one of the roughs, a kosmos." The book opened on a portrait of the author. Who else?

Those who have had access to the original edition report that this was an engraved daguerreotype of a bearded man in his middle thirties. He is slouching under a wide-brimmed and high-crowned black felt hat that has "a rakish kind of slant," the engraver said later, "like the mast of a schooner." "His right hand," Malcolm Cowley reported, "is resting nonchalantly on his hip; the left is hidden in the pocket of his coarse-woven trousers. He wears no coat or waist-coat, and his shirt is thrown wide open at the collar to reveal a burly neck and the top of what seems to be a red-flannel undershirt. It is the portrait of a devil-may-care American workingman, one who might be taken as a somewhat idealized figure in almost any crowd."

There was also a long, madly assertive preface, announcing the on-coming presence of a great native poetry that would be equal to the sig-

nificance of the United States in history. It is so rhapsodic that William
Everson has arranged it as verse, which does not keep it from being a series of inflamed declarations. There is no need to look for a coherent argument. The voice is everything here, and nothing like that voice had
been heard before in American poetry. Whitman was replaying the na-
tionalist orations he had been giving as a radical Democrat in Brooklyn:

> The Americans of all nations at any time upon the earth have
> probably the fullest poetical nature. The United States themselves
> are essentially the greatest poem. In the history of the earth hith-
> erto the largest and most stirring appear tame and orderly to their
> ampler largeness and stir. Here at last is something in the doings of
> man that corresponds with the broadcast doings of the day and
> night.

The tone of the preface is pitched very high. It makes many claims
(and rhapsodically repeats them) line after line about the greatness of
the United States and the hovering greatness of the poetry that is natural to such a creation as the United States. To be rhapsodic in this defiant voice the writer has clearly had to gather himself together as he
never has before. He is plainly determined to force something on the
reader—and it's not just these "states," or the "common people," or the
promise that "the American poets are to enclose old and new." Whitman
celebrates himself as an individual personifying all he sees and honors,
from the common street life to the incipient poets entwined with the
country that has made it all possible. To write on such a scale and in
such a voice is to thrust oneself upon the world. He is "one of the
roughs, a kosmos." He is like nothing and no one else.

"Of all mankind the great poet is the equable man." One doesn't argue with that, or with the man capable of saying that. One bows to the
power of personality that enables him to dominate wherever he situates
himself, to play so many roles that add up to one—Walt Whitman. Although the preface to the 1855 poems is so insistently general, and has
nothing of what makes "Song of Myself" "work"—America in its var-
iousness, the love play, the tenderness mixed with a view of human existence projected onto the universe at large—it prepares us for
Whitman the truly representative man as he made himself. "I am the
man. . . . I suffer'd. . . . I was there."

Nevertheless, the preface is suffused with religion as a great fact about this society that mounts an even greater hope. Whitman has written the great psalm of the Republic in singable lines.

> *The largeness of nature or the nation were monstrous*
> *Without a corresponding largeness and generosity*
> *Of the spirit of the citizen.*

> *A live nation can always cut a deep mark*
> *And can have the best authority the cheapest . . .*
> *Namely from its own soul. This is the sum*
> *Of the profitable uses of individuals and states.*

> *Nothing too close, nothing too far off . . .*
> *The stars not too far off.*

> *As he sees the farthest he has the most faith.*
> *His thoughts are the hymns of the praise of things.*
> *In the talk on the soul and eternity and God off of his equal plane*
> *He is silent.*
> *He sees eternity less like a play with a prologue and denouement.*

> *Dismiss whatever insults your own soul.*

> *Did you suppose there could be only one Supreme?*
> *We affirm there can be unnumbered Supremes,*
> *And that one does not countervail the other.*

There is no one supreme Deity, no hierarchy, no heaven. It is here on earth and nowhere else that we live out the divine in ourselves to which we are called. We are as gods when we recognize all things as one. Spiritually, we are sovereign—entirely—thanks to our culture of freedom. As we dismiss whatever offends our own souls, so we can trust our own souls for knowledge of the infinite.

So Whitman played companion to all the gods from Osiris to Christ, and tied God to the ecstasy of sexual love. Everything human was on an equal plane. In the first 1855 edition of "Song of Myself" he equated the passing "influx" of divinity with God as "a loving bedfellow, the perfect provider night and morning. *"Mon semblable, mon frère!"*

> *I am satisfied. . . . I see, dance, laugh, sing;*
> *As God comes a loving bedfellow and sleeps at my side all night and*
>   *close on the peep of the day,*
> *And leaves for me baskets covered with white towels bulging the house*
>   *with their plenty,*
> *Shall I postpone my acceptation and realization and scream at my*
>   *eyes,*
> *That they turn from gazing after and down the road,*
> *And forthwith cipher and show me to a cent,*
> *Exactly the contents of one, and exactly the contents of two, and*
>   *which is ahead?*

Like so many of his countrymen in the nineteenth century, Whitman was drenched in religion; he positively swam in it, without having to believe in much of it. There was no personal God. He was not a Christian. He was to add nothing to the many public "revivals" of faith storming around him. Even in his childhood among Long Island Quakers, he owed his spiritual aloofness, his independence from orthodoxy, to his father's admiration for Tom Paine and the father's adherence to Elias Hicks, whose belief in the sufficiency of the "inner light" separated him from most Quakers. On the other hand, Whitman *fils* was no eighteenth-century Deist; in his easy embrace of the universe (and of its diverse creeds) he was the most fervid example imaginable of what Whitehead meant when he said that "Romanticism is spilled religion." "Religion" was in Whitman's blood, as in all his American generation (and after), but it was not central to his attempt to incarnate himself as the "divine literatus" (as he would call himself in *Democratic Vistas*)—the poet as world-embracing witness to all that was now profane in America but still sacred because of the limitless progress it embodied. Whitman, personifying this American optimism, presented himself at the center of everything material and "spiritual." In old age, when he was still fighting for recognition, he called religion essential to the ultimate design of *Leaves of Grass*.

There would be wholeness but no intended "design" to his final edition. Everything in Whitman's thirties followed from personal appetite, ambition, and the strident radicalism of both his political and religious background, which promoted the faith in universal benevolence that carries one along in "Song of Myself"—Here Comes Everybody! This was before the Civil War, before the Gilded Age, and before the worship of a few heated disciples cast him in his last role—as "the Good Gray Poet," the elegist of Lincoln and of the democracy that had never recognized him as its most fervent apostle. But "young" or old—and as a writer he made the most of both—he never had as much interest in "God" as he did in replacing conventional religion with himself as all-seeing poet. "The priest departs, the divine literatus comes."

Why "divine" and why "literatus"? Because, lordly as Whitman paraded himself in "Song of Myself," the metaphor that opens the poem, insinuates itself everywhere back into the poem, and recurs at the end leads to a conclusion perfect in tenderness:

Failing to fetch me at first keep encouraged,
Missing me one place search another,
I stop some where waiting for you.

When Whitman says "I," there is always another in wait. He said it in the most comprehensive way, the most loving. There is never a direct reference to the other he seeks, loves, is making love to. The "nigh young men" who boisterously, familiarly greet him in the street remain just that. In the unusually intimate poem "Out of the Cradle Endlessly Rocking" the boy on the beach recognizes himself as a poet-to-be, "uniter of here and hereafter," in the mating songs of "Two feather'd guests from Alabama, two together." But one disappears, forsakes the other, so that it must be in loss and loneliness, the boy weeping yet ecstatic, that the emerging poet recognizes

Now in a moment I know what I am for, I awake,
And already a thousand singers, a thousand songs, clearer, louder and
*   more sorrowful than yours,*
A thousand warbling echoes have started to life within me, never to
*   die.*

O you singer solitary, singing by yourself, projecting me,
O solitary me listening, never more shall I cease perpetuating you.

Whitman in "Song of Myself," guardedly, evasively describing inter-course and hinting at fellatio, was never so true, for once truly personal, as when he ended the "solitary singer" passage with

Never more shall I escape, never more the reverberations,
Never more the cries of unsatisfied love be absent from me,
Never again leave me to be the peaceful child I was before what
*   there in the night,*
By the sea under the yellow and sagging moon,
The messenger there arous'd, the fire, the sweet hell within,
The unknown want, the destiny of me.

That first arousal is backed up by the mother-sea, "the fierce old mother incessantly moaning," and the maternal breasts represented by "The yellow half-moon enlarged, sagging down, drooping, the face of the sea almost touching." The mother as the everlasting sea, the sorrow-fully "moaning" sea, is the only other human person—represented as a force of nature—in the poem. One wonders if, after all the parading of his masculine charms, Whitman as *seeker* of love was not more real than the lover he portrays as so publicly irresistible that

I am satisfied. . . . I see, dance, laugh, sing;
As God comes a loving bedfellow and sleeps at my side all night and
*   close on the peep of the day.*

However that was, Whitman the lover in general was at first suffi-ciently recognized by Emerson when he said that Whitman's book "has the best merits, namely of fortifying and encouraging." Emerson turned his back on Whitman when it became clear with "Children of Adam" and "Calamus" that the poet was "fortifying," all right, but not in the direction that Concord thought worthy of public print. "It was as if the beasts spoke," said Thoreau (who was charged up by the book for rea-sons his purity did not recognize). In Amherst, Emily Dickinson, who never saw a line by Whitman, was told he was "disgraceful." It was all too early for anyone to tell her that some of her poems, silently seething in her bedroom drawer, were in a sense more "sexual" than his, since they were fed by a direct passion for one particular man after another. It was more *natural* for Whitman (not just more discreet) to embrace the universe. To name a "hugging and loving bed-fellow" as "God."

In the 1881 version of "Song of Myself" "God" got replaced by someone we know as little—"the hugging and loving bed-fellow sleeps at my side through the night, and withdraws at the peep of the day with stealthy tread." Whitman in the overflowing heedless spontaneity of the first version (before "Song of Myself" became so overladen an epic journey through America that the original sexual connection was submerged in inventory) was in such rapture of self-creation that "God" was just as lovable and nameable as anything else. Perhaps that is the real point of naming God, including God in his many personae. The whole world of existent phenomena is open to Whitman's general lovingness, which is boundless affirmation. Nothing may be excluded; nothing is higher or lower than anything else. He is the perfect democrat, in religion as in love and politics. There is no hierarchy in his determination to love everything and everyone in one full sweep.

The essential point is that almost despite himself, Whitman made something infinitely precious of *Leaves of Grass*. The essence of it is a call for infinite harmony, harmony relating all things to the poet at the center. It is remarkable: every great Whitman poem grows out of itself, *on* itself as nature does. What runs through *Leaves of Grass* and turns a collection of poems into a *book* (a word Whitman always insisted on; it was his American testament) is his genius for evoking love, sympathy, "comradeship" and for receiving them in turn. Starting with the acceptance of homosexual love for himself, he transformed individual love into a love for everything natural that finally made not "God" sacred but the world.

The most beautiful expression of this is in "Crossing Brooklyn Ferry," with its vision of the future in the present. T. S. Eliot would not have agreed that Whitman on the East River (of all people and of all places!) anticipated the lines with which "Burnt Norton" opens *Four Quartets*:

> *Time present and time past*
> *Are both perhaps present in time future,*

And time future contained in time past.
If all time is eternally present
All time is unredeemable.

Whitman positively embraced the future to show that all times joined in being equally human. His "indiscriminate" love of life made this possible:

The impalpable sustenance of me from all things at all hours of the
    day,
The simple, compact, well-join'd scheme, myself disintegrated, every
    one disintegrated yet part of the scheme,
The similitudes of the past and those of the future,
The glories strung like beads on my smallest sights and hearings, on the
    walk in the street and the passage over the river.

This interweaving of different worlds in time is radiant *and* secular. It is our ability to imagine a future that gives permanence to what surrounds our temporal existence. We die, the world does not. Hence the lasting appeal of

Closer yet I approach you,
What thought you have of me now, I had as much of you—I laid in
    my stores in advance,
I consider'd long and seriously of you before you were born.

Who was to know what should come home to me?
Who knows but I am enjoying this?
Who knows, for all the distance, but I am as good as looking at you
    now, for all you cannot see me?

The sum of it is a love of the world that imparts sacredness to objects and people connected to us by the future. For Eliot time is circular in a way that would have shocked Whitman the radical democrat. The past, he liked to say in praise of his native land, was "feudal." It was exactly his own past in St. Louis along the Mississippi and summers off the Atlantic that entranced Eliot in the personal memories that pervade *Four Quartets*. To bring back the past was to transcend it into the larger circle of God's will that crowned belief in the Incarnation (another interweaving of past and future, based on the union of spirit and flesh).

Nevertheless, Whitman and Eliot are characteristically American in thinking of time as a promise, of something to be fulfilled. They can't wait "to get on with it." They both look forward to a world made secure by their imagination. "Little Gidding" ends *Four Quartets* with

We shall not cease from exploration
And the end of all our exploring
Will be to arrive where we started
And know the place for the first time.

Whitman would have laughed, "Tom, *I* never left—have been here all the time!" Eliot says "we" because he regards himself as a Christian speaking for Christians. Whitman can say "I" because he is in touch with everything he sees. Loves it all. How wonderful to see "glories strung like beads on my smallest sights and hearings, on the walk in the street and the passage over the river." It is this love that carries him into the future:

It avails not, time nor place—distance avails not,
I am with you, you men and women of a generation, or ever so many
*   generations hence,*
Just as you feel when you look on the river and sky, so I felt,
Just as any one of you is one of a living crowd, I was one of a living
*   crowd.*

By identifying with the "living crowd," Whitman really enters into the future—of a people's America crowded with men and women no different from himself. By admitting that "I too felt the curious abrupt questionings stir within me," he gains our trust—our love—he is talk-ing about us—a century and a half yet to come! It is his constant call to himself to "merge and merge again"—by no means just as a lover—that has won me all my life to Whitman's rapture here. "Crossing Brooklyn Ferry" brings together earth, water, and sky into a wonder of space that alternates time now and time future like the tidal rise and fall of the East River. As the future awaits the present, so there is something in *looking* that enables us to recognize our own soul. This is what Emerson did for Whitman. This is what we can at last call proof of an American religion. It matters not that poets in Europe were also "transcendental." This was from Brooklyn, on a ferryboat, 1856.

You have waited, you always wait, you dumb, beautiful ministers,
We receive you with free sense at last, and are insatiate henceforward,
Not you any more shall be able to foil us, or withhold yourselves from
    us,
We use you, and do not cast you aside—we plant you permanently
    within us,
We fathom you not—we love you—there is perfection in you also,
You furnish your parts toward eternity,
Great or small, you furnish your parts toward the soul.

The very homeliness of this went to make Whitman lovable. The response to Whitman, creating an aura, went right into his work. One did not need to posit a supernatural Deity—Whitman did not—to be a "religious" poet. It was enough to *become* a religion. The more in his time he languished for attention as a poet, the more he presented himself as a unique example, the prophet of a wholly new age to come, an American of Americans. A "screamer" as he might be to the Establishment, something vaguely sacred, a touch of authority clung to someone who was, as a poet, so many things at once. Perhaps the "nigh young men" he describes in "Crossing Brooklyn Ferry" flirtatiously calling to him as he crossed Broadway helped form his idea of himself as irresistible. But crucial as liberated sex was to his self-developing legend, it was only a prelude to the comprehensive "vision" he gained from sex:

Swiftly arose and spread around me the peace and joy and knowledge
    that pass all the art and argument of the earth;
And I know that the hand of God is the elder hand of my own,
And I know that the spirit of God is the eldest brother of my own,
And that all the men ever born are also my brothers . . .
And the women my sisters and lovers,
And that a kelson of the creation is love;
And limitless are leaves stiff or drooping in the fields,
And brown ants in the little wells beneath them,
And mossy scabs of the worm fence, and heaped stones, and elder and
    mullen and pokeweed.

Pokeweed! A perennial herb better than its name, but it was a name that only a truly folk poet would have come up with to conclude the most exalted passage in "Song of Myself." So the rough earth and true personal spirituality (our American genius) came together. Not altogether, even in Whitman's old age. No other American writer made such a thing of being "old" at forty-six. With his great beard and the various slouches to which he put his hat, he was such a favorite of photographers that he was virtually a professional model. He willingly posed holding a "butterfly" on one finger. (It was wood, a contraption.)

Of course the "average" Americans Whitman was always calling to paid no attention. Nothing was farther from the reality of Whitman's emerging reputation than the resounding conclusion of his preface to *Leaves of Grass.*

> The soul of the largest and wealthiest and proudest nation may well go half-way to meet that of its poets. The signs are effectual. There is no fear of mistake. If the one is true the other is true. The proof of a poet is that his country absorbs him as affectionately as he has absorbed it.

Whitman's appeal was to the young, to rebels and "progressives," the sexually liberated, the freethinkers and socialist utopians (especially in Germany) who anticipated that the twentieth century would at last be "theirs." He was admired in England by Tennyson, Swinburne, Hopkins, Edward Dowden, W. M. Rossetti, Edward Carpenter, and John Addington Symonds, and in Germany by young radicals and poets who were fated to die in the "Great War" with pocket editions of Whitman in their uniforms. Of course the "real" Whitman had to tell the German Jewish socialist Horace Traubel, who in 1873 became an intimate friend of Whitman's and who meticulously recorded every last thought of the great man after 1888 in the six volumes of *With Walt Whitman in Camden*, "Be radical, be radical, be not too damned radical!"

But Whitman happily agreed with everything his admirers and disciples said about him. His time had come, his life was finally crowned. By 1872, summing up his career in "As a Strong Bird on Pinions Free," he generously admitted that in his poetry "one deep purpose underlay the others, and has underlain it and its execution ever since—and that has been the religious purpose." "Purpose" was certainly yielding to convention in a way that undercut the actual subtlety of his "purpose" as an *artist*. And he did not have to declare his faith in "immortality" when all his greatest poems, especially his one triumph as a truly "old" man, "Passage to India," made "immortality" less a password than a vision:

> *All these hearts as of fretted children shall be sooth'd,*
> *All affection shall be fully responded to, the secret shall be told,*
> *All these separations and gaps shall be taken up and hook'd and link'd*
>   *together,*
> *The whole earth, this cold, impassive, voiceless earth, shall be*
>   *completely justified,*
> *Trinitas divine shall be gloriously accomplish'd and compacted by the*
>   *true son of God, the poet. . . .*
>
> .   .   .   .
>
> *Nature and Man shall be disjoin'd and diffused no more,*
> *The true son of God shall absolutely fuse them.*

Of course the poetry was not enough for those who wanted to be not admirers but disciples. How Whitman, the supposedly broken and half-paralyzed Whitman in Camden, actually furthered his legend as a cosmic figure is shown in the way he took over the adoring biography of him by the Canadian alienist Dr. Richard Maurice Bucke. Bucke, on encountering *Leaves of Grass* in 1867, became an instant "convert" thanks to the divine capabilities he saw in Whitman. Bucke's *Walt Whitman* (1883) is so rapturous in celebrating *Leaves of Grass* as "revealer and herald" of a religious era not yet reached that one sees in its most enthusiastic form the Romantic belief that poetry would rescue religion by replacing it.

> With the incoming moral states to which it belongs, certain cherished social and religious forms and usages are incompatible; hence the deep instinctive aversion and dread with which it is regarded by the ultra-conventional and conservative. Just so, in their far-back times, was Zoroastrianism, Buddhism, Mohammedanism, Christianity, and every new birth received. . . . So also our church-going, bible-reading, creeds, and prayers, will appear from its vantage-ground mere make-believes of religion. . . . *Leaves of Grass* . . . is the preface and creator of a new era. . . . What the Vedas were to Brahmanism, the Law and the Prophets to Judaism, the Avesta and Zend to Zoroastrianism, the Kings to Confucian-

ism and Taoism, the Pitakas to Buddhism, the Quaran to Mohammedanism, will *Leaves of Grass* be to the future of American civilization.

Whitman, after his best work was done, never tired of summing up self and career, interpreting both in weary but friendly new perspectives. He never tired of self-portraits, especially when he discovered readers who thought him as wondrous as he did himself. A year before his death he wrote to Dr. Bucke likening himself to Lear as he went over the complete *Leaves of Grass* once again. "From my own point of view I accept without demur its spurty (old Lear's irascibility)—its offhandedness, even evidence of decrepitude & old fisherman's seine character as part of the *artism* (from my point of view) & as adherent as the determined cartoon of personality that dominates or rather stands behind all of *L. of G.* like the unseen master & director of the show. W. W."

Not without his blessing, he became a church. In Bolton, Lancashire, a group of "adherents" met weekly to read his poems aloud. This was a great source of cheer to people who habitually suffered from "despondency." On May 29, 1891, he wrote to one of its leaders, J. W. Wallace, that he was "badly prostrated, horrible torpidity" but went on to say, "I guess I have a good deal of the feeling of Epictetus & stoicism—or tried to have. They are specially needed in a rich & luxurious, & even scientific age. But I am clear that I include & allow & probably teach some things stoicism would frown upon & discard. One's pulses & marrow are not *democratic & natural* for nothing."

6

Lincoln: The Almighty Has His Own Purposes

I claim not to have controlled events, but confess plainly that events have controlled me. Now, at the end of three years struggle the nation's condition is not what either party, or any man devised, or expected. God alone can claim it.

LINCOLN TO ALBERT G. HODGES (April 4, 1864)

O N M A R C H 4, 1865, Abraham Lincoln for the second time took the oath of office as president of the United States. As was the custom then, he was sworn in after delivering his inaugural address. On taking the oath, he kissed the open Bible. After the ceremony, Chief Justice Chase presented the Bible to Mrs. Lincoln and pointed to the pencil-marked verses kissed by the president, Isaiah 5:27–28:

> None shall be weary nor stumble among them; none shall slumber nor sleep; neither shall the girdle of their loins be loosed, nor the latchet of their shoes be broken.
>
> Whose arrows are sharp, and all their bows bent, their horses' hoofs shall be counted like flint, and their wheels like the whirlwind.

On this day Lincoln delivered the most remarkable inaugural address in our history—the only one that has ever reflected literary genius. Its last paragraph, beginning "With malice toward none; with charity for all," is universally famous, but the heart of the address is the long preceding paragraph, which concludes (perhaps to the surprise of Lincoln himself, the firm rationalist in all things) in open wonder that perhaps, after all, God's hand could be seen settling "the slavery question."

There was good reason for the leader of a "Union" broken by three years of civil war—the North called it "the Great Rebellion" and the

Confederacy "the War for Southern Independence"—not to be weary or stumble or sleep, but to be ready for battle with arrows sharp and bows bent. The previous November, Lincoln had been reelected, despite widespread disapproval of emancipation and bitterness that the war was taking so long. Lincoln had made sure that soldiers in the field would get to vote. He had triumphed over the dismissed head of the Army of the Potomac, George B. McClellan, whose Democratic party platform, which McClellan had repudiated, advocated negotiations with the South leading to a compromise peace. There would have been no end to slavery in the foreseeable future.

Lincoln had for a long time expected defeat in the 1864 election. A series of smashing Union victories kept him in the White House despite the lack of sure national support for the Emancipation Proclamation or the hundred thousand ex-slaves in the Union army and navy. In March, Grant—at last a general "who fights," Lincoln rejoiced—had been made general-in-chief. In September, Sherman had captured Atlanta, going on to the sea to capture Savannah in December, and early the next year would rip the Confederacy apart as he stormed into the Carolinas. Sheridan in September and October triumphed in the Shenandoah Valley at Winchester, Fisher's Hill, and Cedar Creek. It was not until the end of 1865 that the Thirteenth Amendment would finally be ratified, giving legal assurance to the long-tortured race that "neither slavery nor involuntary servitude . . . shall exist within the United States."

Victory was in the air, after three heartbreak years of frustration, incompetence, and defeat which must have made Lincoln grit his teeth as he was successively let down by McClellan, McDowell, Burnside, Hooker, and how many other generals quickly shown up by Lee, Jackson, Johnston, and Nathan Bedford Forrest. Sherman thought Forrest the most remarkable man to come out of the fighting.

Still, on March 4, 1865, despite anger among Radical Republicans in Congress because Lincoln was so eager to get states like Louisiana back in the Union with only 10 percent of the people professing loyalty, Lincoln was confident enough to say that "the progress of our arms, upon which all else chiefly depends, is as well known to the public as to myself; and it is, I trust, reasonably satisfactory and encouraging to all. With high hope for the future, no prediction in regard to it is ventured."

Lee was to surrender to Grant at Appomattox Court House on

April 9. In masses too great to be resisted by their dispersed masters, the slaves had been voting for freedom with their feet. The South was soon to think of itself not as a defeated army but as a martyred civilization "baptized in blood," a cause made forever sacred by the struggle it had put up on its own soil against greater numbers and resources. Antislavery opinion might feel, in the words of Ulysses Grant, that slavery was "the worst cause for which men ever fought." The inextinguishable need of the master class to dominate showed itself in a furious hatred of the ex-slaves. In two years the Ku Klux Klan would form in Tennessee under the leadership of the same Nathan Bedford Forrest whose troops had massacred black Union soldiers at Fort Pillow. By sheer force of circumstances, the war to end "the Great Rebellion"—Lincoln's official policy—had become a second American revolution leading to the end of slavery. Lincoln's prime aim was to save the Union, "with or without slavery." In the first years of the war he had no more anticipated a holy war for human freedom than most Union soldiers expected or desired. Yet without the Civil War, slavery might have continued into the twentieth century. The Southern cause became so desperate that some Confederate leaders proposed arming the slaves. Lincoln responded that any slave who fought to preserve slavery deserved to be a slave.

Revisionist historians, far removed in time and spirit from the struggle for emancipation, like to worry the facts leading up to the Civil War in order to show that human slavery was not the root cause of the war. Even when academics allow that by the 1850s the agitation over slavery had become the prime disturbance of American life, "wiser heads" could somehow have fashioned some compromise or other that would have settled the matter without war. Ultimately, said the Lincoln expert David Herbert Donald in *Lincoln Reconsidered*, the problem was "an excess of democracy."

Abraham Lincoln knew better. As he said in the second inaugural, "One eighth of the whole population were colored slaves, not distributed generally over the Union, but localized in the Southern part of it. These slaves constituted a peculiar and powerful interest. All knew that this interest was, somehow, the cause of the war." The Lincolns in Kentucky had nothing but the ground they cleared; they were utterly removed from slaves and slave owners. They crossed the Ohio into southern Indiana, said George Dangerfield, with the "irremediable status of poor whites." "Ten years later, Thomas Lincoln heard the call of the Illinois prairies, and he and his family crossed the Wabash and the Sangamon. Their struggles and tragedies were those of all but the most fortunate migrants."

Lincoln grew up with the country, passing one frontier after another into the American heartland and finally settling in Springfield. As a constantly tested young man in pioneer territory with barely a month's formal schooling, self-educated, dependent on the hardest physical labor for the slightest claim to a better life, he was as much at home with American beginnings as Thomas Jefferson, who was his lifelong idol. Parson Mason Weems's life of George Washington was no fable to someone for whom the American Revolution was holy as the creation. Lincoln's zeal for the Union over everything else was at the root of his political opposition to the extension of slavery, of his war policy, of his loyalty to the "republican system" in general, and of his concern for the American future. Confederate Vice President Alexander Stephens, who knew Lincoln when they were both in Congress, said that Lincoln's feeling for the Union amounted to "religious mysticism." That recognizes the passion Lincoln brought to the subject. What is really interesting about it is Stephens's wonder at something so far removed from his own willingness as a slaveholder to destroy the country in order to protect his property rights in human beings.

Lincoln was not a sanguine man by nature, nor did he ever lose the melancholy and superstitious belief in "omens" that afflicted life on the frontier. He was a restlessly ambitious self-made man, a political animal to his fingertips who found himself in the law. That was his salvation, his career, his creed. Its name was reason, a faculty that relieved him of useless emotional upheavals and kept him stable, superior to the mob spirit of the frontier. Above all, reason linked him to his idol Thomas Jefferson and to the Revolution that was fading in the minds around him.

In his early address, 1838, to the Young Men's Lyceum of Springfield, he said that "the pillars of the temple of liberty . . . must fall, unless we, their descendants, supply their places with other pillars, hewn from the solid quarry of sober reason. Passion has helped us; but can do so no more. It will in future be our enemy. Reason, cold, calculating, unimpassioned reason, must furnish all the materials for our future support and defence."

As a young man, creating himself out of the few books available to him, Lincoln came to trust his own mind. The hysterical religious revivals that relieved the loneliness of the frontier had no effect on him, especially when roaring young men assured their audience that each person could ensure his own salvation. Neither did the "Free-Will" or Separate Baptists his parents joined when his mother was still alive, nor the Pigeon Baptist Church to which his father and stepmother subscribed. He was just not interested in any particular creed; nothing he ever said on man in relation to God reminds one of Emerson's faith that man in himself is religious enough. Something of the Calvinism so natural to the hardships of the frontier clung to the churchless and fatalistic Lincoln—nothing was assured in this life, and everything good in it was a surprise, a gift—the only hint that there may yet be a Providence. For a long time he held to "the doctrine of necessity"—no one came to his own views freely! As president, he patiently endured hatred and threats of violence that he considered inevitable to his severe sense of life as well as to his position. But everything had to be tested by his own mind. Beyond that—the shadows. "This too will pass."

Lincoln, for all his theoretical loyalty to Jefferson, was far removed from the abstractions of the Virginia gentry who first wrote the laws. He made an idol of "the great compromiser" Henry Clay and became a highly successful lawyer for the dominant railroad in Illinois. He was prudent enough to be a Whig, that party of complacent successes divided by slavery that eventually vanished into the new Republican party. The law, operating in oral argument and written documents, was Lincoln's mature schoolroom and helped to form the cogency and directness of his writing. His law associate Leonard Swett said after Lincoln's death that "his whole life was a calculation of the law of forces and ultimate results. He believed the results toward which certain causes tended; he did not believe that those results would be materially hastened or impelled. . . . He believed from the first, I think, that the agitation of slavery would produce its overthrow, and he acted upon the result as though it were present from the beginning." Lincoln's partner William H. Herndon described Lincoln's perceptions as "slow, cold, clear and exact." It has often been noted that he had "a countryman's mind." He was slow to make it up, but tenacious once he had made it up.

His fierce rationalism can also be seen as a reaction to the violence always surrounding blacks. The same man who when rejected by a woman could describe himself as "the most miserable man living" had no trouble standing up to ruffians. The speech to the Young Men's Lyceum in Springfield calling for "reason, cold, calculating, unimpassioned reason," also shows him deeply affected by attacks on blacks in free Illinois.

So in the debates with Senator Douglas that made him nationally famous, he easily made an appeal from one self-made man to others as the justice due free white labor. Lincoln, despite his one informal use of "nigger," would not stoop to the demagoguery that allowed Douglas, all too alert to the prejudices of his audience in southern Illinois, to horrify it with the news that Frederick Douglass, the runaway slave who had become the leading black abolitionist, had actually been seen riding in a carriage with a white woman.

Lincoln repeated the Free-Soil case from town to town in the seven debates with Douglas. Slavery was wrong, morally and humanly wrong, and imprisoned masters along with their slaves. As Jefferson had feared, it was as disturbing as "a firebell in the night." Lincoln charged that Douglas, along with a majority of the Supreme Court under Taney and accommodating Northern Democratic presidents Pierce and Buchanan, were conspiring to make the whole country safe for slavery.

Douglas won the Senate race, but Lincoln's was substantially the majority view in the North. Many (perhaps most) Northerners were as indifferent to slavery and abolitionist zeal as they were to the defense of slavery based on Scripture put up by Southern clergymen. They could not be indifferent to the South's determined effort, decade after decade, to nationalize its "peculiar institution." This, which the South believed to be the only way of safeguarding slavery, was the ultimate cause of the Civil War.

As president, Lincoln resisted the attack on Fort Sumter by calling for seventy-five thousand troops. But as early as his special July 4, 1861, message to Congress, he said that the war to save the Union would establish a future in freedom for all.

This is essentially a People's contest. On the side of the Union, it is a struggle for maintaining in the world, that form, and substance of government, whose leading object is, to elevate the condition of men—to lift artificial weights from all shoulders—to clear the paths of laudable pursuit for all—to afford all, an unfettered start, and a fair chance, in the race of life.

At Gettysburg he transcended the war to proclaim a "new birth of freedom." Saying "*we* are met, *we* have come to dedicate . . . *we* can not dedicate, *we* can not consecrate, *we* can not hallow," he ended by perceptibly rising on his toes when he came to the word "people"—as in "government of the *people*, by the *people*, for the *people*." Karl Marx in his articles on the war for the New York *Tribune*, the young Henrik Ibsen in his furious elegy on the murder of Lincoln (for which he blamed the kings and potentates of Europe)—both understood, with Lincoln, that the victory of liberal democracy in America could be the supreme event of the century. "Thanks to all," Lincoln was to write in August 1863 after Grant's victory at Vicksburg cleared the Mississippi. (This to a man from Illinois who opposed the Emancipation Proclamation.) "The Father of Waters again goes unvexed to the sea. . . . Thanks to all. For the great republic—for the principle it lives by, and keeps alive—for man's vast future—thanks to all."

By March 4, 1865, with slavery disintegrating and the South about to capitulate in just one month, the president of the United States, reviewing the course of "the great contest," found it natural, at last, to declare for himself how utterly wrong and sinful he thought the whole system of slavery. To say this as president was to put many things behind him—not least his failure early in the war to countenance the immediate emancipation of slaves in the Confederate territory under their control won by antislavery generals Hunter and Frémont. This was the influence of New England, when, as Henry Adams remembered of the "dark days of 1856," "Concord glowed with pure light." But Lincoln was too worried about the border states remaining in the Union to agree with abolitionist and Transcendentalist New England ministers who theologized the war as God's own justice and demanded immediate and total emancipation. (They went to the White House to tell Lincoln they were carrying this message from God Himself. Lincoln replied, "Don't you think, gentlemen, He might have spoken first to *me*?") And of course the Emancipation Proclamation granted freedom only to slaves whose masters were in rebellion.

There had been great religious "awakenings" before the Civil War, but never afterward would Americans North and South feel that they had been *living* Scripture. For once, and for both sides, "God" and "country" truly came together. The victory of the Union would be the emancipation of the nation. But in the hymns and songs created by the war, the North clearly had the edge. The favorite hymn of its soldiers in the field was

> *Stand up, stand up for Jesus*
> *The trumpet call obey,*
> *Forth to the mighty conflict*
> *In this His glorious day*
> *. . . the strife will not be long.*

There was nothing in even the most fervid Southern patriotism, like Henry Timrod's "Ethnogenesis," written during the meeting of the first Southern Congress, at Montgomery, February 1861, to compare with the "Battle Hymn of the Republic," the words of which had roused Julia Ward Howe out of sleep. Where Timrod had proudly written,

> *Hath not the morning dawned with added light?*
> *And will not evening call another star*
> *Out of the infinite reaches of the night,*
> *To mark this day in Heaven? At last, we are*
> *A nation among nations; and the world*
> *Shall soon behold in many a distant port*
> *Another Flag unfurled!*

Mrs. Howe made (and can still make) the flesh tingle with what *she* had seen in the night—our God was back, and like the God of old, a God of righteousness in thunder, a God who "hath loosed the fateful lightning of His terrible, swift sword; / His truth is marching on." Jefferson Davis in Richmond frenetically worried that only sinfulness in the South's ranks could explain loss in the field. But the daughter of the Puritans saw God in the field as when David put the holy ark at the head of his troops.

I have seen Him in the watch-fires of a hundred circling camps;
They have builded Him an altar in the evening dews and damps;

> *I can read His righteous sentence by the dim and flaring lamps.*
> *His day is marching on.*

Exultate! Because God Himself was now on the march. "His" day and the new day of freedom were one. God's will could not be doubted.

> *He has sounded forth the trumpet that shall never call retreat;*
> *He is sifting out the hearts of men before his judgment seat:*
> *Oh! be swift, my soul, to answer Him! be jubilant, my feet!*
> *Our God is marching on.*

In this "People's contest," the righteous feelings were all with the people, not with the ministers who discovered only after Lincoln's murder that he had been a saint all along.

In Northern churches the lack of fervor in the battle against slavery (as among New York's cotton merchants in the too gentlemanly Episcopal Church) exasperated the diarist George Templeton Strong as it had Harriet Beecher Stowe in *Uncle Tom's Cabin*. He broke out on October 3, 1863:

> The church in which I was brought up, which I have maintained so long to be the highest and noblest of organizations, refuses to say one word for the country at this crisis. Her priests call on Almighty God every day, in the most solemn offices at her liturgy, to deliver His people from "false doctrine, heresy and schism," from "sedition, privy conspiracy and rebellion." Now, at last, when they and their people are confronted by the most wicked of rebellions and the most wilful schisms on the vilest of grounds, the constitutional right to breed black babies for sale, when rebellion and schism are arrayed against the church and against society in the unloveliest form they can possibly assume—the church is afraid to speak. How would she get on were there a large, highly respectable minority sympathizing with adultery, or homicide, or larceny?

Of course such moral sloth in the upper class of New York City (no dependable friend to the Union during the Civil War) was nothing compared with the positive violence of Southern opinion when it did not defend slavery by Scripture. George Fitzhugh, the bellicose Virginia lawyer who thought slavery would be easier on white workers than laissez-faire, was demonstrably race-mad. He explained that the Puritans in the North were descended from Saxon serfs, a natural slave race, while the "Cavaliers, Jacobites and Huguenots" who settled the South were Mediterranean descendants of the Romans, natural rulers. "The Saxons and Angles, the ancestors of the Yankees, came from the cold and marshy regions of the North; where man is little more than a cold-blooded, amphibious biped."

To defend slavery by Scripture was a great exercise for Southern ministers. The star in this endeavor was the South Carolina Presbyterian James Henley Thornwell, who in December 1861 justified the secession of Southern Presbyterians from their national assembly:

> The only rule of judgment is the written word of God. The Church knows nothing of the intuitions of reason or the deductions of philosophy, except those reproduced in the Sacred Canon. . . . She . . . has no right to utter a single syllable upon any subject except as the Lord puts words in her mouth. . . . Her creed is an authoritative testimony of God and not a speculation. . . .
>
> The general operation of the system, is kindly and benevolent; it is a real and effective discipline, and without it we are profoundly persuaded that the African race in the midst of us can never be elevated in the scale of being. As long as that race, in its comparative degradation, coexists, side by side with the white, bondage is its normal condition.

Slavery, alas, was a positive exception to the golden rule of Moses and the apostles: "Treat slaves as bound to obey and inculcate obedience as an office of religion—a thing wholly contradictory if the self-authority exercised over them were unlawful and iniquitous."

Never before the second inaugural had Lincoln condemned the whole system of slavery so totally, without qualification and with so much emotion. In the debates with Douglas, knowing that voters especially in the south of Illinois were antagonistic to blacks, he had, for all his clear and severe opposition to the extension of slavery, not been above demagogic reference to "the nigger." "Racism," as we have learned to call it, then meant not "prejudice" but simple and total hatred of the black, a refusal to grant him, even when free, basic civil rights and civility. The more he was in the dust, the more he was despised. The more he was despised, the more he was open to every cruelty and indignity. The South closed itself around slavery as Nazi Germany closed itself around hatred of the Jew. It permitted no public criticism, no public qualms, no occasional commiseration from the slave owners, whose wives were forced to "bite their tongues," as Mrs. James Chesnut, wife of the Confederate leader, complained in her diary as they walked among their husbands' bastards on the plantation.

Lincoln was so avid a politician that one of his law partners said his ambition gave him no rest. He grew up entirely apart from blacks and as a rising lawyer and public figure had no social reason to feel kinship—not many whites did, not even the New England abolitionists who had Frederick Douglass speak on their platform. Lincoln had learned early to restrain his feelings about the misery he had seen. He once wrote to his proslavery friend Joshua Speed, "I hate to see the poor creatures hunted down, and caught and carried back to their stripes, and unrewarded toils; but I bite my lip and keep quiet." He reminded Speed that years before, traveling from Louisville to St. Louis, they had seen slaves "shackled together with irons. That sight was a continual torment to me; and I see something like it every time I touch the Ohio, or any slave border."

Debating with Douglas for the Senate in 1858, Lincoln was outraged by Douglas's "declared indifference" to slavery. The trouble was not just Douglas's expediency, the folly of believing that "a house divided" *could* stand, but Douglas's "covert real zeal for the spread of slavery." Lincoln's passion on the subject here marks the moral leadership from the White House on the race question which seems to have died with him. Imagine any of our recent presidents breaking out like this:

I hate it because of the monstrous injustice of slavery itself. I hate it because it deprives our republican example of its just influence in the world—enables the enemies of free institutions, with plausibility, to taunt us as hypocrites—causes the real friends of freedom to doubt our sincerity, and especially because it causes so many good men among ourselves into an open war with the very fundamental principles of civil liberty—criticizing the Declaration of Independence and insisting that there is no right principle of action but *self* interest.

In a time when Southerners mocked the statement that "all men are created equal" in the Declaration of Independence as "absurd, contrary to fact," Lincoln's only counter to this, his supreme emblem of reason, was to go back to what was self-evident.

Lincoln's belief in the rationality of the law helps us to understand the nonconformity of his religious views. Then as now, a majority of Americans professed belief in God, went to church, and, whether they knew or admitted it, surely thought of their church as a way of belonging and surviving in a violently divided society.

Lincoln never joined any organized church. His law partner in Springfield William H. Herndon saw him reading such Enlightenment skeptics as Voltaire, Tom Paine, and Count Volney—the latter thought morality the only point of religion. Whatever his indifference to frontier revival meetings and the primitive Baptist churches his parents attended, Lincoln's perfect confidence in his own mind (emotionally he was a depressive; as president he dreamed of his own death and state funeral) explains his religious independence.

Lincoln had been right to fear, in his first debate with Douglas on August 21, 1858, that "there is no peaceful extinction of slavery in prospect for us." Seven years later, when he stood in front of the Capitol to deliver his second inaugural, all his positing of the issue on the territories alone, all general hopes for compromise with the South, had become ancient history. The most dramatic thing about the second inaugural, what makes its historical candor so surprising against the usual official rhetoric, is that it says modern history in America begins with and because of the Civil War. Lincoln can now say openly that "the Negro" is the issue of the time and slavery the cause of the Civil War.

Of course this same "Negro" is still just an object, exists entirely within the context of slavery, and is as much a symbol to Lincoln as he is to everyone else. For all politicians, as for most American citizens, he is never an individual human person. But through the impassioned biblical evocations of the second inaugural, slavery has somehow been moved from the political struggle over the territories between North and South to the condemnation of slavery itself. Such condemnation could arise only from principles already known to a Christian nation thanks to the one text most Americans regarded as the abiding interpretation of their existence.

The Bible was still an essential personal resource for this generation of Americans. South and North each found in the Bible justification for its struggle, its own self-declared holiness. Never again in American history would there be so much honest, deeply felt invocation of God's purpose in supporting one or the other side. Everything so long festering in the American heart over the need to believe that God does intervene in history—everything that was to be threatened after the war by the idea of nature as a self-operating mechanism—now flamed out with all the passion of war itself. The Bible was still a bridge between life and death. The Christian promise of salvation offered the one testimony to which people had access that there is "surely" a life beyond this one, a judgment superior to the earthly judgment. And this was burningly proved by the sacrifice of life itself, as shown by the unprecedented, once improbable determination of hundreds of thousands of Americans to mutilate and destroy one another because of loyalties that North and South believed to have the sanction of the Almighty Father, Creator of the Universe, who between 1861 and 1865 was still sitting in judgment on each individual creature.

More than one American was now remembering the Book of Numbers. "Would to God all the Lord's people were prophets." John Brown's body lay a-mould'ring in the grave, but his soul went marching on. Was not the terrible war a carrying out of what Brown in his last letter from Charlestown Prison, December 2, 1859, had defined as the "active" principle of religion "pure and undefiled"? Were there vengeful antislavery and black soldiers who approvingly remembered that in bleeding Kansas, Brown had justified taking out and killing proslavery people because "without the shedding of blood there is no remission of sins"?

Sin? Harriet Beecher Stowe had represented the "pure" conscience of abolitionism when she had written in *Uncle Tom's Cabin*, "What is peculiar to slavery, and distinguishes it from free servitude, is evil, and only evil, and that continually." On the next page she added, "The great object of the author in writing has been to bring this subject of slavery, as a moral and religious question, before the minds of all those who profess to be followers of Christ, in this country." But Southern preachers, poets, politicians, and editors had no trouble defending slavery by the New as well as Old Testament, and in this they were not simply rationalizing their economic interests and social structure. They, too, were loyal to a religious tradition. They, too, were believers. "Sin" was a critical issue of the time, on both sides of the slavery question. The appeal to righteousness and the sense of moral guilt were more vehement and impassioned than anything Germans expressed over Auschwitz, Russians over the Gulag, Americans over the "wasting" of peasant hamlets in Vietnam.

But when before the war, impossible then to imagine so terrible a civil war, had any national leader, not just some wild and vehement William Lloyd Garrison publicly tearing up the Constitution and professing that he was speaking for God's own truth in its simplicity and power—when had it been possible for any national leader, much less the president himself, to call slavery an offense against God and to suggest that the war was God's own punishment of those who had profited from the pain and exploitation of their slaves?

The age of *belief* reaches its culmination in the second inaugural, but with a subtlety and humility that make words from a war president on this public occasion all the more astonishing.

Lincoln begins calmly, almost wearily, reviewing the struggle over slavery that had inevitably ended in war. He is magnanimous enough to say, despite the South Carolina "fire-eaters" who opened the war by firing on Fort Sumter, "All dreaded it—all sought to avert it." Without mentioning the threats to himself, he recalls the dangers under which he had delivered the first inaugural in 1861, describes insurgent agents in Washington "seeking to *destroy* the Union without war—seeking to dissolve the Union, and divide effects, by negotiation. Both parties deprecated war; but one of them would *make* war rather than let the nation survive; and the other would *accept* war rather than let it perish. And the war came." It came, Lincoln says categorically, because one eighth of the whole population were colored slaves. These slaves constituted "a peculiar and powerful interest. All knew that this interest was, somehow, the cause of the war. To strengthen, perpetuate, and extend this interest was the object for which the insurgents would rend the Union, even by war; while the government claimed no right to do more than to restrict the territorial enlargement of it."

After this forthright summary of how the war came (Southerners still insist the issue was one of states' rights), Lincoln notes, "Neither party expected for the war, the magnitude, or the duration, which it has already attained. Neither anticipated that the *cause* of the conflict might cease with, or even before, the conflict itself should cease. Each looked for an easier triumph." To which he added a perfect description of the war—of all great wars—"and a result less fundamental and astounding."

Suddenly we move from the surprise and havoc of war to what—in 1865—was still central to any invocation of God—God as the one true judge, who alone makes the final judgment:

> Each looked for an easier triumph, and a result less fundamental and astounding. Both read the same Bible, and pray to the same God; and each invokes His aid against the other. It may seem strange that any man should dare to ask a just God's assistance in wringing their bread from the sweat of other men's faces; but let us judge not that we be not judged. The prayers of both could not be answered; that of neither has been answered fully. The Almighty has his own purposes.

No president before Lincoln had thought it imperative to discuss a divisive social issue in a religious context, and this with such passion and tribulation. Never before had America been in a war whose immediate effects were so "fundamental and astounding." The general sorrow of the war brought to a peak of intensity not seen before or after a whole people's trust in God. Never again would a consensus in America reach such depths of religious urgency.

God was not yet dead in 1865, nor was He yet entirely identified with what Puritans, who thought the divine mystery more interesting than petty behavior, called "the filthy rags of righteousness." He was the presence and the destiny, the ever-living God of religious seekers and zealots, absolutists of the spirit. The greatest of them led His disciples to pray that the Father's will may yet be done on earth, as it is in heaven. He was the God not of correct behavior but of fire in the hearts of men.

Like all honest men on the subject who value their freedom from orthodoxy, Lincoln had had his doubts about the very existence of God. But he was now president of the United States in the most terrifying crisis. It was up to him to unite his country morally as well as in war. He was carrying it all on his shoulders, aware at every excruciating moment that the country could survive only by the sacrifice of hundreds of thousands of young men.

In a little more than a month after his inauguration, April 14, Good Friday, he would be shot to death by a mad actor who had been driven to frenzy at hearing Lincoln in his last speech, April 11, envision the possibility of Negro suffrage. Lincoln never got over the superstitions of the primitive frontier. He had witnessed the violence that never leaves American life. His life had been threatened by Confederate partisans as he had made his way to Washington to take office. It would not have seemed strange to him, who had sent so many other men to death, that he might have to give up his own life.

"This mighty scourge of war" had made him more truly a man of sorrows than this haunted man had been before. But it had liberated him from his prewar compromises and his enforced declaration that he claimed no right to do more about slavery than restrict the territorial enlargement of it. He had said that "the great body of the Northern people do crucify their feelings in order to maintain their loyalty to the Constitution and the nation." Belabored on all sides in the first years of war for seeming "vacillating," he was now able to speak out with a passionate clarity of heart and mind when so many doubts had been burned away by the emergence of Grant.

Lincoln now had the freedom to say about Southerners praying for the continuance of slavery, "It may seem strange that any men should *dare* to ask a just God's assistance in wringing their bread from the sweat of other men's faces." Lincoln the flatboatman, carpenter, cabin builder, Indian fighter, farmer, hunter, rail-splitter had known a good deal more about sweat than the leading Southern Presbyterian divine, the Reverend James Henley Thornwell. Slaves were *lucky* to have been "redeemed from the *bondage* of barbarism and sin."

Lincoln's opposite number, President Jefferson Davis of the Confederate States of America, a West Point graduate and a Mississippi slaveholder, had in early proclamations asked Southerners to observe days of humiliation and prayer in full confidence that "it hath pleased Almighty God, the Sovereign Disposer of events, to protect and defend the Confederate States hitherto in their conflict with their enemies, and to be unto them a shield."

The seemingly built-in religiosity of the South comes through to us, almost amusingly, in the fundamentalism of that expert killer General Thomas Jonathan Jackson—the immortal Stonewall—who in battle cried "Kill them! Kill them!" but who was not sure it was proper to fight on the Sabbath.

General Edward Porter Alexander, head of Confederate artillery, is hard on Jackson in his memoirs *Fighting for the Confederacy*. Alexander bitterly criticizes him for his action at the Seven Days' Battles (June 26–July 2, 1862). Alexander emphasizes Jackson's "incredible slackness, and delay, and hanging back, which . . . decidedly slackened his own exertions, with the result that General Lee's victory was shorn of the capture of McClellan's entire army."

> The question naturally arises, what was the matter with him? . . . For myself, I think that the one defect in General Jackson's character was his religious beliefs. He believed with absolute faith, in a personal God. . . . It is customary to say that "Providence did not intend that we should win." But Providence did not care a row of pins about it. If it did, it was a very unintelligent Providence not to bring the business to a close—the close it wanted—in less than four years of most terrible and bloody war. . . . It was a serious incubus upon us that during the whole war our president and many of our generals really and actually believed that there *was* this mysterious Providence always hovering over the field . . . and that prayers and piety might win its favor from day to day.
>
> We had the right to fight, but our fight was against what might be called a Darwinian development—or an adaptation to changed and changing conditions.

By the time he wrote this, the irreverent general of artillery did not have to say that the South in defeat recouped itself religiously as "the Religion of the Lost Cause, Baptized in Blood." This creed became a favorite way of preserving, in its own eyes, the godliness of the South.

By contrast, Lincoln the supremely self-made man, the assiduous politician whose ambition knew no rest, had learned in war all too much about the limitations of the human will. His doubts accorded with his sense of a universe not made exclusively for man's self-interest. He was interestingly unlike the divines, South and North, who were perfectly assured that God spoke to them and acted entirely in their behalf. He said in his address that he found particularly "strange" whatever upheld human bondage. In humility he quoted Matthew 7:1: "But let us judge not that we be not judged." He concluded his third paragraph: "The prayers of both could not be answered: that of neither has been answered fully."

In his torturing responsibility to the nation, to the future of democratic government in the world, Lincoln had come through a terrible experience to submit to a power higher and greater than anything his political ambition had prepared him for. Now he felt himself responsible before God for whatever he did and said to guide the nation.

The most compelling sentence to me of the second inaugural is the one that leads to the essence of the speech in the fourth paragraph. There is a troubled searching here of God's will, a startling admission by a man who was as self-trusting in religion as he was in law and the art of writing. *The Almighty Has His Own Purposes.* And it is all he has to say with any confidence about God's will.

He then turns to what he *is* sure of—the sinfulness of slavery. He draws on Matthew 18:7: "Woe unto the world because of offences! for it must needs be that offences come; but woe to that man by whom the offence cometh!" Jesus is here speaking of offenses against children. It is typical of Lincoln's literary acumen as well as his sense of urgency that he seized on the word "offences"—so much more striking than "temptations" or "hindrances" in post–King James translations—to launch into a passage so awesome, a great public cry from the heart:

> If we shall suppose that American Slavery is one of those offences which, in the providence of God, must needs come, but which, having continued through His appointed time, He now wills to remove, and that he gives to both North and South, this terrible war, as the woe due to those by whom the offence came, shall we discern therein any departure from those divine attributes which the believers in a Living God always ascribe to Him? Fondly do we hope—fervently do we pray—that this mighty scourge of war may speedily pass away. Yet, if God wills that it continue, until all the wealth piled by the bond-man's two hundred and fifty years of un-

requited toil shall be sunk, and until every drop of blood drawn with the lash, shall be paid by another drawn with the sword, as was said three thousand years ago, so still it must be said "the judgments of the Lord, are true and righteous altogether."

This is extraordinary, but so long buried in official marble with other American scriptures that unless its conditionals are noted, one is likely to miss the religious hesitation in it, Lincoln's actual reserve. "Let us suppose," he says in effect, that slavery is an offense that God inexplicably allowed into human history. Let us even suppose that he allowed just so much time for it. To suppose anything like this is actually to suppose a very peculiar God. But since it all happened as described, and believers hold God accountable for all things, one can only yield to the enigma of having such a God at all. It is clear that the terrible war has overwhelmed the Lincoln who identified himself as the man of reason. It has brought him to his knees, so to speak, in heartbreaking awareness of the restrictions imposed by a mystery so encompassing it can only be called "God." Lincoln could find no other word for it.

On April 4, 1864, writing to a Kentuckian who was troubled by the enlistment of ex-slaves in the Union forces, Lincoln explained how his views of slavery had evolved to the point where he now fully approved the enlistment of 130,000. He had always been naturally antislavery, quoting himself: "If slavery is not wrong, nothing is wrong." But as president he initially felt that he had "no unrestricted right to act officially upon this judgment and feeling." Early in the war, he had not allowed Generals Frémont and Hunter to free slaves under their control. He had permitted measures, clearly unconstitutional, to become lawful so as to preserve the country. Nothing was so imperative as to avoid the wreck of government, country, and Constitution altogether. Since the border states, like Kentucky, had declined his proposal for compensated emancipation, he had no choice but that of "laying a strong hand upon the colored element." Those who objected to these soldiers, seamen, and laborers could not now, in the same breath, claim to support the Union.

Lincoln added: "I attempt no compliment to my own sagacity. I claim not to have controlled events, but confess plainly that events have controlled me. Now, at the end of three years struggle, the nation's condition is not what either party, or what any man devised or expected. God alone can claim it. If God now wills the removal of a great wrong, and wills also that we of the North as well as you of the South, will pay fairly for our complicity in that wrong, impartial history will find therein new cause to attest and revere the justice and goodness of God. Yours truly, Abraham Lincoln."

Lincoln's God was born of war. It would not have survived without him, since only Lincoln understood Him. Lincoln had nothing to say about Jesus as redeemer and intervener in this life. What was personal to Lincoln was a sense of divinity wrested from the many contradictions in human effort. God came to him through a certain exhaustion. Faith was still deep and intense enough to allow doubt and survive it. The sense of Providence during the Civil War—there was still no alternative—was of a kind we cannot now fully take in.

In Lincoln's own "fiery trial" we see a refusal to "know" God and to see Him directing all one's hopes and ambitions in life. What we have in the second inaugural is religiously tentative, like our own effort to say that there is no peace. We live on a precipice.

The close of the second inaugural—charity for all and malice toward none—is memorable because it is noble and surprising to come out of so ghastly a war. But nothing to my mind is so worth repeating as the veritable outcry earlier over the iniquity of slavery: "Yet, if God wills that it continue, until all the wealth piled by the bond-man's two hundred and fifty years of unrequited toil shall be sunk, and until every drop of blood drawn with the lash, shall be paid by another drawn with the sword, as was said three thousand years ago, so still it must be said 'the judgments of the Lord, are true and righteous altogether.' "

To the New York political boss Thurlow Weed, who had complimented him on the address, Lincoln on March 14 admitted, "I expect it to wear as well as—perhaps better than—anything I have produced; but I believe it is not immediately popular. Men are not flattered by being shown that there has been a difference of purpose between the Almighty and them. To deny it, however, in this case, is to deny that there is a God governing the world. It is a truth which I thought needed to be told; and as whatever of humiliation there is in it, falls most directly on myself, I thought others might afford for me to tell it."

The North triumphed, leaving behind it such idealism as Lincoln, Harriet Beecher Stowe, Julia Ward Howe, and abolitionists like the two younger brothers of William and Henry James (both wounded in the war) had contributed to the Union cause. The crass triumphalism in which the war ended for the North, plus the intoxication of riches, the emergence of a scientific culture, and the settling of the West, abetted the erosion of religious sentiment among writers and scholars. Skeptical veterans of the war like Oliver Wendell Holmes, Jr., and Ambrose Bierce were ironic about a society in which a John D. Rockefeller righteously declared, "God gave me my money."

The triumphant North needed proof of its saintliness, and found it in the consecration of Abraham Lincoln. The civil religion that came out of the war turned America itself into a sacred object and ritual and demanded that America be its own religion—and that everybody had to believe in it. The Lincoln who never joined the Church became the god of a godless religion. Under the smug Republican administration of Calvin Coolidge, a great temple in Washington was built around a statue of Lincoln seated on a throne. Now the people truly had someone eternally to worship.

Lincoln had been assassinated on a Good Friday. The overwrought sermons that followed on Easter Sunday of course turned the dead president into an American Christ. His body went home to Springfield on a journey that stopped in city after city so that Lincoln could lie in state over and over again.

> *Coffin that passes through lanes and streets,*
> *Through day and night with the great cloud darkening the land,*
> *With the pomp of the inloop'd flags, with the cities draped in black,*
> *With the show of the States themselves as of crape-veil'd women*
>   *standing,*
> *With processions long and winding and the flambeaus of the night,*
> *With the countless torches lit, with the silent sea of faces and the*
>   *unbared heads,*
> *With the waiting depot, the arriving coffin, and the sombre faces.*

His body, thought safely interred in Springfield, was briefly stolen, bringing more associations with the Christ who did not remain in His tomb. Lincoln had become the divine Son he never publicly addressed. A Lincoln never less than kindly was imposed on every association with the Civil War.

A visitor to Gettysburg notes that with the exception of the Gettysburg Address, there is no explanation of how the war came about, no mention of slavery. But on display are swords in profusion, cannons, rifles. Robert E. Lee in a small diorama is shown holding the reins of his beloved horse Traveller and comforting the survivors of Pickett's charge. This does not exactly get to the substance of what Lincoln called a new birth of freedom.

A century and a half later it is possible to say that religion and America as a religion are in the minds of many people synonymous. Lincoln said America was a proposition. Religion was to him a matter of the most intensely private conviction. Did he suspect that a wholly politicized religion would yet become everything to many Americans? It was different during the agitation over slavery and the outbreak of fratricidal slaughter. A great many people were certain that they lived and died overseen by God, for purposes instilled in them by God. One cannot think of the long, long story of black bondage and the war that ended it without a shiver of awe. It is the one chapter in American life that brings us back to biblical history.

7

Emily Dickinson: The Alone to the Alone

> *One need not be a Chamber—to be Haunted—*
> *One need not be a House—*
> *The Brain has Corridors—surpassing*
> *Material Place—*
>
> #670

WHITMAN'S *Leaves of Grass* is openly self-praising and self-advancing, familiarly advertised by him as a great American product. One can hardly miss Whitman's effort to make a career out of his pursuing a work of art. Emily Dickinson did not have a career, a publisher, or an audience in her own time. Her almost two thousand poems present a life, *are* her life. Of course the "I" that begins the greatest number of her poems, being created as a character on paper, is not identical with the living, feeling, artful person who by devising the poem separated herself from it. But whose experience, whose tumult of feeling, whose catch-as-catch-can negotiations with what was left in nineteenth-century Amherst of the old Puritan God did she describe but her own? Who were the (not always unnamed) people in her poetry but her family, friends, the inaccessibly beloved?

What silence she lived in once she closed herself in to write. Her more "personal" poems break through this silence in bitterness not always resigned.

> *Dare you see a Soul* at the White Heat?
> *Then crouch within the door—*
> *Red—is the Fire's common tint—*
> *But when the vivid Ore*
> *Has vanquished Flame's conditions,*
> *It quivers from the Forge*

Without a color, but the light
Of unanointed Blaze.

#365

What shall I do—it whimpers so—
This little Hound within the Heart
All day and night with bark and start—
And yet, it will not go—
Would you untie it, were you me—
Would it stop whining—if to Thee—
I sent it—even now?

#186

How many times these low feet staggered—
Only the soldered mouth can tell—
Try—can you stir the awful rivet—
Try—can you lift the hasps of steel!

#187

She gives us few actual details of her life, for she was not writing *to* anyone even when she addressed her sister-in-law, Sue Gilbert, and (in time) the "Master." What unites all her writing—the thousand letters as well as the few poems she tossed off to friends when she began—are the power and depth of her solitude. Religion was habitually at the center of her intelligence, but God was alone in her thought, another "character" in her universe, popping up from time to time because she had no name but "God" for so much power over her life, so many promises, so much remoteness.

Hawthorne, Emerson, and Stowe had at least this in common: each had a belief consistent with itself. Melville drove himself near crazy, "not able either to believe or disbelieve." After them, God, though not yet "dead," was to be taken or to be left just as you please. The question of His reality was no longer a burning one. For Dickinson the question did not come up, since God and the absence of God, the mercy of God and the horror of God haunted her thought just as death did. Her starting point was always mortality and her protest against it. She never got over the impermanence of everything she saw, the fragility of human relationships, the flight of the seasons, the taste of death in winter. But

God, if only as a name, a tradition, a hope, a symbol, a word so recurrent that we no longer ask where it came from, was her *association* with immortality. He had been around so long that doubting His existence or justifying it had the same resonance in words. The language of her poetry, wavelike and whirling, made it easier to deal with our life in His shadow than religion did. He had so many faces (and often no face at all) from poem to poem:

> *Of Course—I prayed—*
> *And did God Care?*
> *He cared as much as on the Air*
> *A Bird—had stamped her foot—*
> *And cried "Give Me"—*
> *My Reason—Life—*
> *I had not had but for Yourself.*
>   #376

But sometimes there was absolutely no one else to turn to:

> *It was too late for Man—*
> *But early, yet, for God—*
> *Creation—impotent to help—*
> *Of our Old Neighbor—God.*
>   #623

She was too much the daughter of Puritan New England to be histrionic like Rilke over "*du Nachbar Gott,*" asking Him if He needed a drink or something to keep Him going. "Our old neighbor God," as she called Him, was there and not there, indisputable but enigmatic, had too many "faces" to wear a single one, created the world—then seemed to leave it. He had always been alone in His unmatchable sovereignty— "*One is one and all alone and ever more shall be so*"—but now He was alone because He was comparatively friendless. Her fathers were big in their own eyes when He was the one Rock on which hope gathered:

> *Those—dying then,*
> *Knew where they went—*

> *They went to God's Right Hand—*
> *That Hand is amputated now*
> *And God cannot be found—*
>
> *The abdication of Belief*
> *Makes the Behavior small—*
> *Better an ignis fatuus*
> *Than no illume at all.*

#*1551*

No question about it, He and she would always circle around each other in the hope of meeting. Better to be deceived by a light where there is no light than to have no light at all. God is forever in our consciousness, and consciousness is what we have of Him. And if all things stop for us in death, where once it was the portal to a new life, a better life, an eternity to be *lived* (with God), "eternity" is still a blessed image for Dickinson, like so many other images embedded in concentration on her own thought.

Death has lost its promise, but it is still the one mystery. Death is the event of events, even when the soiled mattress is flung out of the window.

> *There's been a Death, in the Opposite House,*
> *As lately as Today—*
> *I know it, by the numb look*
> *Such Houses have—alway—*
>
> *The Neighbors rustle in and out—*
> *The Doctor—drives away—*
> *A Window opens like a Pod—*
> *Abrupt—mechanically—*
>
> *Somebody flings a Mattress out—*
> *The Children hurry by—*
> *They wonder if it died—on that—*
> *I used to—when a Boy—*
>
> *The Minister—goes stiffly in—*
> *As if the House were His—*

> *And He owned all the Mourners—now—*
> *And little Boys—besides—*
>
> *And then the Milliner—and the Man*
> *Of the Appalling Trade—*
> *To take the measure of the House—*
> *There'll be that Dark Parade—*
>
> *Of Tassels—and of Coaches—soon*
> *It's easy as a Sign—*
> *The Intuition of the News—*
> *In just a Country Town.*

#389

That was written in 1862, when Amherst's dead returning from the Civil War shocked her solitude. She had known many of them. Death was a very present fact. And yet—and yet—Dickinson would never have self-pleasingly said, like Wallace Stevens in his great cold poem "Sunday Morning," "Death is the mother of beauty." Stevens seemed relieved to have gotten the unpleasantness of death out of his system. It all turned into an aesthetic proposition, like so much in Stevens. In its finality and futile heartbreak, death remained all too real to Dickinson, its ancient promise turned about in her ultimate recognition of life's limits—and the limits of death:

> *Because I could not stop for Death—*
> *He kindly stopped for me—*
> *The Carriage held but just Ourselves—*
> *And Immortality.*

#712

The question the faithful asked of death was once comfortably answered: There is no death. It is only a passing from one "room" to another. But for Dickinson the artist the denial or affirmation of another life was all hypothesis by contrast with the drama of consciousness lingering and dying. "Because I could not stop for Death" triumphs over death—the death of time in us—by prolonging the last day into the "surmise" that there will be no other. Until *that* shudder of recognition everything has been politesse.

We slowly drove—He knew no haste
And I had put away
My labor and my leisure too,
For His Civility—

We passed the School, where Children strove
At Recess—in the Ring—
We passed the Fields of Gazing Grain—
We passed the Setting Sun—

Or rather—He passed Us—
The Dews drew quivering and chill—
For only Gossamer, my Gown—
My Tippet—only Tulle—

We paused before a House that seemed
A Swelling of the Ground—
The Roof was scarcely visible—
The Cornice—in the Ground—

Since then—'tis Centuries—and yet
Feels shorter than the Day
I first surmised the Horses' Heads
Were toward Eternity—

We know because we are in life, not death. Nothing is grander to our perception and yet more astonishing than the realization that there is no turning back. What fascinated Dickinson in all her greatest poems about death coming was exactly its coming. This is finally all we know, and as happens in life, it is the knowing we cannot escape. And on that topic she triumphed. Dickinson was able in one poem after another to convey in the homeliest, most familiar details *what* we are leaving as the supreme experience unfolds:

I heard a Fly buzz—when I died—
The Stillness in the Room
Was like the Stillness in the Air—
Between the Heaves of Storm.

#465

It is hard to give up earth, but only Dickinson in another, jolly poem would have complained that surviving an almost fatal illness made her touch heaven without being able to stay:

> *Just lost, when I was saved!*
> *Just felt the world go by!*
> *Just girt me for the onset with Eternity,*
> *When breath blew back,*
> *And on the other side*
> *I heard recede the disappointed tide!*
>
> *Therefore, as One returned, I feel*
> *Odd secrets of the line to tell!*
> *Some Sailor, skirting foreign shores—*
> *Some pale Reporter, from the awful doors*
> *Before the Seal!*
>
> *Next time, to say!*
> *Next time, the things to see*
> *By Ear unheard.*
> *Unscrutinized by Eye—*
>
> *Next time to tarry*
> *While the Ages steal—*
> *Slow tramp the Centuries,*
> *And the Cycles wheel!*
>
> #160 (1860)

The poem deliciously plays life and death against each other. The other world, too, was something she could describe! Last time she "lost" heaven by being returned to this life. She is glad to think that next time she will not lose it by being saved. "The onset with Eternity"—what an adventure it was just skirting "those foreign shores" like a sailor, or being some frightened reporter just getting a glimpse of the "awful doors" before they were sealed.

"Next time," she stays. Next time, there will be things to see and hear undreamed of on earth. Next time, to "tarry" is to be so far beyond the time allotted to us on earth that one will experience the ages stealing away, and the centuries, as the eternal cycles wheel round and round and round. All these are tropes, but delightfully establish another world as she pretends to regret her survival in this one.

It was all metaphysical play, as when she says (#76),

> *Exultation is the going*
> *Of an inland soul to sea,*
> *Past the houses—past the headlands—*
> *Into deep Eternity.*

Yet in #153 she confesses:

> *Death is the only Secret—*
> *Death, the only One*
> *You cannot find out all about*
> *In his "native town."*

After a lot of fun personalizing Death as the stranger in town who remains unknowable though he seems to have the right qualities— "Industrious! Laconic! / Punctual! Sedate!"—the poem ends amazingly on the image that while Death "Builds, like a Bird, too! / Christ robs the Nest— / Robin after Robin / Smuggled to Rest!"

This power of *running* metaphor, the linking of incommensurables to satisfy us with what could never have been anticipated, is the genius of her poetry. It is her special quality as someone roaming this world as if it were interstellar space. All things earthly and heavenly brush each other in her mind, to represent just what it is to be Emily Dickinson in this room, this house, this town, this universe when she has such power of attention.

> *Some things that fly there be—*
>
> *These the days when Birds come back—*
>
> *A Bird came down the Walk—*
>
> *After great pain a formal feeling comes—*
>
> *My Life had stood—a Loaded Gun—*
>
> *A narrow Fellow in the Grass*
>
> *I like a look of Agony.*

The power of attention is for Dickinson a truer, more spontaneous way of thinking than having "ideas."

> *A Bird came down the Walk—*
> *He did not know I saw—*
> *He bit an Angleworm in halves*
> *And ate the fellow, raw.*
>
> #328

She would have liked Simone Weil's "Attentiveness without an object is the supreme form of prayer."

Other people had faith absolute. She had mind.

Most Dickinsons before her thought heaven real enough—and on the whole thought well enough of themselves to sustain faith that heaven expected them. The Dickinsons came to Massachusetts in the 1620s. For almost a hundred and fifty years in Amherst, they epitomized in their secluded village Puritan New England's reverence for its own apartness. But as the tide of honest belief receded, there was panic in Emily's own family. Her grandfather Samuel Fowler Dickinson, who began as a rationalist in eighteenth-century style, became so intent on founding Amherst College to counteract the dangerous Unitarian heresies disseminated at Harvard that he went bankrupt and fled to the Middle West. Emily's famously stern father, Edward Dickinson, became Amherst's leading citizen, revived the family's fortunes, and led family prayers that Emily usually managed to avoid. When she couldn't escape, she privately made fun of the solemn occasion. Amherst had five Congregational churches, but Emily Dickinson was not to be seen in any of them. Even as a fragile teenager at Mount Holyoke Female Seminary, she had refused to go up to the communion table.

Still, she inherited with her name a religious past that was as much a part of her as being a woman. She did not believe in "God" and His mysteries so much as she possessed them for her own purposes. What to others were articles of belief were to her way stations along the imagination in which she lived her life. They had become *hers*—a great compliment to the centrality of the individual in the Christian faith, for whom salvation was so urgent a matter that everything revolved around the health of his soul.

This central sense of self was Protestant Christianity's gift to her—bestowed, absorbed in the deepest crevices of her being without the old Puritan warning and hovering curse: use for God's purposes, not your own! She did not use her poetry as prayer; she did not write to mollify God, to ward off evil; she wrote because she and she alone could find in religion the adventures of her utterly independent, endlessly speculative soul.

Thomas Carlyle said of Whitman, "He thinks he is a big poet because he comes from a big country." Whitman did indeed believe that the signs of the times were in his favor as a poet. The very idea of being a "big" poet—a national poet, the epic poet of "these states," in a style expansive, oratorical, boastfully confessional (the country as his other self)—had everything to do with the continental grandeur and unrelenting historic push of the United States. To alert the world to a slender sheaf of *poems*, he announced, "Here at last is something in the doings of man that corresponds with the broadcast doings of the day and night. . . . Here is action untied from strings necessarily blind to particulars and details magnificently moving in vast masses."

A hundred years after Emily Dickinson's body was carried from "The Homestead" on Main Street by Irish laborers working on "my father's ground," the broadcast doings of her big, ever-bigger, more triumphantly commercial and wasteful country would have baffled her as much as did the aggressive push of the United States and the sectional war over slavery. When the country, under President James Polk, was making war on Mexico so that we could grab our present Southwest, Emily Dickinson was briefly a student at Mount Holyoke Female Seminary. She archly inquired of her brother Austin: "Do you think the Mexicans will besiege South Hadley?"

Dickinson owed her "perfect literary situation," as Allen Tate put it, to her coming in at the end of Puritanism, absorbing a tradition without having to obey it. Nothing so marks the absence of religious intelligence, knowledge, or concern at the end of the twentieth century as the everlasting attempt of groupies in every camp to turn Dickinson into a stereotype like themselves. Her main literary sustenance was Shakespeare, whom she clutched as her Bible. The widest spectrum of language was there. After that she haltingly named "the Brownings" and—once—Keats. We know that she read Rebecca Harding Davis's "Life in the Iron Mills" in the *Atlantic Monthly*. But fiction seems to have been as foreign to her as it was to Emerson. She was so far from belonging to any literary sorority that she would not have understood Hawthorne's rage at best-selling women novelists crowding him out of public favor: "A damned lot of scribbling women, I wish they were forbidden to write on pain of having their faces deeply scarified."

Dickinson was alone, imaginatively separate from her contemporaries—and assuredly from ours. The intensest privacy, solitude, and loneliness of the Puritan experience in America were still hers even when the theocracy ceased to command. It had been virtually cut off from the sprawling continent until the Revolution. But in the little college town deep in the Connecticut Valley, Emily Dickinson could retain the aloneness central to Puritanism by sheltering herself in her own family. The Dickinsons were leaders of Amherst. Edward Dickinson the father—lawyer, treasurer of the college, state legislator, and sometime congressman—so stern that he was his daughter's favorite subject for raillery, became financially sound after *his* father had gone bankrupt and fled in disgrace. Edward was one of the Connecticut Valley's "river kings."

The father's money and importance—to which brother Austin succeeded in such a whirl of activity that his death was attributed to it—shielded Emily from such possible distractions as the agitation over slavery. She was to write desperate poems mourning young friends killed in the Civil War. But the war as such was as remote from her prime instincts and interests as the contemporary American writers she might have noticed. She does refer once to Whitman—she was told he was "disgraceful." Though her response to an Emerson lecture was pure awe, she had nothing in common with Emerson's message of liberation from the Church and the strenuous individualism that must follow that. Emerson's lectures were so hortatory and assured that she would have found their self-confidence simply curious. In its economy and gnomic style his poetry can remind us of hers. But Emerson in poetry as in prose always gives us his positive conclusions on every topic, as when he grandly wrote, "The stars, the stars are fugitive also." (Yeats thought this the most beautiful line he had ever read.) Dickinson in poem after poem is openly thinking her way through. Where Emerson's lines are classic in feeling, lapidary, as if written to be inscribed on a monument, hers are full of intense personal outcries—"wrecked, solitary, here." They have nothing in common with Emerson's cool mythologizing of general subjects, his professional good nature, and above all his sly preachiness.

What, she says in poem after poem, do I have in common with others? What, on so many terrible days, do *I* have in common with myself? My body, my fate in life, my death?

> *The Soul selects her own Society—*
> *Then—shuts the Door—*
> *To her divine Majority—*
> *Present no more—*
>
> *Unmoved—she notes the Chariots—pausing—*
> *At her low Gate—*
> *Unmoved—an Emperor be kneeling*
> *Upon her Mat—*
>
> *I've known her—from an ample nation—*
> *Choose One—*
> *Then—close the Valves of her attention—*
> *Like Stone—*

#303

An arrogant, totally romantic, flamboyantly Yankee poet writing in Greenwich Village against the rumble of Sixth Avenue life, e. e. cummings, liked to say—and how often he said it—a poet's "supreme country" is himself. That was not selfhood but lack of any material to write about but "himself." Dickinson never celebrated herself as an individual, and certainly not as a type—not of New England, not even of ancestral Amherst and her distinguished family. She certainly did not celebrate poets who constantly wrote about one another because they were all women. She did not come from anyone else's big country. Which may be why so much of our hindsight about her leaves out her shattering sense of what pure being is like that made the Italian critic Paolo Milano, a refugee here during the war, say, "She is the only one of your classic Americans who gives me the satisfaction that the best European poets do."

Still, she had a locality and a whole series of subjects occupying her that became leading themes in her work—nature, God, love, immortality, death.

> *Some things that stay there be—*
> *Grief—Hills—Eternity—*
> *Nor this behooveth me.*
>
> *There are that resting, rise.*
> *Can I expound the skies?*
> *How still the Riddle lies!*

Never political, even during the Civil War, her most creative period, she admitted the devastation of seeing local boys brought back in coffins. Not a poet of big "ideas" like Whitman, she was more intensely reflective on the immediacies of life and death (especially death) than anyone else except Melville. She was the subject—above all to herself—of a religious enclosure. This was dying out in Amherst even as she was dying in the eighties. But it is intensely vivid in her work as it is nowhere else.

> *No Rack can torture me—*
> *My Soul—at Liberty—*
> *Behind this mortal Bone*
> *There knits a bolder One—*
>
> *You cannot prick with saw—*
> *Nor pierce with Scimitar—*
> *Two Bodies—therefore be—*
> *Bind One—The Other fly—*
>
> *The Eagle of his Nest*
> *No easier divest—*
> *And gain the Sky*
> *Than mayest Thou—*
>
> *Except Thyself may be*
> *Thine Enemy—*
> *Captivity is Consciousness—*
> *So's Liberty.*

> *#384*

In the Puritan heyday no form of writing was more important to the anxious elect than the diary that rendered up to God at the end of each year one's moral accounts. Prayer and sermon also led to dialectic, expostulating with oneself. Stylistically, the effect of the Bible, the derivative influence of its grammar, which like all ancient tongues practiced a condensation and contraction peculiarly suitable to man's constant interrogation of himself, was to find its ultimate performance in New England's preference for what Emerson called "dry light and hard expressions." The Puritan way to God could be complicated, even tortured, but it was direct.

The New England saints and sages were to live not by good deeds but by style—always stripping life down to fundamentals and essentials, to aphorisms, parables, seeming riddles. The absolute in Thoreau's style personifies the absolute he tried to live; he said he wanted to drive life into a corner. He certainly got what he wanted. *Walden* describes a personal pilgrimage that convinces us—as it convinced Thoreau—by the exhaustingly achieved economy of its style, not Thoreau's housekeeping.

That passionate being Emily Dickinson also got what she wanted through style, little as she may have *wanted* to live her life in the circular second-story bedroom. For as necessary containment, the compression of lapidary phrases, exclamations, rhapsodies, playful riddles, her style of abruptness and emotional indentation represents some kind of ultimate poetry for the heart's immediacies. Even her punctuation—dashes between words, dashes marking off one line from another, the dashes enabling her (and the reader) to breathe—can remind us, as only the greatest poets do, of our inner despair of words, mere words, crying out against the silence of the universe.

But no poet dominated by the Church as institution could have written, "It is true that the unknown is the largest need of intellect, although for this no one thinks to thank God." No other New Englander forever hearing God praised could have added, for her part, "We thank thee, Father, for these strange minds that enamor us against thee."

> *One need not be a Chamber—to be Haunted—*
> *One need not be a House—*

> *The Brain has Corridors—surpassing*
> *Material Place—*
>
> #670 (c. 1863)

She called God a "Force illegible," while admitting "All Circumstances are the Frame / In which His face is set." From a casual letter: "I was thinking today—as I noticed, that the 'Supernatural' was only the Natural, disclosed." From another letter: "God was penurious with me which makes me shrewd with Him." Another:

> The seeing pain one can't relieve makes a demon of one. If angels have the heart beneath their silver jackets, I think such things could make them weep, but Heaven is so cold! It will never look kind to me that God, who causes all, denies such little wishes. It could not hurt His glory, unless it were a lonesome kind. I must conclude it is.

The humor of Dickinson's verbal relationship with God—she had no other—is not antic or spectacle but supple. God is a name, a tradition, an inheritance—"Father." But how else, where else, does He show His hand except as a circumference—the perfect word—that encloses us? The Old Testament tradition is that God's universe is one of deeds, not words. But only words are left to the modern poet—she was the first to come out of New England—as the rim of circumference recedes further and further from our sight.

Her sense of enclosure set physical limitations as necessary relations. Obviously these were not hindrances to her intellect; one cannot imagine a mind less constrained, more playful about her surroundings. Still, the poet was brought into the local net. When her neo-Calvinist father took her to hear the Swedish soprano Jenny Lind in Northampton, she described Father, not Jenny Lind:

> Father sat all the evening looking mad, and yet so much amused you would have died a-laughing. It wasn't sarcasm, exactly, nor it wasn't disdain, it was infinitely funnier than either of those virtues, as if old Abraham had come to see the show, and thought it was all very well, but a little excess of monkey!

Emily's refusal to follow the Church's paths of accommodation and solace, her very seclusion physically as she settled into her art, suggests independence from pride of station. Just as her grandfather went through his money helping to found Amherst College, so she visited Boston twice—to see an eye doctor. "We," she said of Amherst—meaning the Dickinsons—"were rich in disdain for Bostonians and Boston."

Even before her thirties, when the stress of the Civil War drove her to write a poem almost every day, she increasingly "kept to home." She stopped visiting brother Austin's wife Susan, three hundred feet away. The two houses were half hidden by evergreens. It is to Susan's prodding, who thought the original second stanza of "Safe in Their Alabaster Chambers" inadequate, that we owe the breathtaking stanza Emily added in 1861:

> *Grand go the Years—in the Crescent—above them—*
> *Worlds scoop their Arcs—*
> *And Firmaments—row—*
> *Diadems—drop—and Doges—surrender*
> *Soundless as dots—on a Disc of Snow.*

In "The Homestead" she was born; there she died at fifty-six. Except for the fifteen years in which the family occupied another house on Pleasant Street, she lived for forty years in one house and on its grounds. Well into the twentieth century her house was surrounded by red barns and extensive fields. Amherst was backed up by farm country on every side. One of the poet's essential activities was registering the effect of the "blue" mountains surrounding her valley, the Pelham hills on the horizon, the changing shades and weight of weather in every season, the light, the insects and snakes in her garden.

Nature was the most physical part of her life. Unlike us, who now know nature as a government park, a preserve to enjoy on holiday, she had it ever around her. Nature was the background of her sensibility, the constant, immitigable procession of reality, the great process unrolling our dreamlike passage through existence.

Not being a Romantic or a Transcendentalist, Dickinson did not look for God in nature. She did not find Nature a consoling facsimile for His absence, or what she concluded was "condensed presence." God was a "distant stately lover." He was one character in the eternal drama of things passing, life passing:

> *I have a King, who does not speak—*
> *So—wondering—thro' the hours meek*
> *I trudge the day away.*
>
> #*103*

On occasion God could even be "Burglar, Banker." She said her father worshiped an "Eclipse." She would not have agreed with Whitman that death was the ultimately erotic-mystical event rejoining us to the elements of which we were first composed. It was just another event, the last—one that ended on this side of the grave, when consciousness ended. But as all fear may be fear of what we cannot know, so Nature sends intimations of death. The very light of winter afternoons in the Connecticut Valley, as I have reason to remember, can strike dread. It struck *her* with a force that only her genius could have split into such different corridors of feeling:

> *There's a certain Slant of light,*
> *Winter Afternoons—*
> *That oppresses, like the Heft*
> *Of Cathedral Tunes—*
>
> *Heavenly Hurt, it gives us—*
> *We can find no scar,*
> *But internal difference,*
> *Where the Meanings, are—*
>
> *None may teach it—Any—*
> *'Tis the Seal Despair—*
> *An imperial affliction*
> *Sent us of the Air—*
>
> *When it comes, the Landscape listens—*
> *Shadows—hold their breath—*
> *When it goes, 'tis like the Distance*
> *On the look of Death.*
>
> #*258*

"Heavenly" has to do with distance, not grace. This extraordinary poem brings us back to what Goethe called man's highest response to the universe, our "shudder of awe." Inside was the little factory in the corner bedroom that produced almost two thousand poems and an almost equal sum of letters. Inside was the writing table, the sleigh bell, the Franklin stove, the dresser, the windows from which she could see the front walk and the driveway, the Seth Thomas clock, the ruby decanter, the hatbox, the portraits of George Eliot, Elizabeth Barrett Browning, and Thomas Carlyle. But

> *Had I not seen the Sun*
> *I could have borne the shade*
> *But Light a newer Wilderness*
> *My Wilderness has made.*
>
> *#1233*

Unlike the rest of Amherst, she had, professionally, nothing to do but *look*:

> *I dwell in Possibility—*
> *A fairer House than Prose*
> *More numerous of Windows—*
> *Superior—for Doors—*
>
> *Of Chambers as the Cedars—*
> *Impregnable of Eye—*
> *And for an Everlasting Roof*
> *The Gambrels of the Sky—*
>
> *Of Visitors—the fairest—*
> *For Occupation—This—*
> *The spreading wide my narrow Hands*
> *To gather Paradise.*
>
> *#657 (c. 1862)*

Yeats said that the death of God is but a play. Free of orthodoxy's clichés, like that other lonely thinker Abraham Lincoln, she would have agreed with Lincoln that life's ultimate grace is—*This too will pass.* Life passing, life as the fullness of our struggle against extinction, life lived to extreme consciousness showing just where we are—soon enough, *where* we have been—

> *These are the days when Birds come back—*
> *A very few—a Bird or two—*
> *To take a backward look*
>
> . . . .
>
> *Oh Sacrament of summer days,*
> *Oh Last Communion in the Haze—*
> *Permit a child to join.*
>
> #*130*

"I would eat evanescence slowly." Such interjections within the stream of being tell us what despair within may signify more than pain and why religious *thinking* survives even when "Father" is not exactly where He used to be in the childhood of the world. Where He made everything up (in both senses of "made it up") all by Himself.

She was just past thirty when she seems to have given up hope that her outward life would somehow be transformed.

> *"Hope" is the thing with feathers—*
> *That perches in the soul—*
> *And sings the tune without the words—*
> *And never stops—at all—*
>
> #*254*

At times she was unhinged. One of her greatest poems describes herself at the close as "wrecked, solitary, here." But finally accepting her life (if she ever did accept it) as the round of life she had always lived—it left her free to write, positively *impelled* her to write—she was able to make some supreme poems out of the return of the seasons, the fall of light, the spring of birds, "the angle of a landscape," the leaves that "like women interchange":

> *There came a Day at Summer's full,*
> *Entirely for me—*
> *I thought that such were for the Saints*
> *Where Resurrections—be.*
>
> #*322*

8

William James: Rescuing Religion

PHILOSOPHERS of considerable reputation are usually more admired than loved, but William James inspired affection even among his fellow philosophers. Alfred North Whitehead referred to him as that "adorable genius." His Harvard colleague and department head, George Herbert Palmer, said, "We found in him a masterful type of human being, developed almost to perfection." No one at Harvard in James's many years there, from 1872, when he was hired by President Charles W. Eliot to teach anatomy and physiology, to 1907, when he resigned as Harvard's world-famous professor of philosophy, ever doubted that his personal charm contributed as much to his legend as his freshness as a thinker and his gift for making himself clear and peculiarly valuable to popular audiences. Eliot prided himself on his hunch in adding to the Harvard faculty a man whose professional degree was in medicine, which he never practiced. Even George Santayana, who observed him for decades all too closely as James's student and colleague, and who in a famous sketch of James in *Character and Opinion in the United States* said, "There is a sense in which James was not a philosopher at all," recalled how in the midst of classroom routine "the spirit would sometimes come upon him, and leaning his head on his hand, he would let fall golden words, picturesque, fresh from the heart, full of the knowledge of good and evil."

In our own day the philosopher Richard Rorty, reviewing Jacques Barzun's rapturous *A Stroll with William James* (1983), observed that "everybody who reads William James's letters falls in love with the man. He seems the companion nobody ever had: the one who never gets depressed or angry or bored, is always honest and open, always thinks you interesting." Somehow James, in his early thirties, managed to shuck off all his neuroses, all those fantasies that lead the rest of us to distort and manipulate other people for our self-protection. After frightening bouts of melancholia during his twenties, accompanied by an inability to harness his own energies, suddenly he changes into Whitehead's "adorable genius"—fluent, focused, and indefatigable.

In *The Varieties of Religious Experience*, a book James published eight years before his death in 1910, James was obsessed with what religion had done and could still do for gifted persons he thought of as psychopathic—a clinical term that he did not hesitate to apply to several crises in his own history. He had by no means "managed to shuck off all his neuroses." Like many another exquisitely and excruciatingly sensitive literary artist, he found much of his material in his so-called neuroses. But it is amusing to find Professor Rorty impressed by the fact, as one philosopher commenting on another, that "even his marriage was happy; even his children liked him." Rorty goes on to recall the extraordinary letter James wrote on December 14, 1882, from London to his dying father:

> The thought that this may be your last illness conveys no very sudden shock. You are old enough, you've given your message to the world in many ways and will not be forgotten. . . . If you go, it will not be an inharmonious thing.

Rorty could also have cited James's astounding letter of 1892 to his dying sister Alice as an example of "the charity and the courage to write we all wished we had or will have."

> When that which is *you* passes out of the body, I am sure that there will be an explosion of liberated force and life till then eclipsed and kept down. I can hardly imagine *your* transition without a great oscillation of both "worlds" as they regain their equilibrium after the change. Everyone will feel the shock, but you yourself will be more surprised than anybody else.

Pace Rorty, it was not some psychic wholeness at last in a frequently disturbed life which made James write with such force, but his genius as a thinker turning his own terror into a message of salvation to a father and sister who shared his intense vulnerability.

James's charm for other people, starting with his brother Henry and his sister Alice, stemmed from the recognition that his extraordinarily complex temperament, whatever its several breakdowns, was a gift. His openness, candor, volatility, and enthusiasm were equaled only by his ranging intelligence and occasional lack of psychic balance. Such disproportionate qualities do not surprise us in the personalities of Carlyle, Melville, T. S. Eliot, D. H. Lawrence, and Ezra Pound. They do surprise us in original philosophers like Nietzsche and Wittgenstein. Nietzsche sufferingly *lived* his thought even when it was a radiant-sounding gospel aimed to turn men back to the freedom that supposedly prevailed before Christianity fostered a slave morality. His Zarathustra was the new man-god driven to relentless eloquence as he rose above the human herd. Wittgenstein never presumed to such self-intoxication in words, and portrayed his dilemma as man captive to language. "A picture held us captive, and we could not escape, for it lay in our language. It pitilessly held us and kept us from getting away."

What James did, very much in the American style, was to *appeal* his life, to open it up with the same candor and directness with which he opened up all his thought in its many successive stages in order to *save* it, literally, by the power of his thought. As experience in all its possible departments and ramifications became the foundation of his teaching as a philosopher, so personal experience became the underlying strength of his work. One reason why he became famous as much for his temperament as for his philosophy is that he pursued his thought—at first desperately, then more and more magisterially—for readers and listeners who perhaps recognized his problems as their own. The most important thing to recognize in this reliance on particular ideas for dealing with oneself as a creature always in crisis—James's particular importance to us—is that it candidly looks on religion as therapy. Not "ye shall know the truth and the truth shall set ye free," but just give your anxious self up for the moment.

> There is a state of mind, known to religious men, in which the will to assert ourselves and hold our own has been displaced by a willingness to close our mouth and be nothing in the floods and waterspouts of God. In this state of mind, what we most dreaded has become the habitation of our safety, and the hour of our moral death has turned into our spiritual birthday. The time for tension in our soul is over.

This is not belief, or even as therapy the search for one's earliest past taught by psychoanalysis. It is pragmatism, the saving element to be found in grasping for one's sake a particular idea, that so impresses us in James's famous sense of deliverance after reading the French philosopher Charles Renouvier. In persistent depression and even fear of insanity, in January 1870, a year after getting his M.D., James was at such a low ebb that he wryly suggested that his friend Dr. Henry Bowditch become the keeper of an insane asylum so that he, William James, could find refuge there. Yet by April 30 James could report: "I think that yesterday was a crisis in my life. I finished the first part of Renouvier's second 'Essais' and see no reason why his definition of Free Will—'the sustaining of a thought *because I choose to*—when I might have other thoughts'—need be the definition of an illusion."

In the same period James wrote in his diary, "In accumulated acts of thought lies salvation. . . . Hitherto, when I have felt like taking a free initiative, like daring to act originally, without carefully waiting for contemplation of the external world to determine all for me, suicide seemed the most manly form to put my daring into; now, I will go a step further with my will, not only act with it, but believe as well; believe in my individual reality and creative power. My belief to be sure can't be optimistic—but I will posit life (the real, the good) in the self-governing resistance of the ego to the world."

The "dark night of the soul," in the phrase of the Spanish mystic Saint John of the Cross, is a familiar feature in those of William James's writings that are supposed to be entirely philosophic when they are not purely scientific and educational. In *The Principles of Psychology* (1890), James's first book and based in part on laboratory research that James started at Harvard, one suddenly comes across statements that echo the most deeply personal sense of crisis, not just reflexes testable and recordable. In the famous chapter entitled "Habit," there is a hint of peculiar urgency when he names habit as society's most precious conservative agent. "It alone keeps us all within the bounds of ordinance, and saves the children of fortune from the envious uprisings of the poor." If this hints of some propertied smugness, James is anything but smug when he declares that "habit dooms us all to fight out the battle of life upon the lines of our nurture or our own early choice, and to make the best of a pursuit that disagrees, because there is no other for which we are fitted, and it is too late to begin again. . . . On the whole, it is best we should not escape. It is well for the world that in most of us, by the age of thirty, the character has set like plaster, and will never soften again."

Yet James came to believe that it is never too late to begin again, that the character—especially his own, which he was in some sense always endeavoring to remake—is not set forever in life. The whole point of *The Varieties of Religious Experience*, a book ostensibly descriptive and objectively psychological, is that the truly religious character begins as a "sick soul," is dominated by a sense of lack, of something basically wrong, but through the mysterious accession of faith in the world opened to the subconscious is given—gives itself—that second chance in life that religion helps to provide. The term "psychopath" did not scare James as it can now scare us.

> In the psychopathic temperament we have the *sine qua non* of mortal perception . . . we have the love of metaphysics and mysticism which carry one's interests beyond the surface of the sensible world.

Notice the quest for security in the ominously prudential sentences I have quoted about habit alone keeping "us all within the bounds of ordinance." I don't know if James knew Santayana's saying that "we are all maniacs held in leash." This was a considerable insight on the part of so essentially conservative and even classical a thinker as Santayana, who practiced wisdom rather than adventurous living, who remained a Catholic at heart without believing in Christianity, and who was so careful a bachelor all his life that near the end of it he thought it was just possible that as an undergraduate he might have had some homosexual inclination.

James said of his old student and colleague that his thinking reminded him of white marble. James knew well enough how close *he* had come to whatever it is we call mania. Years ago the famous Harvard psychologist Henry A. Murray told me that at one point in his life James had put himself into McLean's, the Somerville asylum famous for its blue-blooded clientele, described by Robert Lowell in "Waking in the Blue" as "figures of bravado ossified young."

This marvelously intelligent and creative thinker William James was not afraid to admit in his *Varieties of Religious Experience* that

> the normal process of life contains moments as bad as any of those which insane melancholy is filled with, moments in which radical

evil gets its innings and takes its solid turn. The lunatic's visions of horror are all drawn from the material of daily fact. Our civilization is founded on the shambles, and every individual existence goes out in a lonely spasm of helpless agony. If you protest, my friend, wait till you arrive there yourself!

The most publicized pathological episode in James's life is noteworthy for several reasons. In the crucial chapter "The Sick Soul" in *The Varieties of Religious Experience* an extreme case of panic fear is described in excruciating detail, but is ascribed to a French source whom James wryly describes as having evidently been in a bad nervous condition at the time of which he writes. Otherwise it has the "merit of extreme simplicity." It is particularly noteworthy because the panic and disorientation described are startlingly similar to that suffered by Henry James, Sr., in England, 1844.

The son admits to having edged out of the worst of the experience by clinging to Scripture texts. The father felt he was saved by a lady who explained his "vastation," his experience of being devastated, as a case familiar to followers of Emanuel Swedenborg and redeemable through his creed.

William James's critical experience was probably in 1872, when he was in a particularly unsteady state trying to decide on his vocation. He related it in the Gifford Lectures at the University of Edinburgh thirty years later, in 1902, when he was at the peak of his fame, with the terrible vividness with which people on the couch recall some particularly wounding psychic episode.

Whilst in this state of philosophic pessimism and general depression of spirits about my prospects, I went one evening into a dressing-room in the twilight to procure some article that was there; when suddenly there fell upon me without any warning, just as if it came out of the darkness, a horrible fear of my own existence. Simultaneously there arose in my mind the image of an epileptic patient whom I had seen in the asylum, a black-haired youth with greenish skin, entirely idiotic, who used to sit all day on one of the benches, or rather shelves against the wall, with his knees drawn up against his chin, and the coarse gray undershirt, which was his only garment, drawn over them inclosing his entire figure. He sat there like a sort of sculptured Egyptian cat or Peruvian mummy, moving nothing but his black eyes and looking absolutely non-human. This image and my fear entered into a species of combination with each other. *That shape am I,* I felt, potentially. Nothing that I possess can defend me against that fate, if the hour for it should strike for me as it struck for him. There was such a horror of him, and such a perception of my own merely momentary discrepancy from him, that it was as if something hitherto solid within my breast gave way entirely, and I became a mass of quivering fear. After this the universe was changed for me altogether. I awoke morning after morning with a horrible dread at the pit of my stomach, and with a sense of the insecurity of life that I never knew before, and that I have never felt since. It was like a revelation; and although the immediate feelings passed away, the experience has made me sympathetic with the morbid feelings of others ever since.

James concludes, "I have always thought that this experience of melancholia of mine had a religious bearing. . . . [T]he fear was so invasive and powerful that if I had not clung to scripture-texts like 'The eternal God is my refuge,' etc. 'Come unto me, all ye that labor and are heavy-laden,' etc. I think I should have grown really insane."

Here we come to the most interesting side of William James as a religious thinker, for it is so unexpected. He was the firstborn and the eldest son of a father who was immersed all his life in writing himself out of the harsh Calvinist Presbyterianism of *his* Irish-born father. William was the child who most duplicated the father's speculative turn of mind. But if Henry James, Sr., despite his winning exuberance, was a curiosity to his contemporaries (he would have been totally forgotten if he had not been the father of Henry and William James), he was an object of powerful resentment to his son.

To begin with, the old fellow was always at home, *writing*. He had lost a leg as a boy trying to put out a fire; he had acquired, not without a struggle, a significant inheritance from his father's fortune in Albany and Syracuse real estate. His son Henry wrote in *Notes of a Son and Brother* that no one in his family was guilty of doing a single stroke of business. Sure that his children could not get a proper education at home, the father impulsively moved them around from school to school in Germany, England, and France. William's fluent German and French were to give him access to new schools of psychology and philosophy in Europe and made him a favorite chairman at international congresses. But the father dominated and oppressed his family as he could not his intellectual contemporaries; he was so fiercely loving and possessive of his children that sooner or later they had to flee.

Worst of all, from the point of view of William James, brought up on the psychology of reflexes he had developed on Darwinism and positivism, was the father's preoccupation not just with religion but with establishing his own brand of self-emancipating Swedenborgianism on a basis of utopian socialism. Every time I read Henry James the elder, who can be vaguely exalting but bogs down just when the argument, if you can locate it, should go forward, I think of Emerson's rueful remark in his journal, "After us, mysticism should go out of style for a very long time."

William was lively like his father, but unlike the father infinitely adaptable to everything under the sun. He had the curiosity of the true doctor, which in time was to make him come to religion not as a creed, religion as theism, but religion as an individual psychological experience, as a way of extending the person's hold on life by giving him the feeling of a second chance, of being twice-born. From James's scientific and psychiatric vantage point as an observer of "the sick soul," a state he knew well, the many different creeds and positions he quoted and examined at such length in *The Varieties of Religious Experience* were precious personal confessions. Religion was no longer a matter of objective certitude and truth. But in the last decades of the nineteenth century, positivism and materialism as a worldview were becoming grossly intolerant in the world of thought. James had established the first psychology laboratory in America and had written his famous *Principles of Psychology*, he said, sentence by sentence "in the teeth of irreducible facts." But laboratory psychology and mechanism in physics and biology could not account for the individual's own sense of the exceptionality of his existence. Religion, as the only field of human thought and endeavor purporting to speak of life and death together, that even claimed to be the one bridge between them, at least satisfied James's belief that the axis of reality goes through personal existence.

James's first book in philosophy was called *The Will to Believe*. He later said it should have been called "The Right to Believe." What he could not call it was "The Ability to Believe." America, despite its high rate of church observance, is a peculiarly secular culture. The proof is the mechanistic and even commercial vocabulary in which, more than ever, Americans talk and write. Even William James, in his most famous book, *Pragmatism*, gave a falsely material reputation to the term by speaking of the "cash-value" of an idea. What he meant—and it was his central idea—is that the true end of life is realization of one's ideas and ideals, not hugging one's internal consciousness. And realization in the deepest sense is the realization of some sense of immortality in those endeavors—commitments, loyalties, and affections that inevitably break the heart through the narrowness of our perspective, the thinness of our belief, the persistence of our childhood egotism.

James understood the power and penetration of scientism because he was so much a part of it, had as a psychologist helped to create it through the pioneer laboratory he had founded at Harvard and his natural adherence to the skepticism of a generation whose emancipation from supernaturalism had been considerably strengthened by the brutal experience of the Civil War. His two younger brothers, Garth Wilkinson (named after an English Swedenborgian) and Robertson, had both been wounded in the war, from which the father had carefully shielded his two older and more promising sons. It was in the hothouse of his parental home, so strangely dominated by an almost too loving father, who was always writing away at ideas that were out of date and, as William duly noted, were always the same ideas from book to book, that William certainly learned what belonged to *his* mind and not to his father's. As a young man so gifted in drawing that he thought of becoming a professional artist, he had to endure his father's stern rejection, as from Mount Sinai, of an aesthetic attitude toward life—hardly William James's weakness! And he could have said, even before Nietzsche brought the news of God's death, that his father's attempt to locate God entirely in man was an admission that he had given up not only Calvinism but the old God who was no longer anyone's father or lawgiver or conscience. God, too, had become a reflex for the faithful, just a slogan to be rejected by the emancipated.

Nevertheless, the sons of ministers like Nietzsche and Emerson, the son of a God-obsessed man like William James, were all haunted by a possible failure in man if the death of God as an objective entity whose existence we can intellectually confirm led to a shallow, materialistic outlook in all things. James saw this more closely than any of his scientific peers at the close of the century. The important side of Nietzsche's dictum is not just that God is dead but that man must now transcend his old dependent self, must in truth become more than man. This is the superman carrying the rest of us to new heights whom the post-Christian Emerson called representative man and the admirer of Prussian *Macht* his friend Carlyle called the hero as original man. The religion-despising Trotsky foresaw under Communism minds exceeding Aristotle and Goethe, but meanwhile regretted the necessity of murdering all opponents.

William James was actually too democratic-minded to fall into the poses of superior wisdom that led Freud, for example, to derogate followers who were no longer, as he says about Otto Rank in *Moses and Monotheism*, "under my influence." Unlike Freud, who treated everyone but himself as a possible patient (thus leaving himself open to posthumous derogation and scandal), Dr. William James regarded himself as a sort of patient to the end, unfinished business. He always felt that he had to make up for the professional indecision of his young manhood, for his deep depressions, and, as his brother Henry did, for having been kept out of the Civil War. "The moral equivalent of war," as he put it in a famous essay, was a big thing in his mind, especially by contrast with the unbearable self-confidence of his friend Oliver Wendell Holmes, Jr., wounded thrice in the Civil War, and his overconfident student at Harvard Theodore Roosevelt, noisy proponent of the strenuous life, which came to mean a love of war.

Still, James identified more with brashly assertive Americans like Holmes and Roosevelt than he ever could have with the pessimist Freud. He believed, like a good American, in remaking himself, something different from making *it*—money. James, always worried about his health, might not have died of heart disease at sixty-eight if he had not strained his heart in mountaineering. And he would not be the James whom readers fall in love with and identify with if he had not written, along with *The Varieties of Religious Experience*, so many other things, even in technical philosophy, that are really tracts for living, guides to wider and deeper experiences of life.

This is where the message of the twice-born, the idea of giving ourselves that second chance in life of which conversion is the paradigm, becomes so important to the *Varieties*. What we may or can convert to is not a new idea of God or faith in Him, but a suddenly charged realization of possibilities in ourselves withheld by the restrictive formulae of our culture—meaning scientism as necessary objective judgment superimposed on and restraining the throb of our actual experience, the truth we come upon only within our individual existence.

According to James, we liberate ourselves first of all by being totally disenchanted with the manner and shape of our lives. This is the great thing about the arduous saints, mystics, penitents, original eccentrics, and whatnot, from Saint Paul to Tolstoy, whose neuroses, if you insist on that Freud-flavored word in disparagement, were really critics of their civilization. Often, as with Tolstoy, you get the remarkable example of a man who had everything—genius, aristocratic position, wealth, who possessed and relished the most crucial experiences of his time as soldier, lover, and national leader in Russia—yet was driven by the wildest dissatisfaction with everything and everyone until, in terms that no one in his family shared, he tried to throw it all away to live the life of a humble pilgrim trudging the earth alone.

James, dying the same year as Tolstoy, missed the slightly comic picture of the world-famous writer and feudal aristocrat dying as a tramp—surrounded by the world press. But if he had known it, he would have pronounced perfect Tolstoy's anguished cry over the misery of the poorest and most rejected, those called "the dark people." "One cannot live so! One cannot live so!"

James helped to found the anti-imperialist league in protest against the brutal suppression of Filipino independence. (Santayana thought imperialism the natural behavior of big powers like his native Spain and scorned James as naïve.) But James was an active citizen, aware of the growing bitterness of the immigrant working class in the big cities. He alarmed his Harvard colleagues by attending séances and investigating psychic phenomena. He alarmed brother Henry by climbing a ladder to have a peek at the garden of G. K. Chesterton, that supermilitant convert to Catholic orthodoxy whom, typically, James thought a pragmatist. He was so unusual a Harvard eminence that he went out of his way to look up Walter Lippmann after encountering a brilliant paper by the young freshman.

These unconventional and remarkably open attitudes in every department of life are not equal to those radical figures in the *Varieties* whose need of God, and whose ability to achieve Him, so to speak, radically enlarged not only their own lives but the lives of many devoted to their example. Enlargement, "more," more to ourselves, is the key word in the conclusion of *The Varieties of Religious Experience*, and for this he relied on evidence of our subliminal faculties. His proof of their existence was the power of revelation, the sudden knowledge of a world other than the one we mistakenly think our only one.

This, fundamentally, was the *use* of religion to James. It was the principal evidence he had, as a psychologist, that while the first step of the significantly religious consciousness is uneasiness, the sense that there is *something wrong about us* as we naturally stand, "the solution is a sense that *we are saved from the wrongness* by making proper connection with the higher powers."

Here at last, after devoting so many acute and sympathetic pages to those who were delivered from their "wrongness," or whatever it was that made them feel that the great universe itself was lacking on *them*, that they were withholding it from themselves by withholding their subconscious belief in transcending to a higher power, James is confronting his own case on the essential question: How can a natural believer like himself believe when the age in its best minds denies everything about belief in God—except its psychological efficacy, which has so impressed James and has transparently applied to himself?

This is a question that does not come up today, when among the intellectual leaders of American society a deeply personal belief in God is tolerated as harmlessly personal, like a taste in food or a loyalty to the Red Sox. Religion even among the faithful, like American literature today, has left cosmology to the physicists. Nobody argues about God today. It is enough for the complacent that Americans go to church and synagogue in record numbers.

But James was writing about religion at the tag end of the nineteenth century, which intellectually brought the issue to rest and so welcomed a descriptive study of *the varieties of religious experience*—the title alone could have put the material into the *Journal of Abnormal Psychology*. Nevertheless, James had to make some positive conclusion of his own. What he comes out with is this:

> The individual, so far as he suffers from his wrongness and criti- cizes it, is to that extent consciously beyond it, and in at least pos- sible touch with something higher. . . . *He becomes conscious that the higher part is conterminous* and continuous with MORE of the same quality which is operative in the universe outside him, and which he can keep in working touch with, and in a fashion get on board of and save himself when all his lower being has gone to pieces in the wreck.

This is not the kind of testimony likely to have assuaged the broken heart of faith in the nineteenth century, but it goes down perfectly in the twentieth. James has not yet arrived at our sublime faith in repression as the only thing to get over. He knows he cannot get away with proclaim- ing the "new life" opening up for those who find new spiritual strength as "a place of conflux where the forces of two universes meet." He has to meet the question of objective certitude, once easy for those who be- lieved that God was more than a metaphor. As he says, "Is such a 'more' merely our own notion, or does it really exist? If so, in what shape does it exist? Does it act, as well as exist? And in what form should we con- ceive of that 'union' with it of which religious geniuses are so con- vinced?"

James's answer is to fall back on the "*subconscious self*" (James's ital- ics) as a "well-accredited psychological entity" and "exactly the mediat- ing term required. Apart from all religious considerations, there is actually and literally more life in our total soul than we are at any time aware of. The exploration of the transmarginal field has hardly yet been seriously undertaken." So we come to the hypothesis that "whatever it may be on its *further* side, the 'more' with which in religious experience we feel ourselves connected with is on its *hither* side the subconscious continuation of our conscious life." So that "starting thus with a recog- nized psychological fact as our basis, we seem to preserve a contact with 'science' which the ordinary theologian lacks. At the same time the the- ologian's contention that the religious man is moved by an external power is vindicated, for it is one of the peculiarities of invasions from the subconscious region to take on objective appearances, and to suggest to the subject an external control. In the religious life the control is felt as 'higher'; but since on our hypothesis it is higher faculties of our own hidden mind which are controlling, the sense of union with the power beyond us is a sense of something, not merely apparently, but literally true."

As James admits, this "doorway into the subject seems to me the best one for a science of religions." As for himself, "Those of us who are not personally favored with such specific revelations must stand outside of them altogether and, for the present at least, decide that, since they corroborate incomparable theological doctrines, they neutralize one another and leave no fixed result."

This is fine for the "science of religions," but if you ask James for bread in this matter, he gives you a stone—meaning an hypothesis. Why should this be in the least a disappointment in a book that offers itself as a psychologist's scientific study of the "varieties" of "religious *experience*"? Because the whole basis of the book is *personal* experience, because the so-called science of religions is not what enters into James's wonderfully close and sympathetic analysis of each experience, because James is too evidently seeking a solution to his lifelong problem, beginning with his relation to a father who, whatever his lack of interest for James as a thinker, most deeply influenced James by seeing himself and no other as the occasion of God's presence and intervention, and thus the proof that He exists.

William James found himself writing to his dying sister Alice that by 1892 he was surprisingly more in sympathy with their father than he had expected. James incorporated into the underlying passion of his "scientific" book what remained of an age of faith: faith is a personal gift, and if you have it, you are beyond argument.

Freud in *The Future of an Illusion* dismissed religion as an outworn form of dependency dating from childhood. Either the Deity was real or He was not: end of the subject, end of hope for those who cannot find any solace in such reductionist psychology. Freud as a Jew was enthralled by the survival of his people and, whether he admitted it or not, attributed the survival not to persistent loyalty to God but to anti-

Semitism, which kept one fighting back. "Being a Jew I knew I would always be in the opposition."

Christianity, being more plastic and openly mythological, not to say polytheistic, made it easier to adapt to the vanishing of Jehovah. As the maverick educator Ivan Ilyich, while still a monsignor, put it to me, "God became smaller and smaller so that we could at last see Him." Jews were not supposed to "see" Him at all. Faith was absolute or, in the name of the only Deity, loyalty to one's history. Kafka to Gustav Janouch: "He who has faith cannot talk about it; he who has no faith should not talk about it." What a difference from Alfred North White-head, who near the end of *Science and the Modern World*, in the chapter "Religion and Science," admitting that "the presentation of God under the aspect of power awakens every modern instinct of critical reaction," went on, in a spirit of hope unknown to Freud on religion as "illusion," to say, "Religion is the vision of something which stands beyond, be-hind, and within, the passing flux of immediate things; something which is real, and yet waiting to be realized; something which is a re-mote possibility, and yet the greatest of present facts; something that gives meaning to all that passes, and yet eludes apprehension; something whose possession is the final good, and yet is beyond all reach; some-thing which is the ultimate ideal, and the hopeless quest."

This is the argument for *The Varieties of Religious Experience* that James did not make, but which explains the power and enduring popu-larity of his book. As the Son became far more real than the Father, so "religion" is forever real, especially to those for whom "God" is not. As things go nowadays, you might almost say that "religion" as a subject of the most intense personal interest has replaced "God," which after all is or is not a matter of objective existence and truth—or so it used to be. But if the triumph of "religion," especially comparative religion, over "God," explains our personal gratitude for James's *Varieties of Religious Experience*, no one seriously interested in the actual content of religion can doubt that James finally wins us as a fellow soul, not as a believer. Which is ironic, since the most impressive case histories he presents are those for whom faith came to be as real as the personal hell from which they were delivered.

9

Mark Twain: The American Funnyman Who Put God on Trial

The calm confidence of a Christian with four aces.

MARK TWAIN

IN THE FRENZIED YEARS of sudden opportunity after the Civil War, a self-declared and self-promoting type emerged from the West calling himself *the* real and only true "American." Part rebel and always the funnyman, he quickly attained success as a folk type but bore no resemblance to the wild men thrown up by the often lawless society of the frontier. It was not his mind or his behavior that was revolutionary—it was his temperament and the circumstances that led him to pursue the frontier from a village on the Mississippi to silver-rich Nevada and California. Mark Twain's father, John Marshall Clemens, was a Virginia patrician unhappily drawn to fail in remote Missouri, where he never stopped dreaming of the fortune to be claimed from his brash investment in Tennessee land. A gentleman's son immersed in "Great Nature" on the Mississippi, Mark Twain was brought up a Presbyterian on the strictest and most punitive ideas of "damnation." A sense of guilt at his natural skepticism never left him. The contrast between theology as American law and his buoyant early skepticism became the foundation of his famous humor. "It ain't necessarily so."

What replaced the early, dutiful, easily terrified Presbyterianism was his sense of himself as an event new and provocative. He chose to be a satirist, a disturber of convention, rather than a hero. He made a game of opposing himself to settled patterns of tradition and culture. Forever on the move (and describing his every move as a fresh hilarity), he was able to persuade his audience—it became enormous—that he was God's favorite child, and so ever new, like the creation.

This "American" began his career with a joke story—"Jim Smiley and His Jumping Frog," or how to win a bet by swindling the other guy—that became a best-seller and universal favorite. As silver miner, freelance journalist, husband to an heiress, and the most popular author of his day (he sold his books by subscription and later became his own publisher), Mark Twain was consumed by the dream of big (but *big*) money. In the end he went bankrupt after investing in a typesetting machine that would be the only one of its kind. (Alas, it was.) He saw his satire on respectable society as a commercial product, a deliberate joke, but he was easily gratified by that society and comfortably settled himself in it. But he was created by the New World when it was still really new, and as "Mark Twain" (a name he patented), genius, greed, and all, he returned the compliment by turning America into an emblem of himself.

Emerson, Thoreau, Whitman, Melville, and Henry James all talked about "the American," and on the whole they assumed him to be something altogether new and unique. But the narrator of *The Innocents Abroad* became this character. The author's second book, it was his first major effort; and it is this awareness, so early in Mark Twain's career (1869), that makes *The Innocents Abroad* in all its glibness and breeziness such a distinct and comic creation. For it is "the American," this wise-cracking type impatient with tradition and culture (still more a temperament than a mind), who has turned the tables on the Old World by showing himself innocent of the past *but of nothing else*. "The American" is now at large, face to face with all those treasures of the past that arouse his derision. Irreverence became Mark Twain's business. Not his only business, of course, for socially he does not consider himself inferior to his fellow passengers on the steamship *Quaker City*, just more observant. He is not overpowered by seeing Europe and the Near East for the first time. He is a professional—the others are on a "pilgrimage" to see the land they know so well from the Bible.

Despite the seeming spontaneity of all the narrator's likes and prejudices, *The Innocents Abroad* was carefully rewritten from the travel letters that Mark Twain sent back to newspapers in San Francisco and New York from the *Quaker City* excursion in 1867 to Europe, the Holy Land, and Egypt. Mark Twain's presence on board was a tribute to the success he had achieved as a correspondent at large; he had started out as a writer for newspapers in Nevada, and after three years there, two months in San Francisco, and four months in the Hawaiian Islands, he was a celebrity of sorts. The consciously roguish style became his trademark and helped to form the professional funnyman who pops up in his greatest books. His travel letters were so popular that a San Francisco paper wanted to publish them as a book. Mark Twain had to go back to San Francisco to head this off before he could sit down to his own book. This was published with the subtitle *The New Pilgrim's Progress*.

The original newspaper accounts of the excursion (edited by D. M. McKeithan as *Traveling with the Innocents Abroad*) show how much the author had to tone down his irritation with the piety of the elders, the majority aboard the *Quaker City*. Brought up the lonely fearful Presbyterian in St. Petersburg along the Mississippi, he was to pretty it all up in *The Adventures of Tom Sawyer* as everyone's church, Sunday school, and schoolroom. Forced at twelve (so goes the rumor) to attend his father's corpse, Mark Twain was distinctly uneasy with the conventional poses struck by well-heeled Christians. He was similarly exasperated by the piety of many of the sixty-five passengers aboard the *Quaker City*, three fourths of whom were much older than he, and so given to prayer meetings that they were called "the Synagogue." Mark Twain deleted from his book this last line: "But that such pleasure excursions as this are calculated to be suffocated with pleasure, I deny; and that a party more ill-fitted, by age and awful solemnity, for scurrying around the world on a giddy picnic, ever went to sea in a ship since the world began, I deny also, most fervently."

The Innocents Abroad (said to be the most popular book of foreign travel ever published by an American) has endured all these years because it wears the national mask in a way that would have embarrassed even Whitman. It revels in an air of uninterruptible self-satisfaction. In the derisive person of one so-called "American" (in another work it became "the American Vandal"), he had only to mutter his doggedly profane, unimpressed opinion about anything venerable to appear what he said he was. Much of the cockiness in *The Innocents Abroad* dates from a time when Americans thought themselves politically virtuous, the only true democrats and egalitarians in the world, since they were mostly Anglo-Saxon and Protestant. Of course Mark Twain always had his eye on his audience and would routinely say anything, no matter what the subject or occasion, to get a laugh. But one must not think that the many insolent opinions he throws out on Old Europe and the Middle East were too low for Mark Twain himself. Up to the Civil War and reaching His apotheosis in the war, God still obsessed the growingly skeptical mind of the nineteenth century. With Mark Twain we are truly in the age of "the American Vandal." Jefferson in Paris, Emerson in Rome, Melville in the South Seas were respectful and even curious about religions not their own. Mark Twain on Catholicism in the Azores is a foretaste of George F. Babbitt:

> The community is entirely Portuguese—that is to say, it is slow, poor, shiftless, sleepy, and lazy. . . . The good Catholic Portuguese crossed himself and prayed God to shield him from all blasphemous desire to know more than his father did before him. . . . The donkey and the men, women and children of a family, all eat and sleep in the same room, and are unclean, are ravaged by vermin, and are truly happy. The people lie, and cheat the stranger, and are desperately ignorant, and have hardly any reverence for their dead. The latter trait shows how little better they are than the donkeys they eat and sleep with. The only well-dressed Portuguese in the camp are half a dozen well-to-do families, the Jesuit priests, and the soldiers of the little garrison.

A Jesuit cathedral nearly two hundred years old represents itself as possessing a piece of the true Cross—and, says our American-with-no-nonsense-about-him, this object "was polished and hard, and in as excellent a state of preservation as if the dread tragedy on Calvary had occurred yesterday instead of eighteen centuries ago."

And yet "rusty" as this Old World is, broken-down, tyrannized by the Church whose only concern is to keep its faithful in order, it is *old*. And history for Mark Twain (who is celebrating the New World of his time as his own story) is a kind of wealth that fascinates like the more obvious kind. His success will eventually keep him and his family in Europe for over a decade, will lead him to adore the Middle Ages in the person of Joan of Arc—and once he reached the Holy Land, the Crusaders at their bloodiest. History is a statistic, it is fame to put into the book of records. Along with disdain for the backward and ignorant there sounds throughout *The Innocents Abroad* a breathless respect for a place in which so much has *happened* that an American can recite back to an American audience. He was starstruck by anything *really* old. He pictures himself in Tangier

before a crumbling wall that was old when Columbus discovered America; was old when Peter the Hermit aroused the knightly men of the Middle Ages to arm for the first crusade; was old when Charlemagne and his paladins beleaguered enchanted castles and battled with giants and genii in the fabled days of the olden time; was old when Christ and his disciples walked the earth; stood where it stands today when the lips of Memnon were vocal, and men bought and sold in the streets of ancient Thebes!

Approaching the Holy Land (the main destination of the passengers), Mark Twain was a shade solemn. He of course showed himself dutiful in relating his youthful Sunday school visions of Palestine to the arid, rocky land before him. The only objects of derision left to him were the lies in current guidebooks about the sacred beauty of the country and the unbelievable comfort that protected these well-moneyed folk against the rigors of the desert. (The exceptionally pious were dying to sail on the Lake of Galilee when they came to it, but when they offered a dollar for the experience, were chagrined to see the boatmen take off without them.)

Shortly after six, our pack-train arrived. I had not seen it before, and a good right I had to be astonished. We had nineteen serving-men and twenty-six pack mules! . . . Five stately circus tents were up—tents that were brilliant, within, with blue and gold and crimson, and all manner of splendid adornment. Then they brought eight little iron bedsteads, and set them up in the tents; they put a soft mattress and pillows and blankets and two snow-white sheets on the bed. . . . It was a gem of a place . . . a tablecloth and napkins whose whiteness and whose fineness laughed to scorn the things we were used to in the great excursion steamer . . . everything in the handsomest kind of style! It was wonderful! And they call *this* camping out!

Of the ultrareligious passengers, those who packed the "Synagogue" aboard the *Quaker City* twice on Sundays, three would not take to the desert on the Sabbath. Mark Twain was not happy with true believers, nor they with him. He was conscious of behaving well—no disputing with anyone if he could help it—but it was "virtue thrown away." "Every time they read me a scorcher of a lecture I mean to talk back in print." He certainly had his revenge—it is one of the high points of the book—when he describes how the pilgrims outfitted themselves against the Syrian sun:

> But of all the ridiculous sights I ever have seen, our party of eight is the most so—they do cut such an outlandish figure. They travel single file; they all wear the endless white rag of Constantinople wrapped round and round their hats and dangling down their backs; they all wear thick green spectacles, with side-glasses to them; they all hold white umbrellas, lined with green, over their heads; without exception their stirrups are too short—they are the worst gang of horsemen on earth; their animals to a horse trot fearfully hard—and when they get strung out one after the other, glaring straight ahead and breathless; bouncing high and out of turn, all along the line; knees well up and stiff, elbows flapping like roosters that are about to crow, and the long file of umbrellas popping convulsively up and down—when one sees this outrageous picture exposed to the light of day, he is amazed that the gods don't get out their thunderbolts and destroy them off the face of the earth! . . . I wouldn't let any such caravan go through a country of mine.

For all his lack of piety and his irritation with those who flourished it in his direction, the "proper" side of Mark Twain came out in his dutifully long guidebook descriptions of Palestine scenes and history. To think that he was standing where Christ had stood! Of course everything scriptural was so much smaller than he had pictured it back in Sunday school. And how *could* those awful Turks, who couldn't abide a Christian anyway, be allowed to keep Palestine "in sackcloth and ashes. Over it broods the spell of a curse that has withered its fields and fettered its energies."

The radiance they told him of back home, where is it now? He is so appalled by Galilee that he cannot bear to linger on its daytime appearance, but must draw over it the shades of night.

Night is the time to see Galilee. Gennesaret under these lustrous stars has nothing repulsive about it. Gennesaret with the glittering reflections of the constellations flecking its surface, almost makes me regret that I ever saw the rude glare of the day upon it. Its history and its associations are its chiefest charm, in any eyes, and the spells they weave are feeble in the searching light of the sun. . . . But when the day is done . . . the old traditions of the place steal upon his memory and haunt his reveries, and then his fancy clothes all sights and sounds with the supernatural.

What a confession! "One can comprehend it only when night has hidden all incongruities and created a theater proper for so grand a drama." But that is the same gloss he put on his early life in *The Adventures of Tom Sawyer*, a "hymn" with the strictest commercial flattery of the past. When William Dean Howells wondered "why we hate the past so," Mark Twain replied, "Because it was so humiliating."

There is no trace of humiliation in Tom Sawyer, no dead father exposed in all his dismemberment after the autopsy, as Robert Penn Warren pictured the ordeal of the eleven-year-old Sam Clemens in his strong poem "The Last Laugh." Warren imagines the boy missing not *his* autocratic father but *a* father, then discovering with relief that as there is no father there is no God, and laughing over the death of God until he, too, dies and God has the last laugh.

Such a religious awakening was too conventional for Sam Clemens the boy and Mark Twain the world-famous author who was deriding God with all his might—and, typically, postponing the news of these effusions until he died. "Only dead men tell the truth." God was forced down his throat so long as he remained with his mother in St. Petersburg, a tribulation he never touched on in *Tom Sawyer* (Tom has no mother). In *The Adventures of Huckleberry Finn*, however, this turned into Huck's struggle against decorum, the show of religion, not the thing itself, because Huck was blameless in his ignorance and outsiderness.

Howells, in his accommodating review of *Tom Sawyer*, noted that "Tom belongs to the better sort of people in it, and has been bred to fear and dread the Sunday school." This happened to Sam Clemens, not Tom Sawyer. Tom never displays the slightest "dread" of the Presbyterian God and, unwillingly cooped up in church and Sunday school as he is at school and at home with his Aunt Polly, is bored with everything when not plotting something "outrageous." If he has a "religion," it is the superstitions known only to boys and the Negro slaves they have borrowed them from.

Mark Twain told Howells he was not sure whether *The Adventures of Tom Sawyer* was a book about boys and girls for adults or for boys and girls themselves. He finally thought he was writing for both. But as he admitted in his preface, "Part of my plan has been to try to pleasantly remind adults of what they were themselves, and of how they felt and thought and talked, and what queer enterprises they sometimes engaged in." His real "plan," in fact, whether he knew it or not, was to throw a veil over his true upbringing as a boy, to make everything and everyone simply and pleasantly representative, like the readers of the book now expected en masse to think of themselves as what "they" once were themselves and "what queer enterprises they sometimes engaged in."

The village in *Tom Sawyer* is too homogeneous to be a real place, and the judge, the teacher, the minister, the Sunday school superintendent, to say nothing of the "boys and girls" collecting around Tom Sawyer because he is always asserting himself as leader, are types that only Mark Twain's immense gift for writing right down to his audience could have created. Here is a mythical past for Americans comfortable in the Gilded Age to identify with. What Mark Twain prods them to believe of themselves when they were "boys and girls"! If he had not followed up this romance of boyhood with *The Adventures of Huckleberry Finn*, which is as honest about being out of society (in a way Tom Sawyer knows nothing about), *Tom Sawyer* would now be just another guidebook for Victorian children who never existed.

Who and what is Tom Sawyer that he makes such a fuss about being Tom Sawyer? It is surely not because he was created—Mark Twain claims in his preface—"as a combination of the characteristics of three boys whom I knew, and therefore belongs to the composite order of architecture." Tom is Mark Twain—always on the move, always up to something, always putting himself forward, futile to contain and impossible to shut up. Yet the objects to be attained or conquered by his restless spirit are trivial when they are not juvenile distortions of "adventures" he has learned from books. As Aunt Polly closes her scolding with a "happy Scriptural flourish," he "hooks" a doughnut when she is not looking; he tricks his pals into whitewashing the fence; he unlooses a beetle in church; he fraudulently collects Sunday school tickets he is supposed to earn by memorizing biblical passages.

Tom Sawyer is boy to the unstoppably fluent man Mark Twain—he lived to "astonish," to be marked by the world, to have opinions about everything and anything, and never to recognize what was sound in the endless gush of words that followed from his tirelessly assertive temperament. So in *Tom Sawyer* superstition is the underground scripture. "Church" is just the way the community of respectable whites keeps together. It has no religious content (as it had none for Mark Twain). It is a social duty, a civic routine that is unquestioned by everyone. One people, one church, one faith in little old Hannibal! A dissembling. What counts for Mark Twain is the image of a boy in perfectly comfortable surroundings always acting up, playing mischief, miscreant, scapegrace, in a game that only he is allowed to win. No wonder he surfaces near the end of *Huckleberry Finn* still using games to keep in captivity a runaway slave who was actually given his freedom.

All this drives us to despair after what Huck and Jim have been through in Mark Twain's one masterpiece. But, having missed the Ohio in a fog and been forced to go ever more south, there was nowhere for Huck and Jim to end up except with Tom Sawyer—the eternal brat at his "games," who when he is not irrelevant is one of life's eternal spoilers. Mark Twain was to know all too much about spoilers.

Tom Sawyer is the perfect idyll, a "hymn" to a mythical homogeneous society seen from on top. Propriety is the only commandment Tom is likely to break. *Huckleberry Finn* depicts frontier society along the great river as lived from the bottom by a boy escaping the respectable society that wants to "sivilize" him and a father who wants to rob him and would kill him if necessary. He is joined by a runaway slave who comes to love him as no one else ever has. So this profoundly subversive book (until Tom Sawyer comes back) significantly begins with Huck's revolt against belonging to society at all: "The widow Douglas, she took me for her son." Mark Twain, when dying, complained of being loaded down with honors, and wanted to be a free spirit again. Huck is that free spirit, as perhaps only a boy of fourteen can be. And funny as he is when trying to assimilate the table manners and Bible lessons the "widder" is joylessly teaching, we remember that Mark Twain had a thing about the Bible—he thought it irresistibly absurd. Huck's derision was something little Sam Clemens in St. Petersburg never had the chance to voice:

> When you got to the table you couldn't go right to eating, but you had to wait for the widow to tuck down her head and grumble a little over the victuals, though there warn't really anything the matter with them. . . .
>
> After supper she got out her book and learned me about Moses and the Bulrushers; and I was in a sweat to find out all about him; but by-and-by she let it out that Moses had been dead a considerable long time; so then I didn't care no more about him; because I don't take no stock in dead people. . . .
>
> . . . That is just the way it is with some people. They get down on a thing when they don't know nothing about it. Here she was a bothering about Moses, which was no kin to her, and no use to anybody, being gone, you see.

And that goes for "the bad place" the widow's sister Miss Watson ("a tolerable slim old maid") tells him of,

> and I said I wished I was there. She got mad, then, but I didn't mean no harm. All I wanted was to go somewheres; all I wanted was a change, I warn't particular. She said it was wicked to say what I said; said she wouldn't say it for the whole world; *she* was going to live so as to go to the good place. Well, I couldn't see no advantage in going where she was going, so I made up my mind I wouldn't try for it.

We laugh at the contrast between Huck, who won't believe in anything he hasn't experienced, and the (significantly sexless) widow and dried-up old maid to whom it is left to hand down the word of God. Mark Twain was so soaked in the Bible that when Huck sees Pap Finn totally drunk, "a boy would a thought he was Adam, he was just all mud." (Adam was a favorite character of Mark Twain's, he was so "natural"; Twain wanted to see a statue put up to Adam.) But Huck is delicious as well as funny simply because he will not accept anything on hearsay. In Chapter III Huck comes back from his romp with Tom

Sawyer all grease and clay. "Then Miss Watson she took me in the closet and prayed, but nothing come of it. She told me to pray every day, and whatever I asked for I would get it. But it warn't so. I tried it."

And for Mark Twain as well, religion is hearsay. By contrast, the river is a place where a dead man is fished up wearing women's clothes. That is the truth of life, not the sky god the widow and Miss Watson preach, "not knowing anything about it." That is the momentum that carries the narrative along the river and truly makes it a river—"a strong brown god," T. S. Eliot remembered from his native St. Louis—bearing, overflowing with, the ruses, masquerades, and treacheries of human experience.

Henry James thought Mark Twain could appeal only to "rudimentary" minds. Exactly. With the "rudimentary" we are at the root of Mark Twain's masterpiece (and of much in American literary experience that in Faulkner went beyond Mark Twain). Here it is with the beautifully unshaped primitive, the unlearned, the spontaneous, the imperiled, through whom we see past the moral order created by inert traditional religion and the traditional justification for slavery that has held Huck captive. He thinks himself damned for not turning Jim in. It is only when you are altogether in danger that you are free to save yourself by deceptions and impersonations inconceivable to those who live in safety and by self-approval. The root of it all is the aloneness in the world (not just on the river) that leads Huck and Jim, together under the stars in Chapter XIX, to wonder, to ask, about God and such big questions—almost everybody else, between hunting one another to death, claims to have the answers.

> Sometimes we'd have that whole river all to ourselves for the longest time. Yonder was the banks and the islands, across the water; and maybe a spark—which was a candle in a cabin window— and sometimes on the water you could see a spark or two—on a raft or a scow, you know; and maybe you could hear a fiddle or a song come over from one of them crafts. It's lovely to live on a raft. We had the sky, up there, all speckled with stars, and we used to lay on our backs and look up at them, and discuss about whether they was made, or only just happened—Jim he allowed they was made, but I allowed they happened; I judged it would have took too long

to *make* so many. Jim said the moon could a *laid* them; well, that looked kind of reasonable, so I didn't say nothing against it, because I've seen a frog lay most as many, so of course it could be done. We used to watch the stars that fell, too, and see them streak down. Jim allowed they'd got spoiled and was hove out of the nest.

We are back to the beginning of the world, before systems replaced the natural man's wonder at the creation. We are back to a "simplicity" of mind that preceded the frontier created by white male Protestants with theologies at the ready like their rifles. We are back to a frame of mind that perhaps existed only among Indians communicating in symbols of the nature they revered. Mark Twain never again wrote like this. *A Connecticut Yankee at King Arthur's Court* (1889) has all his old charm, but is a muddle. The triumph of technology over the medieval is mechanical and unfelt. The book ends in the profound sadness of an irretrievable love that was more and more to darken Mark Twain's mind in the last decades of his life. "And as for me, all that I can think about in this plodding sad pilgrimage, this pathetic drift between the eternities, is to look out and humbly live a pure and high and blameless life, and save that one microscopic me that is truly *me*."

The old booster of American naturalness was beginning to laugh at the sanctity of American progress. In his novel of 1874 he had named the period "the Gilded Age," dominated as it was by open corruption from Washington down and the most brazen corporate plunder. As good Baptists like John D. Rockefeller brazenly monopolized the oil business as if competitors had no right to exist, it was clear that the country was increasingly in the hands of great wealth. Mark Twain naturally liked to think of himself as an enemy of plutocracy, but he hobnobbed with millionaires like Andrew Carnegie whom he secretly detested and he worshiped Rockefeller's partner Henry Huddleston Rogers, who saved him financially after Twain lost a fortune on the ill-fated Paige typesetting machine. As the United States brutally suppressed the Filipinos seeking their national freedom after Spain had lost the islands in the Spanish-American War, Mark Twain was "in eruption," denouncing our generals for their cruelty. But this was disclosed long after his death. He never meant to lose the audience that doted on him.

Before he was engulfed in personal tragedy—he was to lose an infant son and two daughters, and to be frightened by the lingering illness of his wife and his impending bankruptcy—Mark Twain prided himself on his objectivity as a literary addict of science. The perfect confidence with which Victorian science put all nature into unassailable law was intensely agreeable to someone brought up on the Calvinist systemization of human nature as essentially depraved, the absolute sovereignty of God, and the inviolable truth of predestination. What the young Sam Clemens had to swallow as God's immutable law, the aging Mark Twain would finally, bitterly accept as laws of necessity. In *Huckleberry Finn* he had already depicted man as the animal with a Bible. Poor, stupidly drunk old Boggs cannot be restrained from challenging haughty Colonel Sherburn, is shot down, and in his last gasp is encumbered by an open Bible on his chest. That is Mark Twain the novelist, who follows this up with the picture of the crowd admiring "one long lanky man with long hair and a big white fur stove-pipe hat on the back of his head" who reproduces the murder scene, playing first Boggs then Sherburn with all their gestures. "The people that had seen the thing said he done it perfect; said it was just exactly the way it all happened. Then as much as a dozen people got out their bottles and treated him."

A curious thing about Mark Twain is that as he became a determinist and polemicist in defense of his "scientific" views, he thought it required a special courage to say so. In a dialogue with a young man called *What Is Man?* (1906) Mark Twain as the old man insists that "the human being is merely a machine, and nothing more. Every such thought was accepted by millions upon millions of men—and concealed, kept private. Why did they not speak out? Because they dreaded (*and could not bear*) the disapproval of the people around them. Why have I not published? The same reason has restrained me, I think. I could find no other." The vast "autobiography" he dictated from bed to his official biographer was not to be published until long after his death. "Only dead men tell the truth."

It never occurred to him that the Boggs-Sherburn scene, among so many others in *Huckleberry Finn*, was a far more integral and drastic picture of human nature than anything he could say in *What Is Man?* by just asserting that "the human being is merely a machine."

Who in 1905 was to be terrified by such popular banalities? Obviously he was arguing (and in a sense supporting) the dogma of absolute necessity that fitted his childhood Calvinism. He had to play the intellectual, the philosopher, instead of saying it all in another narrative like *Huckleberry Finn*. But that was all part of the Mississippi legend through which he re-created his youth, a legend he had exhausted despite his narrative genius. What remained of his youth was really the old Presbyterian scare world of personal sin, and for this he was unquenchably mad at God. One of the most imperial personages of his time, Mark Twain could not abide his fellow egotist Theodore Roosevelt. His own attacks on the traditional God were as majestic as the bearlike post TR took in front of the beast he had just slain. From the notebook of Mark Twain (1887):

I believe in God the Almighty.

I do not believe he ever sent a message to man by anybody, or delivered one to him word of mouth, or made Himself visible to mortal eyes at any time in any place.

I believe that the Old and New Testaments were imagined and written by man, and that no line in them was authorized by God, much less inspired by Him.

I do not believe in special providences. I believe that the universe is governed by strict and immutable laws. If one man's family is swept away by a pestilence and another man's spared it is only the law working: God is not interfering in that small matter, either against one man or in favor of the other.

I cannot see how eternal punishment hereafter could accomplish any good end, therefore I am not able to believe in it. To chasten a man in order to perfect him might be reasonable enough: to annihilate him when he shall have proved himself incapable of reaching perfection might be reasonable enough; but to roast him forever for the mere satisfaction of seeing him roast would not be reasonable—even the atrocious God imagined by the Jews would tire of the spectacle eventually.

I believe that the world's moral laws are the outcome of the world's experience. It needed no God to come down out of heaven to tell men that murder and theft and the other immoralities were bad, both for the individual who commits them and for society which suffers from them.

If I break all these moral laws I cannot see how I injure God by it, for He is beyond the reach of injury from me—I could as easily injure a planet by throwing mud at it. It seems to me that my misconduct could only injure me and other men. I cannot benefit God by obeying these moral laws—I could as easily benefit the planet by withholding my mud. (Let these sentences be read in the light of the fact that I believe I have received moral laws *only* from man—none whatever from God.) Consequently I do not see why I should be either punished or rewarded hereafter for the deeds I do here.

From Mark Twain's notebook, May 30, 1898:

The Being who to me is the real God is the One who created this majestic universe and rules it. . . . He is the perfect artisan, the perfect artist. Everything which he has made is fine, everything which he has made is beautiful.

The happiness (God gives us) seem to be traps, and to have no other intent. . . . This to discipline us? ("What Is the Real Character of Conscience?," 1898)

Man is a machine, made up of many mechanisms, the moral and mental ones acting automatically in accordance with the impulses of an interior Master who is built out of born-temperament and an accumulation of multitudinous outside influences and trainings; a machine whose *one* function is to secure the spiritual contentment of the Master, be his desires good or be they evil; a machine whose Will is absolute and must be obeyed, and always *is* obeyed. (*What Is Man?*)

The same unflinching "determinist" let it slip that "I think the goodness, the justice, and the mercy of God are manifested toward me in this life; the logical conclusion is that they will be manifested toward me in the life to come, if there should be one." He was too obsessed with God to be consistent about Him. If ever there was a Calvinist whose theology survived his faith, it was Mark Twain. From the eighties on to just before his death in 1910, he so steadily pursued his quarrel with God, his "wrestling with God," as the Russians once put it about their more outlandish saints, that one wonders how he found time to write anything else. Here is a partial list of Mark Twain's essays on God, man, and religion put together by Jane Wilson:

As Concerns the Deity
At the Funeral (from an unfinished burlesque of books on
    etiquette)
Bible Teaching and Religious Practice
The Dervish and the Offensive Stranger
The Intelligence of God
Letter to the Earth (from the recording secretary)
Letters from the Earth
Little Bessie
Little Nelly Tells a Story out of Her Own Head
The Lowest Animals
Notebooks (various entries)
Papers of the Adam Family
Reflections on Being the Delight of God
Slave Catching from the Slave's Point of View
Sold to Satan
Something about Repentance
The Synod of Praise
The Ten Commandments
Thoughts of God
To My Missionary Critics
The War Prayer
Was the World Made for Man?
What Is Man?

These attempts to keep God around for the sake of argument went hand in hand with his outrage over the vanity of persons too powerful in politics and society, the corruption of Congress ("the only native criminal class"), "the United States of Lyncherdom," King Leopold's enslavement of the Congo for his personal wealth. As Bernard De Voto said when he was finally able to bring out Mark Twain's fulminations (thirty years after the man's death!), Mark Twain in this period was in "eruption." He would not have been displeased to think of himself as a volcano. But volcanoes do not argue, they erupt; and Mark Twain could have gone on arguing, arguing forever to get the Deity off his pedestal, thus eliminating whatever it was that so infuriated him.

Fortunately, his last word on the subject—*The Mysterious Stranger*—took the form of storytelling. Of course he could not let the subject drop even there, and tried four different versions that survive in three manuscripts. Between 1902 and 1908, William M. Gibson reports in his editing of the manuscripts (University of California Press, 1969), Mark Twain worked on Version III, the only one that he called "The Mysterious Stranger." Satan's nephew, "Young Satan," also known as "44," comes to a hidebound Austrian village in the Middle Ages and, despite his slight appearance and boyish charm, turns out to know everything, including the future. It turns out that predestination is just as real as John Calvin said it was. The difference is that it is all, all of no account. Life is nothing but a vision, a dream. What a friend we have in Satan—if it is nothingness we now desperately seek after life's crushing hour!

> *Nothing* exists; all is a dream. God—man—the world—the sun, the moon, the wilderness of stars: a dream, all a dream—they have no existence. *Nothing exists save empty space and you!*
>
> And you are not you—you have no body, no bones, you are but a *thought.* . . . In a little while you will be alone in shoreless space, to wander its limitless solitudes without friend or comrade forever—for you will remain a *Thought*, the only existent Thought, and by your nature inextinguishable, indestructible.

Whatever this meant—Mark Twain alone through eternity imagining a universe that doesn't really exist—it is comforting to find Satan—Satan!—taking up Mark Twain's indictment of God:

> Your universe and its contents were only dreams, visions, fictions! Strange, because they are so frankly and hysterically insane—like all dreams: a God who could make good children as easily as bad, yet preferred to make bad ones; who could have made every one of them happy, yet never a single happy one; who . . . gave his angels

eternal happiness unearned, yet required his other children to earn it; who gave his angels painless lives, yet cursed his other children with biting miseries and maladies of mind and body; who mouths justice—and invented hell—mouths mercy, and invented hell; mouths morals to other people, and has none himself . . . who created man without invitation, then shuffles the responsibility for man's acts upon man, instead of honorably placing it where it belongs, upon himself; and finally, with altogether divine obtuseness, invites this poor abused slave to worship him! . . .

You perceive, now, that these things are all impossible, except in a dream.

Yes, but who, by this confession, had this dream that God had a plan, a dreadful, insanely *total* plan for mankind but someone brought up like Mark Twain himself? Why blame God for becoming man's "supreme fiction"?

10

T. S. Eliot: The Pilgrim from St. Louis

I will show you fear in a handful of dust.   *The Waste Land*

In France we remain Catholic after we have ceased to be Christians.
CHARLES-AUGUSTIN SAINTE-BEUVE

T. S. ELIOT'S GRANDFATHER the Reverend William Green-leaf Eliot was born 1811 in New Bedford and died 1887 (a year before his grandson was born) in remote Mississippi. Had he gone down to Mississippi as a Unitarian missionary? The Reverend Dr. Eliot was so committed to the Unitarian Church that when barely twenty-three he left the Harvard Divinity School to establish Unitarianism on the frontier in rough, partly French, still largely Catholic St. Louis. Emerson met him when he lectured in St. Louis, and had nothing but admiration for this "Saint of the West." Emerson was certain that "no thinking or reading man" was to be found "in the city's 95,000 souls."

As if to prove Emerson a bad prophet, the Reverend Dr. Eliot founded Washington University in St. Louis (he declined to have it named after himself), three schools, and a poor fund. During the Civil War he established the Western Sanitary Commission that put order into army hospitals. It is said he had written the history of a black slave, and that his grandson "cherished" it. William Greenleaf Eliot's old-fashioned belief that a Christian was needed by the poor, the helpless, and the uneducated would not kindle the slightest fire in the heart of his grandson, who was to re-create himself in England on the basis of his antipathy to the very American Protestantism on which he had been raised in St. Louis. In 1927 he became a British subject and a member of the Anglican Church. In England he was to explain, "A Church is to be judged by its intellectual fruits, by its influence on the sensibility of the most sensitive and on the intellect of the most intelligent, and it must be made real to the eye by monuments of artistic merit." Eliot never included the Father or the Son in his adoration of the Church itself. The Church was authority, orthodoxy, a safe bastion. Admitting that he was a "resident alien" in England, he was careful to establish positions that were more royalist than the king, and so fixed that they made him a curiosity to the English. He made a point of defining himself as "monarchist in politics, classicist in literature, Anglo-Catholic in religion." So in a late lecture on Goethe he was to explain, again, that Goethe was antipathetic to "anyone like myself, who combines a Catholic cast of mind, a Calvinist heritage, and a Puritan temperament."

But there was no other "like myself." Behind the public man who established himself as a poet of startling originality and a critic given to the most subtle discriminations was a man susceptible to terror, so bound up with himself and psychologically fractured that he could see a better, other life only in literature. The world became sordid and pressed its meaninglessness on him to the point where only authority, hierarchy, some absolute never to be doubted, promised to relieve him of the sense of his own oddity in the democratic mass world. Nothing could have been more in the American literary tradition than Eliot's obsession with self and his solitude when he was caught in England by the war. But America remembered as his cherished childhood in St. Louis and his summers on the Massachusetts coast furnished his emotional capital as a poet. America in its constant democratic upheavals, its religiously pluralistic mass civilization, was in the abstract, far from home, something he meant to free himself from, so he was always disdaining and rejecting in modern thought what he liked to call "heresies." Tradition, authority, orthodoxy had sanctity in themselves. This was far from what actual society in England was like in the twentieth century, when the emptying Church of England was struggling to reach the masses. The rigor and coldness of Eliot's social opinions resembled the gifts for impersonation that astonished the first readers of "The Love Song of J. Alfred Prufrock."

Poetry was everything to him, for poetry alone could display the "bits and pieces" that he saw the modern world reflecting in himself, the "many voices" in the disordered modern world he was to echo in the interstices of consciousness. Poetry organized the fragments of being and triumphed over them through its supremacy as sound. Sound was the lovable greater voice in the world that harmonized and took over. Even as a boy he was excited by poetry in French before he understood the words, aroused by their sheer sound. This emphasis on sound, on the tonality fused by rhyme and repetition that comes first in our sensuous experience of poetry, was to become Eliot's way of capturing the reader even in the most unsettling "modernist" poems. Rhyme gave a mocking banality and a deceptive lilt to situations (as in "Prufrock") that were awful but not serious. Eliot's mother constantly read poetry aloud in her own pursuit of a literary career in poetic epics. Eliot's instinct for sound led him to internalize exemplary passages from other poets—his first instinct before he became absolutist enough in his views to dismiss the Romantics and virtually the whole nineteenth century in English poetry. (He paid no attention to American poets of the period.) Even in his devotion to poetry, a sacred order that became his model of tradition and led to his hierarchical views in religion and politics, he was the divided man. He became categorical in his judgments even as his poems found their initial subject in the fear of his own weakness in himself. Where the psyche was so uncertain, the critical intelligence so incisive in public, it was no wonder that the single work that made him famous, *The Waste Land*, a mosaic of quotations in text and notes coldly establishing the deterioration of the contemporary age, turned out to be something less severe. This Eliot confessed in the mellowness of his second marriage, and was another show of his genius for impersonation, but it was too late to turn *The Waste Land* into "a piece of rhythmical grumbling." One can hate the poem, as William Carlos Williams did, because it was so reactionary in principle and despairing in tone. Williams said it was taking poetry in exactly the wrong direction; it was selling out the future. But to hate it was to confess its power. The truest line in *The Waste Land*, straight from Eliot's heart despite his many convolutions, is "I will show you fear in a handful of dust."

So with Eliot's contempt and positive hatred for Jews, which insinuated themselves into "Burbank with a Baedeker: Bleistein with a Cigar," which included the vile lines "The rats are underneath the piles. / The Jew is underneath the lot." (The "j" was in lowercase; Eliot later capitalized it.) In "Gerontion" the line "And the Jew squats on the window sill, the owner," is properly interpreted by Anthony Julius as connected with defecation. "The squatting Jew perched in a window sill [is] in a state of precarious quarantine . . . kept apart because he is unclean, unwelcome even in the house that he owns, wretched yet monied. These lines are a horror picture, drawn with loathing." But "Gerontion" is so exact in its horror of what the "little old man" recalls, poetically so clever in its fleeting images, that many a Jew has been seduced into admiring it. Eliot wrote before the Holocaust, and even at the war's close in 1945 managed to commemorate the victims in a dirge without mentioning the Jews. Isaiah Berlin persuaded Eliot to include "Israel" in the poem in a general sense. So it goes in a world where forever, it seems, Jews are regularly abominated and even demonized in works they cannot help admiring and whose authors they are proud to call friends. After a lecture I gave to a college audience, a non-Jewish professor gently reproached me for quoting with evident pleasure lines from *Four Quartets*. "How can you admire such an enemy of the Jews?" I replied that if I had to exclude anti-Semites, I would have little enough to read.

Eliot was a decisive thinker who on many issues, literary as well as social and religious, simply fabricated the world on which he made so many pronouncements. In his most famous essay in criticism, "Tradition and the Individual Talent" (1917), he instructed the reader, "What is to be insisted upon is that the poet must develop or procure the consciousness of the past and that he should continue to develop this consciousness throughout his career.

"What happens is a continual surrender of himself as he is at the moment to something which is more valuable. The progress of an artist is a continual self-sacrifice, a continual extinction of personality." Of course a writer "surrenders himself" to the character on paper merely based on himself. But when Eliot "insisted" on the "extinction of personality," all he possibly meant was the contrast of "the man who suffers" as opposed to the "mind that creates." The modern writers Eliot most admired were not afraid, as evidently he was, of speaking in their own personae. Baudelaire called the reader of *Les Fleurs du mal* "*mon semblable, mon frère.*" Flaubert admitted, "I am Madame Bovary." Henry James said openly, "The port from which I started was loneliness." No one doubts that James Joyce meant to portray himself as Stephen Dedalus. Of course Eliot is thinking not of "those poets Homer," as Max Beerbohm called them, or of Shakespeare, who was too busy writing plays to leave his name on all of them. It is only Eliot himself he is describing,

Eliot in his occasional dread of himself, not the artist who was to end his career with *Four Quartets*, the most beautiful, the most openly personal and successful quest for lost time by a great artist since Proust. The "self-sacrifice," the "extinction" of personality refer not to literature but to the hard-driven Eliot's hope to find peace in the authoritarianism of the Action Française and the venerability of the Church of England. As he was to say in *After Strange Gods* (1934), "At the moment when one writes, one is what one is, and the damage of a lifetime, and of having been born into an unsettled society, cannot at the moment of composition be repaired." What a strange expectation of human experience. Whose life has ever escaped "damage"? What society about which we know anything has not been "unsettled"?

All this pertains not to Eliot organizing the bits and pieces of his private disorder to triumph as a poet of internal consciousness but to his private literary myth that for the poet (it can hardly be this for anyone else) the past exists as a literary tradition intact and continuous. To have "the historical sense involves a perception, not only of the pastness of the past, but of its presence; the historical sense compels a man to write not merely with his own generation in his bones, but with a feeling that the whole of the literature of Europe from Homer and within it the whole of the literature of his own country has a simultaneous existence and composes a simultaneous order."

Only an American could have dreamed up such a perfectly ordered fantasy of Europe as a single order that overlooks the human discordance and revolutions routine in life. For this literary pilgrim Europe was without friction, without politics, without gaps in its memory of itself. Everything stable and perfectly "settled." "The existing order is complete before the new work arrives; for order to persist after the supervention of novelty, the *whole* existing order must be, if ever so slightly, altered; and so the relations, proportions, values of each work of art toward the whole are readjusted; and this is conformity between the old and the new." Everything just had to come together, like the top of the tapestry looking to the bottom to complete it.

Without ever becoming a *Roman* Catholic, Eliot was claiming the Middle Ages as his true spiritual home. Eliot's idea of "order" is as unworldly as a seminarian who confronts life with nothing but theology.

As a dogma about the unresting presence of literature—not true even for someone so devoted to poetry as Eliot—it was so static and sanctimonious as to be interesting only for its air of total certainty. When Eliot included "the whole of the literature of his own country," he did not mean that poor thing the open, democratic, hopeful America in which he had been brought up. In 1919 he wrote a scornful review from England of *The Education of Henry Adams* which was as contemptuous of New England, all passion spent on Puritanism, as it was of Adams for becoming a skeptic. "A skepticism which is difficult to explain to those who are not born to it. This skepticism is a product, or a cause, or a concomitant, of Unitarianism; it is not destructive, but it is dissolvent." Eliot's awful condescension to *The Education* did not keep him from borrowing the beautiful passage in Adams's Chapter XVIII about the sensuousness of Washington's Rock Creek in summer: "the dogwood and the judas-tree . . . passionate depravity." In "Gerontion" this turned up in a spirit just the contrary of Adams's joy. "In depraved May, dogwood and chestnut, flowering Judas" was used up and down by Eliot's devotees to describe a world fallen, fallen without repair (except by an established church), and as yet unquickened by desire for redemption.

> *Signs are taken for wonders. "We would see a sign!"*
> *The word within a word, unable to speak a word,*
> *Swaddled with darkness. In the juvescence of the year*
> *Came Christ the tiger*
>
> . . . .
>
> *To be eaten, to be divided, to be drunk*
> *Among whispers.*

By strangers (otherwise unknown) with foreign names and sinister (sexual) intentions. How Eliot could transcribe other writers' innocent images into the woefulness of his own existence! Eliot's 1919 review of *The Education* is insolent, clever, destructive. One would never have guessed that Eliot, positively sneering at Adams for his "skepticism," had recognized in it something like his own despair. Adams, too, was the victim of a tragic marriage. In America, Eliot could never have put down Adams with such lordliness. But in England he was safe. Ensconced in an ever-present and visible "tradition" of which he said, "It cannot be inherited and if you want it you must obtain it by great labor."

He was on his way to the top in neo-orthodoxy. Everything there was to be grist to his mill. "Reasons of race and religion" combine, he wrote in *After Strange Gods*, to make "an excessive number of free-thinking Jews undesirable." He never republished this but never retracted it either. In 1921 he confessed to Richard Aldington that he had such a profound hatred for democracy that he had to describe it "as a continuous physical horror, a horror to be sane in the midst of all this, it was too dreadful, it goes too far for rage." Long before the French were defeated in 1940 and the triumph under Pétain of the "national order" that owed its chauvinism and genocidal racism to Charles Maurras and the Action Française, Eliot declared his homage to Maurras. With the peculiar coldness that was necessary to his public persona, he even (in 1934) published another writer's unsigned note in *The Criterion* that mocked bishops of the Church of England, *his* church, for publicizing Hitler's persecution of Jews. No wonder that as late as 1982 *Spearhead*, the organ of the British Fascist party, still acclaimed Eliot their "Great British Racialist" and *The Waste Land* a masterpiece because it "represents this civilization as a thing of barren materialism pulled up by its race-cultural roots."

Eliot as an Anglican and a royalist pronounced his preference for fascism; his fundamental objection was merely that it appeared pagan. With his "carelessness of public utterance," as Michael Hastings put it, he also said that the great majority of human beings should go on living where they were born. So Eliot said. He said so many things! Yet this seeming zealot for "order" (at any price?) was the most personally indrawn, haunted, and haunting of "modernist" poets—and everything in his poetry went back to America.

The Eliot family regularly spent summers at Gloucester. Sailing (often alone) off the Massachusetts coast gave the young Eliot his one abiding sense of freedom, an imperishable sense of connection with the natural world that went into his early poetry even before he gave full breath in "The Dry Salvages" to his love of the sea off Cape Ann. There he was removed from industrially sulfurous St. Louis, where even the ultrarespectable Eliots lived in areas that were turning into slums. St. Louis at the turn of the century figured heavily in Lincoln Steffens's exposé of urban corruption, *The Shame of the Cities*—"Hell with the lid off." Theodore Dreiser (it is impossible to imagine Eliot knowing this) was then a working journalist in St. Louis. Dreiser was not charmed by the foul-smelling industrial pile where Eliot's father was the leading manufacturer of bricks.

Of course there was the great river that Eliot commemorated as a god—"without some kind of god man is not even very interesting"— when he came to write about *Huckleberry Finn* amazingly late in life. In "The Dry Salvages" he rapturously remembered the river as

> *a strong brown god—sullen, untamed and intractable,*
> . . . .
> *the brown god is almost forgotten*
> *By the dwellers in cities—ever, however, implacable,*
> *Keeping his seasons and rages, destroyer, reminder*
> *Of what men choose to forget. . . .*
> . . . .
> *His rhythm was present in the nursery bedroom,*
> *In the rank ailanthus of the April dooryard,*
> *In the smell of grapes on the autumn table,*
> *And the evening circle in the winter gaslight.*

In later life, buoyed by fame nowhere greater than in America, he fondly admitted at the university his grandfather had founded, "I am very glad to have been born in St. Louis."

This was certainly news to students of his career in England. He left St. Louis at sixteen to prepare for Harvard at Milton Academy outside Boston. He was to say after marrying Valerie Fletcher in 1957 that he had recovered happiness he had experienced only as a child. But in St. Louis, Eliot's Puritan father was as distrustful of sex as his mother was all too reverential toward the literary culture that was to become Eliot's only key to an unmanageable world. It was in order to rise above the real St. Louis, with its terrible sewers, that his family first imprisoned him in the genteel tradition he was to satirize at Harvard in poems about emotionally stifled literary hostesses on Beacon Hill. These blossomed into Eliot's first great literary impersonation. There were to be many, beginning with "The Love Song of J. Alfred Prufrock." Artistically, this was revolution, thus the very contrary of the self-restrictions that almost extinguished Prufrock ("Prudent frock").

The expatriate who late in life was "very glad to have been born in St. Louis" was dissembling yet again. He was actually so alienated that he was to pretend that because of the conflict between his Northern ancestry and Southern birth he did not "believe [himself] to be an American at all." Southern birth! The Eliots were hardly Confederates. But the disclaimer was typical of the Eliot who could turn at a moment's notice against any solid sense of his identity. As a would-be Englishman he took positions in art, politics, and religion stridently negative in their rejection of "America." He complained that he had been brought up "outside the Christian fold," that without belief in the Incarnation one could not be a Christian. With that he rejected as well everything open and tolerant in his grandfather's rock-rooted belief that God was more than the Church. The only thing Eliot could say for Emerson—a believer on his own terms, as was Eliot—was that he had "dignity." Yes, but that was born of a positively rapturous confidence in his heresies that Eliot never knew in his adherence to orthodoxy. No doubt Emerson deluded himself that his leaving the Church pointed to a more committed religious future. But as an American, Emerson of course believed in a future. Compare the conclusion of Eliot's "Thoughts after Lambeth" (1931) on an Anglican conference made imperative by the dwindling numbers of worshipers. With his usual contempt for liberals and meliorists in and out of the Church, Eliot insisted that "in spite of the apparently insoluble problems with which it has to deal, the Church of England is strengthening its position as a branch of the Catholic Church, the Catholic Church in England." Then, grimly, Eliot concluded "Thoughts after Lambeth" by complaining that Christianity was no longer "official." Was an established church everywhere in the West, as in the Middle Ages, the only way to restore faith in the modern world?

> The World is trying the experiment of attempting to form a civilized but non-Christian mentality. The experiment will fail; but we must be very patient in awaiting its collapse; meanwhile redeeming the time: so that the Faith may be preserved alive through the dark

ages before us; to renew and rebuild civilization, and save the
World from suicide.

The individual supplicant, hesitating on the threshold of the Church
for reassurance in this life and the next, could not feel that *he* was being
addressed by Eliot. Eliot did not extend his Christianity to others possibly suffering like himself. But he was possessed by the verbal spell of
poetry, the reverberations that became intrinsic to his modernist agility.
These provided Eliot's security—his guide to the literary devotions always before him in his search for a faith that would become "the one
still point in a turning world." But it was through his individual art, not
his easily proclaimed public faith, that he would attain that "one still
point" in this madly rushing world. From earliest youth he lived in poetry as he did nowhere else. By 1906, when he entered "the Harvard of
the aesthetes," he was as compact in his sense of what mattered in his
passion for poetry as he would ever be. He was in all senses formed
early, he formed *himself* terribly early. At Harvard he sought out not the
poet-philosopher Santayana (William James was just retiring, but they
would have disapproved of each other anyway) but Irving Babbitt, the
rigid-minded prophet of a "humanism" based on the "inner check."

Of course one wonders what Eliot's career would have been if he had
not been caught in England when war began in 1914, if he had been accepted for the commission he sought from American naval intelligence
in London, if he had not in 1915 married unstable Vivien Haigh-Wood,
if he had not lived most of his life as a "resident alien." He remained in
England, by his own account, because he did not want to present Vivien
to his parents, just as he chose not to take ship in wartime in order to accept his Harvard doctorate in philosophy. But he had a sense of fatality
in all this necessary to his career. He shuddered at the thought of becoming an academic in America. Imagine him in any department with
his copycat admirers! It is obvious from his sticking to England in
wartime, and this as a solitary American, a paradox in a foreign country,
that he knew what would support his originality—his aloneness—as
America never could. His father thought him perverse, a failure, and in
disapproval of his independence cut him out of his will. There was a
Puritan background for you! Eliot became a harried, underpaid school-
master and part-time lecturer in workers' evening classes. (He was not

sympathetic to workers and derided Gray's "Elegy Written in a Country Churchyard" as sentimental.) For years, until he joined the Faber and Faber publishing firm, he dutifully bent his back working in a bank. But while little known, he knew what he thought and so knew what he was doing and was about to do. The force of rejection behind all this is remarkable. After first reading Eliot's poems in 1915, Pound in some astonishment reported to *Poetry*'s Harriet Monroe in Chicago, he "has actually trained himself *and* modernized himself *on his own*." The hardheaded, fully conscious element of intellectual self-knowledge in Eliot's makeup contributed to his prominence as an expatriate. His external assurance as a critic and cultural guru still in his twenties was remarkable and dramatic.

But it becomes even more dramatic when one contrasts the seeming positiveness of his views with the plaintively broken world described in his poetry. As he liked to say, poetry describes the world as it is, criticism as it should be. An indissoluble sense of terror clings to the "heap of broken images" on which he relied to convey the sense of fragmentation in his life and immediate surroundings. The supercilious lawgiver in public could be the most driven, the most affecting of modern poets. The despair was real, as the Absolute to nullify it he was always reaching for was more symbolic than real—a "position" rather than the living God. As Jonathan Edwards said in his *Treatise Concerning Religious Affections*, "What makes men partial in religion is, that they seek themselves, and not God, in their religion." Eliot was so divided from himself that in the mocking disorder of "The Love Song of J. Alfred Prufrock," objects in the external world spoke to the poor fellow in ominous proof that he was several people at once.

The volume *Prufrock and Other Observations* is dedicated to Eliot's French friend Jean Verdenal, 1889–1915, "mort aux Dardanelles." A memorial note quotes Dante in hell praising a love for the departed so real that it makes his "shadow" real. Then the inevitable epigraph to the poem from Dante (*Inferno*, Canto XXVII, lines 61–66) in which Guido, count of Montefeltro, asked to identify himself, can tell his life story since "none did ever return live from this depth." But Prufrock feels no such love for an individual, lost or alive, as Eliot did for Jean Verdenal. What we get from the opening, immediately, is uncertainty; pervasive, made here into a principle. We do not know who "you" is from the first line:

> *Let us go then, you and I,*
> *When the evening is spread out against the sky*
> *Like a patient etherised upon a table;*
> *Let us go, through certain half-deserted streets.*

We will not locate this "you" again until we realize (with a gasp) that it may very well be the other half, the "shadow" of Prufrock himself. Yet all this is so musically told—

> *Let us go, through certain half-deserted streets,*
> *The muttering retreats*
> *Of restless nights in one-night cheap hotels*
> *And sawdust restaurants with oyster-shells*

—that we are hypnotized by Prufrock's projection in his divided state of external objects speaking in human voices—and with human complaints. Ventriloquism is turned on its head. Eliot's incipient triumph is to turn Prufrock's alienation from the real world back on this world itself, to turn the real world Prufrockian. His inner consciousness is so externalized that "the evening . . . spread out against the sky / Like a patient etherised upon a table" becomes sickeningly numb and flat. Restless nights in one-night cheap hotels become "muttering retreats." And streets—streets!—"follow like a tedious argument / Of insidious intent." All this is made comically "merry," tinkling, by Eliot's captivating use of rhyme as closure, line by line. In a poem so built on ominous disorder, we need the easy compensation that rhyme provides. The ice here is so thin that reader and Prufrock alike keep their balance by *hearing* through rhyme reminders of the real world Prufrock has left:

> *Oh, do not ask, "What is it?"*
> *Let us go and make our visit.*

Terror made melodious is no less terror—when one hears the inner scream of Prufrock's hesitation (and even fright) preparatory to his visit. The yellow fog rubs its back, its muzzle, licks its tongue, makes a sudden leap, falls asleep. Poor Prufrock! Telling himself

> *There will be time, there will be time*
> *To prepare a face to meet the faces that you meet.*

As rhyme is echo deceiving the speaker that he is not alone (but he is
alone), so the repetition of whole lines (it was to express Eliot's sense of
emotional urgency) was to give "The Love Song of J. Alfred Prufrock"
the effect of some wonderful music swerving from line to line on a jin-
gling piano. The reverberations in "Prufrock" bring out the insistency
of Prufrock's self-imprisonment. And mock it.

> *And I have known the eyes already, known them all—*
> *The eyes that fix you in a formulated phrase,*
> *And when I am formulated, sprawling on a pin,*
> *When I am pinned and wriggling on the wall,*
> *Then how should I begin*
> *To spit out all the butt-ends of my days and ways?*

We laugh; the sheer cleverness of *how* everything is said makes it impossible for us to be anything but a spectator (as Prufrock sinks into becoming a spectator of himself). We do not identify with Prufrock, we
are too absorbed by Eliot's workmanship. Prufrock's fate is total, but in-
sidiously comic. The last lines compel our admiration, so *rapturously* do
we move between the upper and lower worlds—between sleep and
death—

> *We have lingered in the chambers of the sea*
> *By sea-girls wreathed with seaweed red and brown*
> *Till human voices wake us, and we drown.*

Eliot said of *The Waste Land* to Harvard's Theodore Spencer, "Various critics have done me the honour to interpret the poem in terms of
criticism of the contemporary world, have considered it, indeed, as an
important bit of social criticism. To me it was only the relief of a personal and wholly insignificant grouse against life; it is just a piece of
rhythmical grumbling." This confession was to the point but came so
late after the poem had established itself as a sweeping indictment of
the modern world that it was funny. What a role-player! The notes were
there in the first place to disguise their makeshift origins in the stream-

of-consciousness drafts, based on many voices, that Ezra Pound cut and dressed to make the poem finally ready for publication in 1922. The elaborate show of learning not only disguised the deep-seated personal lament (hardly just "grousing") behind the poem, but was surely intended to give him authority in a turbulent postwar world that still looked to writers for moral leadership. The whole poem was a powerful act of negation, marvelous in the spacing and timing with which it arranged contrasting sections. It moved in powerfully alternating rhythms, putting the poem together out of the "heap of broken images" that established the "dissociation" Eliot thought the essence of modern life. By "dissociation" Eliot also meant, as he said in his essay on Dante, that the love of man and woman is only made possible by a higher love, that of God; or else it is simply "the coupling of animals." Such sordid, loveless copulation was for him as much an example of dissociation as the divide between emotion and intellect that followed from the rise of science in the seventeenth century. And how fitting that in his obvious suspicion of sex Eliot should decide (*after* the poem had been cut down by Pound to its final size) that Tiresias the blind man-woman prophet who has been changed from man to woman and back to man again should be the central figure in the poem. Tiresias is understandably weary of sex, knows all the moves in advance:

> *I Tiresias, old man with wrinkled dugs*
> *Perceived the scene, and foretold the rest—*
> *I too awaited the expected guest.*

Who, of course, turns out to be a "young man carbuncular,"

> *One of the low on whom assurance sits*
> *As a silk hat on a Bradford millionaire.*

Apparently this squalid routine occurs only in the lower classes, who to cap the horror wear carbuncles that no doubt exude pus. For a fellow from St. Louis, Eliot had certainly absorbed the facility with which the proper Englishman finds another class disgusting. But in point of fact the poem, with its ominous monotone of sexual failure, reaches its stunning apotheosis in Part V, "What the Thunder Said," with its emphasis on dryness, on mountains of rock without water, on sandy places, on dry, sterile thunder without rain. But here we are not in the biblical desert where gods thrive, but in the end-place, the acedia and nullity in which civilizations once formed by religious enthusiasm now die. The towers once encasing church bells are now "upside down in air," and in "this decayed hole among the mountains . . . / There is the empty chapel, only the wind's home."

Eliot never wrote anything more evocative of his heart's belief that the world is desiccating in spiritual emptiness. He himself thought that the "water-dripping song" in Part V,

> *Where the hermit-thrush sings in the pine trees*
> *Drip drop drip drop drop drop drop*
> *But there is no water,*

were the best-*written* lines in the poem. But here is the great prophetic passage in Part V, beginning at line 367:

> *What is that sound high in the air*
> *Murmur of maternal lamentation*
> *Who are those hooded hordes swarming*
> *Over endless plains, stumbling in cracked earth.*

This is Eliot at his truest, most emotionally piercing, as the aria rises "Over endless plains . . . / Ringed by the flat horizon only," asks, "What is the city over the mountains" that "Cracks and reforms and bursts in the violet air" only to end in the litany of judgment:

> *Falling towers*
> *Jerusalem Athens Alexandria*
> *Vienna London*
> *Unreal.*

That is the true climax of the poem before it ends in a wizardry of quotations from diverse sources that testify to the submission—peace at any price—that takes us back to the epigraph from Petronious in the *Satyricon* with which the poem opens: "I saw with my own eyes the Sibyl at Cumae hanging in a cage, and when the boys said to her: 'Sibyl, what do you want?' she answered: 'I want to die.' "

The message was not exactly loud and clear, but clearly Eliot needed to move on, past the despair and parody of despair in "The Hollow Men," 1925. The more withered Eliot's domestic situation became, the more he made a point of displaying his repertory of skills. The assumed lightness of "This is the way the world ends / . . . Not with a bang but a whimper," became popular. Eliot's avid public recited this ending as if it were the latest ditty. It stuck in a reader's memory more than Eliot's astonishing ability to equate *post coitum omne animal triste* with remoteness from "the kingdom." *This* was the end of the world? For a poet who had adjured the "continuous self-sacrifice of personality," even "its extinction," Eliot was clearly using poetry to follow his own traces, to mark every stage in his pilgrimage.

"Ash-Wednesday" (1930) is a lyrically tortured evocation of the halts and starts in Eliot's longing to find certainty in the Church. At times it is Eliot at his most open and confiding, straight in his appeal. Here, for once, he writes out of his own heart. The tonality he makes of precious memories brings us to the threshold of *Four Quartets*, where "end" and "beginning" revert to childhood.

> *And the lost heart stiffens and rejoices*
> *In the lost lilac and the lost sea voices*
> *And the weak spirit quickens to rebel*
> *For the bent golden-rod and the lost sea smell.*

In such a passage Eliot is closer to himself than he has ever been before. But the poem is essentially a dramatic soliloquy in which everything in Eliot's personal repertory (including quotations from Scripture and the Book of Common Prayer) is used to bring home the twistings and turnings of a penitent not yet at home in the Church.

Struggle is everything in "Ash-Wednesday."

> *Because I do not hope to know again*
> *The infirm glory of the positive hour*
> *Because I do not think*
> *Because I know that I shall not know*
> *The one veritable transitory power*
> *Because I cannot drink*
> *There, where trees flower, and springs flow, for there is nothing again.*

The poet seeks not belief but "peace." As Pascal said that man's troubles stem from his inability to sit still in his own room, so Eliot asks, "Teach us to care and not to care / Teach us to sit still." The inquietude that presses him is pervasive enough to divest the very texts he seeks for authority, meaning consolation.

> *. . . And God said*
> *Prophesy to the wind, to the wind only for only*
> *The wind will listen.*

What is left when the hallowed texts written by God or His exegetes seem to mock themselves? The third and final part gives the answer: an ascent straight out of Dante (though it is only up three *stairways*, which of course stand for hell, purgatory, and paradise). As the struggle in the first and second parts of "Ash-Wednesday" was hell on him to get as far as this! so on the second stairway he must still struggle, but with "the devil of the stairs who wears / The deceitful face of hope and of despair." At the second turning of the second stair "There were no more faces." Climbing the third stair, he finds "strength beyond hope and despair," for here,

> *beyond the hawthorn blossom and a pasture scene*
> *The broadbacked figure drest in blue and green*
> *Enchanted the maytime with antique flute.*

Is this heaven? Jacques Maritain, in America during the war, was most strongly attracted to "Ash-Wednesday." Of the last eleven lines he would say, "In these lines I hear the beauty of pure sound, such as the *poètes maudits* strove to create. The words are so clear. It is a chant, a ritualistic chant, which we don't really have in the French language."

> *Blessèd sister, holy mother, spirit of the fountain, spirit of the garden,*
> *Suffer us not to mock ourselves with falsehood*
> *Teach us to care and not to care*
> *Teach us to sit still*
> *Even among these rocks,*
> *Our peace in His will*
> *And even among these rocks*

Sister, mother
And spirit of the river, spirit of the sea,
Suffer me not to be separated

And let my cry come unto Thee.

The *Four Quartets* are more literally a "*recherche*" in the sense of an "inquiry" into "*temps perdu*" than Proust's great novel. Proust gives us a comprehensive picture of French society as seen through the prodigious intellect that, even more than his homosexuality and half-Jewish inheritance, made Marcel an outsider. It is only in the last of Proust's seven novels, when time is "recovered," is seen to be all of a piece, when the aging man sees the single truth that transcends his experience, that the narrator is no longer "searching" but finally united with himself.

Eliot begins in "Burnt Norton" by positing the circular nature of time. Time present and time past "Are both perhaps present in time future," but while they are all united in the mind by fleeting scenes from childhood, the poet sees no real end, no "purpose" to time. "What might have been and what has been" jointly end up in a present full of regret. "Human kind / Can not bear very much reality." And in fact, as is Eliot's way, there is not much "reality" in the external world to describe. We read the poem in delight and of course the usual apprehension as Eliot roams his "first world"—

> *Footfalls echo in the memory*
> *Down the passage which we did not take*
> *Towards the door we never opened*
> *Into the rose-garden*

only to fret over the fragments left in the mind. These recoveries of experience come and go as portents of the thesis that time, far from being ever "lost," does not yet give forth its meaning, is still "unredeemable." Everything remains scattered, longing for "the one still point in a turning world" promised in Scripture and to be exemplified on earth as it is in heaven.

> *The trilling wire in the blood*
> *Sings below inveterate scars*
> *And reconciles forgotten wars.*

One wants to talk back to Eliot here for all his virtuosity. Not all wars are "forgotten" and "reconciled." But we are held by the subtle movement of Eliot's remembrances and the skill with which he stops them dead in time to pursue his "inquiry" into the cycle of time.

Eliot gratefully accepted Pound's cutting and redressing of *The Waste Land* because the final product was "effective" no matter what Eliot first had in mind with "He do the police in different voices," the recurrent "heap of broken images." So the *Four Quartets* are effective more for "the beauty of pure sound," line after line searching to connect with each other, than for his worrying his life back and forth. Writing at the supposed culmination of his life (he was forty-seven when "Burnt Norton" appeared in 1935), the famous man frets over the betrayal that lies in the nature of words. Mortality is in the way everywhere.

> . . . *Words strain,*
> *Crack and sometimes break, under the burden,*
> *Under the tension, slip, slide, perish,*
> *Decay with imprecision, will not stay in place.*

"To be still" in the midst of living! That is the fixed point Eliot is always steering for. As he said in "Ash-Wednesday," "Teach us to care and not to care." Though "Burnt Norton" ends, "The detail of the pattern is movement," Eliot does not really want "movement." With his usual severity—the supercilious negative, the rejection ex cathedra, the chilling riposte—he informs us, "Desire itself is movement / Not in itself desirable," and ends, "Ridiculous the waste sad time / Stretching before and after."

Four Quartets has been seen as a "religious" and even mystical poem because it does move, finally, to the devotional spirit that gives Eliot peace at Nicholas Farrar's humble old church. All comes together with "Sin is Behovely," in the eternal constitution of things. The past, no longer mere event when seen under the aspect of eternity assured by the Christian past, unites everything. Martyred Charles I and his Puritan regicides—all now "Accept the constitution of silence / And are folded in a single party."

So "all shall be well."

But there is no God of comfort and love where the poem ends, just the dazzling rhetoric as Eliot brings in the Holy Spirit, "The dove descending . . . With flame of incandescent terror," in order to proclaim "The one discharge from sin and error." "The only hope, or else despair / Lies in the choice of pyre or pyre— / To be redeemed from fire by fire."

Four Quartets is for me the great elegy that Eliot wrote in order to forgive himself at last. So much is forgiven, or can happily be overlooked. What has so long been divided in himself is now united—as in the Incarnation of God in man. In "The Dry Salvages" Eliot wrote in rapture of the Incarnation, "Here the impossible union / Of spheres of existence is actual."

All this follows from the ambiguity Eliot set out to resolve. And so he did, in the most beautiful music:

> *All manner of things shall be well*
> *When the tongues of flame are in-folded*
> *Into the crowned knot of fire*
> *And the fire and the rose are one.*

Mary McCarthy once said to Flannery O'Connor of the Eucharist, "Of course it is only a symbol." To which Flannery responded, "If it is only a symbol, to hell with it." Were the fire and the rose as actual to Eliot as they were necessary to "crown" the poem? All I know is that the intense pleasure I get from *Four Quartets* is mostly in the ravishing lines, not in the supposed coming together of the Trinity in which the poem ends. It is most beautiful in a reverence for early experience that literally brings Eliot back to St. Louis and then the sea off Cape Ann.

> *The salt is on the briar rose,*
> *The fog is in the fir trees.*
> *The sea howl*
> *And the sea yelp, are different voices*
> *Often together heard.*

"He do the police in different voices." This quotation from Dickens's *Our Mutual Friend* was how Eliot originally began *The Waste*

Land. How Eliot was haunted yet made as a poet by his ability to summon up "different voices"! Always the many voices that intone the disharmony in Eliot that led him to cry for peace. Where perhaps there is no peace. Between midnight and dawn "the past is all deception."

11

Robert Frost: The Survival of the Fittest

> *The intense concentration of self in the middle of such a heartless immensity, my God! who can tell it?*
>
> MELVILLE, *Moby-Dick, Chapter 93, "The Castaway"*

A T AMHERST COLLEGE in the middle 1950s Robert Frost was often in evidence. One of the great sights in that small, narrow place was the beaming, heavily triumphant, rumpled Frost, now in his eighties, "saying" his poems in Johnson Chapel to worshipful crowds and between poems saying anything that came to mind about the universe at large. Starting in 1917 he had been the first American poet-in-residence at any American college. Over the years, reading and lecturing everywhere in a conversational style as direct as his poetry, he came to depend on an immediate audience to confirm his hold on the public, which identified with him as it did no other poet—"you can read *him*." He needed this audience to lift him above his often shaky morale.

Several times I was his only audience. After dinner at our house on Woodside Avenue—where a little Cinzano vermouth, which he claimed never to have encountered before, set him up for a night's excited talking—I walked him back to his room at the Lord Jeffrey Inn. Telling me frankly that he was often afraid to go to bed, he insisted on walking me back; I would have to walk him back still again.

In the dark Amherst night we worked our way past the football stadium, the shaky bridge, and the mud everywhere underfoot. Frost never seemed to notice anything, least of all my shivering yawns, in the rambling, fiercely resentful trance into which he fell as soon as we set off for his hotel. He talked about his early life in San Francisco, his erratic, often violent father dying of tuberculosis when Frost was eleven, leaving the family with eight dollars, his mother taking the body of his father back to New England, the aborted term at Dartmouth, his "second try at education," that one unfinished time at Harvard. To my amazement, he was reciting his life—to someone accidentally present for him—as if I had never known all this, as if nothing existed but his struggle. The world was all Robert Frost. His soul was crowded with ghosts. His life was unrelieved. Despite his immense fame and the "baby critics" at the universities interested not in his values but in "explicating" his every line for dear life, *his* life at two in the morning, trudging through Amherst, was still his early life—a cry for appreciation, an effort to throw off a curse. So it had been when he was alone with his family on the New Hampshire farm his grandfather had given him as a last resort, and he was trying to eke out not a living but a life by writing poetry. And this when New England was being given up by its own in the rush to the West. He, too, had been left behind in old, craggy, surly New England, like the desperate farmers who recur in his poetry with their maddened wives.

At about this time it was announced that a radar signal had bounced off the moon. Frost's startling personal confidences, bulking in the dark like his body swollen in old age, reminded me of that outer beep in outer space. His wife Elinor had died twenty years before, and he kept circling around her name, their flighty, hazardous family life, his fear that all Frosts were somehow off-balance. His father had beaten him like a madman.

A very old, enlarged, slowly moving man (he actually apologized for his heaviness, growling, "Can't do anything about *that*"), Frost seemed to be defending every particle of existence left to him. He remembered his griefs with a kind of rage. The subtlety and hardness of his thinking—at the same time emotionally more open than that of other poets—struck me again when I saw him in the company of professors who carefully weighed everything they said. Those nineteenth-century men who (once) dominated the twentieth by having grown up with that ancient, ferocious self-assertion! Edmund Wilson, with whom I was always arguing about Frost—Wilson crankily dismissed him as a publicity hound—would travel by taxi from Wellfleet to his friends all over the Eastern Seaboard. He visited me in Amherst, resting himself on the porch like a squire out of Gogol, and suggested we steal into the registrar's office to look up the grades of his grandfather Thaddeus, who had gone on to the Presbyterian ministry. Wilson was teaching himself Hebrew from his grandfather's old Hebrew grammar in divinity school, but derided anyone who spoke up for "religion." In his most emphatic no-nonsense style he would declaim, "We must simply live without religion."

Frost was also from this species, where people were harder, more fundamental, and not afraid to suffer. He was a Darwinian by instinct, and one all by himself. He greatly admired Thomas Hardy's poetry, even saw him as a forerunner, but in the hard American style of rugged individualism that advanced with fame, he lacked Hardy's compassion, *sunt lacrimae rerum*, "the tears of things" that come with being mortal. Frost had the wary physical repulsion of milder temperaments which often comes with powerful imaginative capacity. He was exactly the opposite of the all-admiring teachers with whom he spent much of his time as he "lectured" from college to college. They could never flatter him enough; otherwise he was by no means prepared even to consider an opinion because it was in the air. His thinking was sharply his own— incisive and harshly self-determined, philosophical about anything on earth that came his way. "Heaven" was simply the place above us he adopted as a poetic convention. As a "good Greek," on occasion he liked to remember the literature he had been early taught, in which men embraced human fate stoically. His thinking was practical and fiercely self-affirming, based on what he had worked out in defense of his creative pride as a poet working inside the spoken language. That was his greatness. "Why can't we have any one quality of poetry we choose by itself?" he asked in his essay "The Figure a Poem Makes." "We can have it in thought. Then it will go hard if we can't in practice, Our lives for it."

Younger poets, he noticed when they evaded the test of skill, lacked dramatic tone and "sparkle." He came to dislike writers who slipped into "radical" postures. This was "defeatism" calling itself idealism. He was always putting on a show of wild strength, even when there was no occasion for proclaiming it, even when he was just fending off fawning questions. Why had he repeated the last line of "Stopping by Woods on a Snowy Evening"?

> *The woods are lovely, dark and deep,*
> *But I have promises to keep,*

> *And miles to go before I sleep,*
> *And miles to go before I sleep.*

"Because I couldn't think of another!" Not true. Poem after poem showed how much he was drawn to those "woods"—and how he fought against this attraction. No wonder "courage" was his highest personal ideal, counting on everything in the "heart" against the fear that arose in the "soul." "Strength" was his test of a man and his opinions. Strength he obviously struggled for more than anything else. "Strength" of character, he could have said with Herbert Hoover, would lift the destitute above their unfortunate situation. This was the merciless individualism straight out of Herbert Spencer's brand of Darwinism—"make it or die!"—that had been discounted by Franklin D. Roosevelt's cowardly, cringing, wasteful New Deal. Elinor Frost was even fiercer in her hatred of all reform measures. This was before President Kennedy took Frost up and Frost remembered that his father in San Francisco had been a Democratic party activist and had run for local office on the Democratic ticket. Robert Frost was "again" a Democrat.

He could not stop talking. He could not stop talking about *them*, early enemies. He could not stop talking about his great friend the English poet Edward Thomas, killed in 1917. He kept coming back to Ezra Pound, now at St. Elizabeths, as he had first met him in London, in 1913. Frost was not drowning, far from it, but his whole life seemed to pass in review as he dragged me through the first springtime mud. He was holding on to life sentence by sentence. The wonderful thing about these much recited yet still pent-up memories was the spell they put on him as he "spoke" them. He was saying the same thing in his letters and even in his public talks in Johnson Chapel. But while he was walking with me, the transitions in his night talks were hauntingly spaced and somehow as stoical, lean, bitten off the edge of the soul as in his remarkable early poems. There the gap between the solitary poet and the "vastness," the new open space he yearns to travel into, promises an adventure that will surely confirm his early sense of what things are about and his love for his own. But the farther world he seeks has "an edge of doom." For Frost there will always be an "edge" off the world, despite his success in it.

A Boy's Will (1913), first published in England, opens with "Into My Own," where

> *One of my wishes is that those dark trees,*
> *So old and firm they scarcely show the breeze,*
> *Were not, as 'twere, the merest mask of gloom,*
> *But stretched away unto the edge of doom.*

Frost was now twice the age he had been when he published those lines, but the old man brooding his memories at me in the night was still the poet who became a farmer just as farmers were giving up on New England. Their lone, deserted farmhouses would reappear in later stricken poems like "The Black Cottage," "The Wood-Pile," "The Thatch." In *A Boy's Will*, in "Ghost House," a "memory" poem, he lives with the dead:

> *I dwell in a lonely house I know*
> *That vanished many a summer ago,*
> *And left no trace but the cellar walls,*
> *And a cellar in which the daylight falls*

and there is a whiff of Thomas Hardy's "In Time of 'The Breaking of Nations' " (Hardy was always important to him) in Frost's concluding "They are tireless folk, but slow and sad— / Though two, close-keeping, are lass and lad." Of course Hardy's "a maid and her wight" are alive and Frost's "lass and lad" are dead. And Frost is passively alone with himself in an American tradition of unavailing solitude that was different from Hardy's, full of neighboring folk and their stories of men and women.

More, there is a desperateness to some of the best poems in *A Boy's Will* which was to become familiar in later books, but there Frost often struggled to end a poem on a note of satisfaction and reconciliation. In "Storm Fear" we meet for the first time the menacing snow and wind that so often return in Frost's winter journey through life to produce startling depths of desolation—and this straight on. Here husband and wife with child huddle together in the night against a wind that works against them in the dark and, pelting with snow the lower chamber window on the east, becomes a beast that "with a sort of stifled bark" whispers, "Come out! Come out!" No, it costs no inward struggle not to go, but everything familiar and comforting has been made distant by the piled-up drifts. And the poem ends in open doubt "Whether 'tis in us to arise with day / And save ourselves unaided."

Frost in later life was to toss the idea of God up and down like a ball—it was always something to play with. He was on the side of the eternal verities, all right, and unlike less traditional Americans never sought or claimed a God that did not belong to everyone in common. But as a countryman always working against the weather, he could not disabuse himself of the glaring neutrality of the universe. As with "snow," so with "stars"—these were fixtures in his poetry. To the first he assigned death, to the other indifference. The early poem "Stars" brings up his enemy snow, "in shapes as tall as trees," which inclines him to give up, to falter with his last steps "As if with keenness for our fate," to "white rest, and a place of rest / Invisible at dawn." While the snow attacks directly, the stars, "like some snow-white / Minerva's snow-white marble eyes," show neither love nor hate, are "Without the gift of sight." We are where we are, closed in.

Still, Frost needed the metaphysical backup—something more than one man's grim wandering—that he found in "The Trial by Existence." The life we live is the life we choose to live, but our fate so little depends on our choice that in the end "are we wholly stripped of pride / In the pain that has but one close, / Bearing it crushed and mystified." Frost would return to his primal fear of being closed in—"Home Burial," "The Black Cottage," "Fire and Ice," "Stopping by Woods on a Snowy Evening," "The Onset," "Acquainted with the Night," "Desert Places." But in many poems his way out was to make a connection with minuscule natural beings in nature—who again and again spoke for a life in nature so vibrant and continuous that Frost felt they spoke for him as well. In "The Tuft of Flowers" Frost, studying the grass all mown by "one / Who mowed it in the dew before the sun," is passed by a butterfly "bewildered" by the newly leveled field, but who in turning away "led my eye to look / At a tall tuft of flowers beside a brook." Whoever had mowed "before the sun" had left this "A leaping tongue of bloom the scythe had spared / Beside a reedy brook the scythe had bared." The mower had done this not for anyone coming after him but "from sheer morning gladness at the brim." And this was a message "The butterfly and I had lit upon." Frost feels in the mysterious mower "a spirit kindred to my own; / So that henceforth I worked no more alone." Such an ending was to make Frost all too agreeable to future audiences still hoping for a moral. But of course what has kept the poem fresh is not "a message from the dawn" but Frost's ability to picture the invisible mower "And hear his long scythe whispering to the ground." This was the connection that could raise him above his fear. It was also, alas, to establish Frost as a "country poet" able and even eager to address the easily pleased.

North of Boston (1914) remains one of the most startling breakthroughs by a modern American poet. *A Boy's Will* was a meditation from within by a man looking for a subject; it was not even a dialogue with oneself. *North of Boston* was regional drama in verse, a triumph in the use of actual speech. Frost was thoroughly in charge now, replacing the wistful melancholy of *A Boy's Will* with a fluid metric line as confident in narrative as in the detachment with which Frost told of a New England crabbier and narrower than ever. It is still remarkable that Frost was able to insinuate his natural lyricism into external dialogue in order to characterize the speaker in an unredeemable situation. In "The Death of the Hired Man" the wife coaxing her husband to take back the man who has so often disappointed him shows her difference from her husband in her connection with the universe:

> *Part of a moon was falling down the west,*
> *Dragging the whole sky with it to the hills.*
> *Its light poured softly in her lap. She saw it*
> *And spread her apron to it. She put out her hand*
> *Among the harplike morning-glory strings,*
> *Taut with the dew from garden bed to eaves,*
> *As if she played unheard some tenderness*
> *That wrought on him beside her in the night.*
> *"Warren," she said, "he has come home to die:*
> *You needn't be afraid he'll leave you this time."*

The connection here is with the real life in nature, which once led Silas the aging hired man to rage lovingly against a college boy haying with him, and which now in the form of death is taking him over completely. Frost the poet is here a naturalist without theory or bitterness. The human intensity of all four characters in the poem is wonderful.

Frost has no design on these people, has no point to make of their situation, does not betray the conscious pride of a Browning in trying a drama in verse or the despair in general of a Robinson Jeffers. He has not yet become the sententious old man I would hear scorning "weakness" and boasting that he was tops in "prowess" and "feats of association." Nothing so confirms Frost's belief that poetry had to be drama, drama as in the total naturalness with which husband and wife shuttle Silas's life story between them as they argue over him. One line leads into and crosses another with the metrical ease that Frost called "playing" against the regular beat. The husband—

> "When was I anything but kind to him? / But I'll not have the fellow
>   back," he said.
> "I told him so last haying, didn't I?
> If he left then, I said, that ended it.
> What good is he? Who else will harbor him
> At his age for the little he can do.
> . . . I'm done."

The wife—

> "Sh! not so loud: he'll hear you," Mary said. . . .
> "He's worn out. He's asleep beside the stove.
> When I came up from Rowe's I found him here,
> Huddled against the barn door fast asleep,
> A miserable sight, and frightening, too—
> You needn't smile—I didn't recognize him—I wasn't looking for
>   him—and he's changed.
> Wait till you see."

Frost was *the* poet of marriage, a central subject for him if not for other American poets. In "Home Burial" the husband has thoughtlessly buried the body of their first child so near the house that the wife feels she is always looking at the grave. The tie between them is badly strained. The "home burial" has come as a last straw. He does not seem to know this. What makes the poem shattering is that everything said and felt between them is as immediate and concentrated in perspective as a film. It begins, "He saw her from the bottom of the stairs / Before she saw him. She was starting down, / Looking back over her shoulder

at some fear." Although we wonder at first that the husband could actually demand "What is it you see?" the wife's terror at his lack of understanding and the husband's terror at losing her completely bring home
the intensity of love turned inside out. The grip of this is Frost's genius; the desperate emotions that can tie a man and woman for life
were all too familiar to him. One morning I saw him alone for the last
time when he summoned me to his room at the Lord Jeffrey. He triumphantly waved a new poem at me. "It's called 'Kitty Hawk' and I'll
bet you can't guess what it's about!" "The Wright Brothers?" "Knew
you would say that! It's about a girl I chased down there in 1894!" The
"girl" was his future wife Elinor, whom he could not persuade to marry
him at once. What Frost did not tell me, and neither did "Kitty Hawk"
when I got to read the poem, was that Elinor's refusal had so disturbed
him that he fled to the Dismal Swamp on the Virginia–North Carolina
border. He actually walked into the swamp, had to be rescued, and managed to return home only by hopping freight trains to Baltimore and
borrowing money for the journey back to Lawrence.

"Kitty Hawk" bounces about in the style Frost finally arrived at as
America's national bard, the universally honored wisdom figure every
congressman had to love. He is genial, even jaunty, in three-beat phrases
remembering

> *When I came here young*
> *. . . I was, to be sure,*
> *Out of sorts with Fate,*
> *Wandering to and fro*
> *In the earth alone.*

"Out of sorts with Fate" is not exactly the tone of "Home Burial." The
husband had buried his child in "The little graveyard where my people
are! / So small the window frames the whole of it." His defense is that
he is used to the sight, even the new mound that marks his child. But
" 'Don't, don't, don't, don't,' she cried." He begs, "Can't a man speak
of his own child he's lost?" but as Frost was to say of the runaway wife
in "The Hill Wife" (*Mountain Interval*), there are "finalities / Besides
the grave." In "Home Burial" the wife opens the door as if to run away,
the husband shouts he will bring her back by force, and there all things
stand, marriage as a story without resolution, will against will.

North of Boston is full of dramatic picture-scenes—"The Black Cottage," "A Servant to Servants," "The Fear" (among others)—created by the flowing naturalness of speech that informs the whole. The characters are grim to the point of being outlandish, as in "The Fear," where a farmwife in deepest night is frightened of something, someone in the barn, only to discover that it is a man who has been walking about with his child. "Every child should have the memory / Of at least one long-after-bedtime walk. / What, son?" Of course this strange parent is Frost himself, who was known for his nighttime prowls, with and without child. But marginal as he felt himself to be all his life, he wonderfully used his idiosyncrasy to describe not his own "poetic soul" but the fear pervading the New England of leftover isolated farms in which character once shaped by religion, weather, and New England's famous intransigence had now become a puzzle and curiosity to itself.

New England's back country was what was left over. In "The Black Cottage" a minister musing over the house long occupied by a widow whose husband had fallen "at Gettysburg or Fredericksburg" recalls that "Nothing could draw her" after the two sons who had left.

> *She valued the considerable neglect*
> *She had at some cost taught them. . . .*
> *. . . She had her own ideas of things, the old lady.*
> *. . . You couldn't tell her what the West was saying,*
> *And what the South, to her serene belief. . . .*
> *White was the only race she ever knew.*
> *Black she had scarcely seen, and yellow never.*
> *But how could they be made so very unlike*
> *By the same hand working in the same stuff?*
> *She had supposed the war decided that.*
> *What are you going to do with such a person?*

This was perhaps less idealism than obstinacy. In Frost's "A Servant to Servants" that obstinacy is a desperate hold on life that no longer sees an opening anywhere, that is simply the fatalism that comes with exhausting routine. "A Servant to Servants" is one of the greatest dramatic monologues I know, and all the more affecting for the long-departed rural idiom in which the hard-pressed woman at the kitchen window recites her life. The regional harshness of the New England back country is centered on the nameless woman who can see a lake through her kitchen window but, endlessly at work in the kitchen, can only envy occasional campers on "our land."

> *It seems to me*
> *I can't express my feelings, any more*
> *Than I can raise my voice or want to lift*
> *My hand (oh, I can lift it when I have to).*
> *Did ever you feel so? I hope you never.*
> *It's got so I don't even know for sure*
> *Whether I am glad, sorry, or anything.*
> *There's nothing but a voice-like left inside*
> *That seems to tell me how I ought to feel,*
> *And would feel if I wasn't all gone wrong*

The "wrong" is that she is exhausted "from doing / Things over and over that just won't stay done." She and her husband "Len" used to live "ten miles from anywhere," but Len insisted on buying the bit of shore along the long narrow lake and building cabins for tourists who hardly ever come. He is now in charge of highway work, and has boarded four of the laborers, crude men living in her house in total indifference to her while piling up more work for her. Her real, deepest trouble is that while she is ailing body and soul, her always optimistic, forthright husband "says one steady pull more ought to do it. / He says the best way out is always through." "Through" is what she feels, all right: "I can see no way out but through— / Leastways for me—and then they'll be convinced."

Len may want "the best for me," but he can't deal with her deepest fear. "I have my fancies: it runs in the family." What follows, surely building on Frost's own terror of traits descending from his father to his sister and two of his daughters (his only son was to commit suicide), is the farmwife's desolate confession that she has been—once—to the state asylum. The unutterable, the most private fact is not that she has had her "fancies" and that even the highway laborers in her kitchen might be afraid of her, but that "you can't know / Affection or the want of it in that state."

Her father's brother, "he went mad quite young. . . . / . . . Anyway all he talked about was love." Rather than send him to the asylum, the father built his brother

> *a sort of cage,*
> *Or room within a room, of hickory poles,*
> *Like stanchions in the barn, from floor to ceiling—*
> *A narrow passage all the way around.*

Her mother as a bride had "to accommodate her young life" to the "creature." "That was what marrying father meant to her. / She had to lie and hear love things made dreadful / By his shouts in the night."

Whatever the self-observed struggle against heredity that made Frost eternally battle for more and more triumph in his life, he never lacked honesty or the courage he called the supreme value. More than eighty years after "A Servant to Servants" first appeared in *North of Boston*, I am still astonished by the deftness with which Frost has the woman touch on every side of the abyss that never leaves her mind, that terrifies her even as she cannot abandon one of the tasks that have become her life in the kitchen. At the end, when the campers leave, she probably wonders if her desperateness has driven them away. There was still a good deal of the old century's "genteel tradition" hanging over Frost in 1915. He does not seem to have noticed it.

Of course it was a kind of ruthlessness about human relations he brought to poetry—something very different from the scorn for the modern mass world which engaged Eliot and Pound. "I don't want to find out what can't be known," the husband says in "In the Home Stretch" (*Mountain Interval*). And his wife:

> *You're searching, Joe,*
> *For things that don't exist; I mean beginnings.*
> *Ends and beginnings—there are no such things.*
> *There are only middles.*

That is pure Frost, as is the great line in "Birches," a poem that delights in a boy's swinging up to "heaven" and down again: "Earth's the right place for love."

Frost never stayed long with the vision he exacted in any one poem. Unlike Wallace Stevens, he did not debate with himself the replacement of religion by art, the relation of the imagination to "reality." He did not think in such abstractions. He was not a leisurely spectator of his own life. He was an almost frighteningly powerful temperament—charged up, overflowing with crotchets, always on the move between such wonder at existence as only genius possesses and his need to supplant everyone else. Other poets did not exist. In such chatty self-celebrations as "New Hampshire," a foretaste of many poems in Frost's triumphant maturity, Frost laughs at "a poet from another state, / A zealot full of fluid inspiration." This one angrily tried to make him write a protest against the act prohibiting the manufacture, sale, and transportation of intoxicating liquors. And "Do you know, / Considering the market, there are more / Poems produced than any other thing." I was once amazed to see Frost impatiently stamping on a book by a new poet he simply did not want to consider. As a young poet Frost felt himself alone in his struggle for recognition. He was now four times the favorite poet of the Pulitzer Prize committee and of a public that did not have to read him to know that he was important. Frost had most arduously earned his success. He was now alone in his superiority—his genially proffered wisdom, his freedom from cant. Breezy, happily confiding in his neighbors,

> *I may as well confess myself the author*
> *Of several books against the world in general.*
> *To take them as against a special state*
> *Or even nation's to restrict my meaning.*
> *I'm what is called a sensibilitist,*
> *Or otherwise an environmentalist.*
> *I refuse to adapt myself a mite*
> *To any change from hot to cold, from wet*
> *To dry, from poor to rich, or back again.*
> *I make a virtue of my suffering*
> *From nearly everything that goes on round me.*

He added, "I know wherever I am, / . . . I shall not lack for pain to keep me awake." And this because he was a "creature of literature." God knows a writer that sensitive is a porous being. In "A Star in a Stoneboat" Frost imagines a farmer picking up a fallen star and, not knowing any better, using it as material to shore up his fence. Frost is wonderfully indignant at this. "It went for building stone, and I, as though / Commanded in a dream, forever go / To right the wrong that this should have been so."

As old-fashioned a romantic gesture as this is, Frost could have stopped there. But he had to bring the subject around to himself—a complacent earthling. No, he does not look at stars so much as he follows walls.

> *Some may know what they seek in school and church,*
> *And why they seek it there; for what I search,*
> *I must go measuring stone walls, perch on perch;*
> *. . . Such as it is, it promises the prize*
> *Of the one world complete in any size*
> *That I am like to compass, fool or wise.*

No fool, Robert Frost. But the poem is discursive in Frost's commencement-address style. And by contrast with the wonderful image of the farmer dragging the star about "at a pace / But faintly reminiscent of the race / Of jostling rock in interstellar space," sadly self-satisfied.

Frost was a greatly mixed creature. At his top, he was such an existentialist that in poems like "The Census-Taker," "Fire and Ice," "Stopping by Woods on a Snowy Evening," "The Need of Being Versed in Country Things," "Acquainted with the Night," "Desert Places," "Neither Out Far Nor In Deep," he does not walk around the subject, he nails it to us. He said in his essay "The Figure a Poem Makes" that "the background is hugeness and confusion." Yes, he had to battle against all that to make the surface flat, straight, keen as a weapon. For once, no opinions! America's "favorite, national" poet turned out to be not a comforter but a writer racked and wrecked enough as the unaccommodating American persona that D. H. Lawrence described as "stoic, isolate, a killer."

> *Some say the world will end in fire,*
> *Some say in ice.*
> *. . . I think I know enough of hate*
> *To say that for destruction ice*
> *Is also great*
> *And would suffice.*

"Once by the Pacific":

> *The shattered water made a misty din.*
> *Great waves looked over others coming in,*
> *And thought of doing something to the shore*
> *That water never did to land before*
> *. . . It looked as if a night of dark intent*
> *Was coming, and not only a night, an age.*
> *Someone had better be prepared for rage.*
> *There would be more than ocean-water broken*
> *Before God's last* Put out the Light *was spoken.*

"Bereft":

> *Where had I heard this wind before*
> *Change like this to a deeper roar?*
> *. . . Summer was past and day was past*
> *Somber clouds in the west were massed.*
> *Out in the porch's sagging floor*
> *Leaves got up in a coil and hissed. . . .*
> *Something sinister in the tone*
> *Told me my secret must be known:*
> *Word I was in the house alone*
> *Somehow must have gotten abroad,*
> *Word I was in my life alone,*
> *Word I had no one left but God.*

For me Frost's greatest poem is "Neither Out Far Nor In Deep" (*A Further Range*). It is a pure distillation of Frost's long-standing identification of the human situation with the act of seeing—so hedged that it keeps us in the middle of things. The people along the sand look just one way. Until a ship passes out of sight, they can see it raising its hull. The "wetter" ground is like glass, reflecting a standing gull.

> *The land may vary more;*
> *But wherever the truth may be—*
> *The water comes ashore,*
> *And the people look at the sea.*
> *They cannot look out far.*

> *They cannot look in deep.*
> *But when was that ever a bar*
> *To any watch they keep?*

The poem is inexorable on human limits. Frost easily moves from stage to stage in his self-embattled thinking. But he cannot afford to be unclear, coming as he does out of "the vast chaos of all I have lived through." In "The Figure a Poem Makes" he wrote that a poem "ends in a clarification of life—not necessarily a great clarification, such as sects and cults are founded on, but in a momentary stay against confusion." "Neither Out Far Nor In Deep" says—in terse lines that capture the limitations of our physical being, of our sight—that such limitations never keep us from looking, continuing, seeking. To live is to keep watch—for our own bare survival. That is the sudden complication in the poem—searching for what we will never find, we save ourselves without perhaps knowing that *this* is the condition that mind (with all its wishes) sets for our lives.

We are the real world. The point of his great poem "Design" (*A Further Range*) is that there really isn't any. In the sight of "a dimpled spider, fat and white, / On a white heal-all, holding up a moth / Like a white piece of rigid satin cloth," Frost sees "Assorted characters of death and blight / Mixed ready to begin the morning right, / Like the ingredients of a witches' broth." After all, "What had that flower to do with being white . . . ? / What brought the kindred spider to that height, / Then steered the white moth thither in the night? / What but design of darkness to appall?— / If design govern in a thing so small?"

Frost liked to pose himself as questioner where other writers (especially in the 1930s) were shouting explanations. Without going into any all-governing determinism or theology, Frost sees the design in nature as inherent, not meaningful. The religious see "design" as directed by God's purpose. Actually, all creatures are such "Assorted characters of death and blight" as they are formed in nature. Frost is playing on contrary meanings of "design"—one is the natural constitution of all living beings, the other the terrible thought that they *intend* to wreak death and destruction. A thought possible only to our narcissism, which confuses freedom of the will with our ability to create effect.

Frost leaves the heartlessness of things as he sees them. As a metaphysician dealing in negatives and riddles, he is superb but encouraging only to himself as someone who could make order in poetry. In 1935 he told Amherst students, "The background is hugeness and confusion shading away from where we stand into black and utter chaos; and against the background any small man-made figure of order and concentration. What pleasanter than that this should be so?" He lived for poetry. The world was Robert Frost. And he could never shut up about anything in it. In the 1960s he was to disturb his patron President Kennedy by arrogantly explaining America to Khrushchev and making dangerous public judgments concerning Soviet policy in his characteristically smug oracular style. In the 1930s he ridiculed the New Deal in "A Roadside Stand"—about victims of the depression pathetically keeping a stand:

> *It is in the news that all these pitiful kin*
> *Are to be bought out and mercifully gathered in*
> *To live in villages next to the theater and store,*
> *Where they won't have to think for themselves anymore;*
> *While greedy good-doers, beneficent beasts of prey,*
> *Swarm over their lives enforcing benefits*
> *That are calculated to soothe them out of their wits.*

Frost at this point was hysterical. "I can't help owning the great relief it would be / To put these people at one stroke out of their pain." It was all "insane." Evidently, Frost (like another brilliant and embittered man in this period, Herbert Hoover, who had risen out of poverty) could not bear to modify in the slightest his self-reflecting portrait of America stern but just. As for Frost's other heritage, the Bible, Frost in *A Masque of Reason* added his own last chapter to the Book of Job. Here God is brought down to earth to confess that He is just part of a process and helplessly rueful about the bullying manner in which He got Job to accept his sufferings.

God now tells Job that He has had the poor fellow on His mind for a thousand years. Job helped Him to "Establish once for all the principle / There's no connection man can reason out / Between his just deserts and what he gets." He didn't tell Job that because "I have to wait for words like anyone." (This, coming out of the Voice of the Whirlwind, is surprising but a good joke in a poem that shows God to be something of a joke—just like us.) Anyway, it was "the essence of the trial" that "It had to seem unmeaning to have meaning. / And it came out all right."

"All right" here means that Job's anguished questioning worked "To stultify the Deuteronomist / And change the tenor of religious thought." Job's resistance released God "From moral bondage to the human race." Man alone knew free will to do good or evil as he chose. God had to follow him "With forfeits and rewards he understood— / Unless I liked to suffer loss of worship." So God did the expected— he prospered good and punished evil until Job, who was punished for no reason other than God's need to impress Satan with His power, changed all that. God was not just, not perfect. And now He is liberated to be just what He is. He always needs someone to work with. The Devil was more original; he alone invented hell. It was Job "and I together / Found out the discipline man needed most / Was to learn his submission to unreason." And that for man's own sake "So he won't find it hard to take his orders / From his inferiors in intelligence / In peace and war—especially in war."

There is supposed to be a reason for things. And now again Job, though "flattered proud / To have been in on anything with You. / 'Twas a great demonstration if You say so," wonders what reason God had for doing all this at Job's expense. Wonderful lines here about their collaboration in the past.

> But, Lord, we showed them what. The audience
> Has all gone home to bed. The play's played out.
> Come, after all these years—to satisfy me.
> . . . Why did You hurt me so? I am reduced
> To asking flatly for the reason—outright.

God, lamely, "I'd tell you, Job—" Job:

> But what is all this secrecy about?
> . . . The obscurity's a fraud to cover nothing.
> . . . We don't know where we are, or who we are.
> We don't know one another; don't know You;
> Don't know what time it is. We don't know, don't we?

To which God, finally, has to admit, "I was just showing off to the Devil, Job, / As is set forth in Chapters One and Two." Later: "I brought him in, / More to give his reality its due / Than anything."

So we are back where we began. God is what He was. Here endeth the lesson for the day. What seems like confusion is not confusion but "the form of forms, / The serpent's tail stuck down the serpent's throat, / Which is the symbol of eternity." All things come round? But that does not satisfy. God comes off here a little *too* human and unsure of Himself. The central character in the celestial drama is not God but Job, who has suffered too long (and meaninglessly). *We* are Job. Frost should have delivered him at last, but was too pleased with his own raillery to come clean.

12

Faulkner: God over the South

The deep sea pressure of Mississippi, otherwise known as the closed society.
BOB MOSES

From a merely artistic point of view, there is no ground, ancient or modern, whose vivid lights, gloomy shadows and grotesque groupings, afford . . . so wide a scope as did the South.
HARRIET BEECHER STOWE, *Dred* (1856)

THE PREAMBLE TO the constitution of the Confederate States of America, March 11, 1861, invoked "the favor and guidance of Almighty God." President Jefferson Davis's biographer William C. Davis* notes that in defeat, in April 1865, President Davis "turned more and more to the Almighty for support. In the closing hours of the Confederacy he revealed an inclination that the Confederate constitution should not have stopped at recognizing God but should have gone on to express its belief in the 'Saviour of Mankind' and perhaps even that the document should specifically have countenanced Christianity. Might this, he may well have wondered, have saved his dying nation?"

The South became for a very long time, up to our day, the Lost Cause, the "Redeemer Nation," "Baptized in Blood," crushed to its soul by an experience of defeat not comprehensible even to Northern dissidents resisting American capitalism at its greediest. But out of defeat, and a sense of guilt not explicit but born out of a sense that life was more genuinely sorrowful and complex than the old South or the new North could take in, rose an extraordinary Southern literature in the twentieth century more religiously intelligent, subtle, and all-encompassing than Northern realists and satirists knew. When Walker

---

Jefferson Davis: The Man and His Hour (1991)

Percy, who began his career with a truly existential novel, *The Moviegoer* (1961), which sprang from a sense of dread and futility in the modern South, was asked why there were now so many significant Southern writers, he replied, "Because we got beat." Percy, a physician who had turned to writing and Catholicism when he was isolated by tuberculosis during the Second World War, was influenced not by other Southern writers but by Kierkegaard, Dostoevsky, and French Catholic writers.

If Lincoln now emerges as the great writer of the Civil War and its sustaining moral force, it is Faulkner who more and more embodies the distortion of life in the South, and as realized after him by Flannery O'Connor. By contrast, Edmund Wilson, who in *Patriotic Gore* wrote an extraordinary book around the Civil War, came to think the war simply a mistake. Bruce Catton said of *Patriotic Gore* that its author knew everything about the Civil War except why it was fought. Perhaps there is some connection between Wilson's despair about American history and his insistence that "we must simply learn to live without religion." But living side by side with religion as part of our inheritance in America, our sense that life is never simply circumstantial, does not mean that we have to believe. No other American writer in our time has put this into fiction with so much passion as Faulkner. The belief in our own righteousness can end on the battlefield.

Faulkner is the greatest writer the South has produced. No one else in our century's fiction has come anywhere close to Faulkner's intense and epic imagination in reacting to the thrust and disorder of American life. If he alone in the American field makes one think of the rich, thick human material in Balzac, Dickens, and Tolstoy, one reason is that he is beset by a religious consensus that explains many of his characters and one that as an independent artist he often travesties. In *Sartoris* and *The Sound and the Fury* some kind of deity is called "the Player." He is a gambler who shakes us out to move us on a board. He is blind, "the blind Dice-Man." The two most obvious "Christ figures" in Faulkner are Benjy, the castrated idiot whose monologue opens *The Sound and the Fury* on his thirty-third birthday, and Joe Christmas in *Light in August*, who murders his white mistress because she is always praying over him as a poor neglected black. But he never knows whether he is black or not. He is shot, then castrated by the white supremacist Percy Grimm, who holds up the bloody knife, gloating, "Now you'll leave white women alone, even in hell." Faulkner's Christ is all victim—"the man things are done to."

If ever a contemporary American took on a subject filled to overflowing with war, violence, pain, cruelty, exclusion, servitude, impoverishment, racial pride, sheer cussedness, resentment of the other America, and delusions of everlasting power over others, it was Faulkner. A great writer and, as Estelle Faulkner said in their many troubles, a man of grace. He was also a deeply afflicted man born at a low point in the history of his region, into a family whose memories of glory he mocked in the self-pity of Mrs. Compson in *The Sound and the Fury* and the crookedness of her son Jason. His own attitude toward Oxford, long after he was derided as "Count No Account" for occasionally drinking himself into the gutter, took the form not of boasting of his world fame but of building up his estate, Rowan Oak, on an ever grander scale.

Because I think of religion as the most intimate expression of the human heart, as the most secret of personal confessions, where we admit to ourselves alone our fears and our losses, our sense of holy dread and our awe before the unflagging power of a universe that regards us as indeed of "no account," I find it hard to think of Faulkner confiding in a personal God. He was by no means as hard-bitten as Joe Christmas, Jason Compson, Mrs. Armstid, Popeye, Percy Grimm, Doc Hines, McEachern, Lucas Burch, the Snopeses, or the many others in his great kingdom of characters who remind us in their hardness of everything inflexible in the Southern character. Faulkner did not look upon his fellow critters as did Lena Grove in *Light in August*, but he was able to create someone so lastingly innocent and good. Seduced, pregnant, and deserted by a passing lover, she still expects a good proper life. And will get it from Byron Bunch, a shy fellow who jolts on a mule all Saturday night so as to help the services in a backwoods church. For me Faulkner reached the heights imagining Joe Christmas's eager-loving and grieving grandmother, Mrs. Hines, who sees in Lena Grove's newborn baby little Joey himself, who never had a chance. Not to forget Ike McCaslin, who out of love of the wilderness and weariness of killing, deliberately puts aside his gun and compass, and comes to argue against the very concept of landownership because of the curse that slavery had put upon the land.

In the everlasting war against evil by the small amount of good in the world, Faulkner chose not religion but art. And such is now the shallowness and aggressiveness of public religion in the service of hardright politics that one wants to thank God that Faulkner was not personally a believer. This was an independent soul in his most tormented moments, who has the imprisoned doctor in *The Wild Palms* say, "Between grief and nothing I will take grief." He wrote to his admirer Malcolm Cowley when Cowley's *Portable Faulkner* helped to make him acceptable, "Life is the same frantic steeplechase toward nothing everywhere and man stinks the same stink no matter where in time."

I don't think it can be said of Faulkner what Tolstoy said to Maxim Gorky: "God is the name of my desire." That is not the way really good American writers today think or talk about religion, if they ever do. On the other hand, the religion of the South Faulkner grew up with, strict churches and stricter doctrine, was dominating. It was a way of life, the most traditional and still most lasting expression of community. And unlike white churches elsewhere, the all-prevailing Baptists in the South were still so much up against their own experience of sin and redemption that by the end of this century they finally and officially apologized for having supported slavery (and straightway launched a campaign to convert the Jews). Unlike a lot of other white churches, the Southerners did not deal in pale, abstract words heard only on Sunday. In black churches immediate issues of life and death were reflected in the words thundering from the pulpit, burned in every heart, and brought home a sense of human existence fraught with the most terrible consequences.

The incisive and traditionalist Southern poet-critic Allen Tate said in *Reactionary Essays on Poetry and Ideas* that slavery was wrong because the owner gave everything to the slave and got nothing in return. Tate believed that whatever the evils of slavery, it made possible "high cultures." "High cultures" are not much seen in *Sartoris*, Faulkner's portrayal of an upper-class family replaying a family history of violence based on their enthusiasm for war. The last Bayard Sartoris, a flying ace who returns from France in 1918, still seeks the death his twin brother John achieved in the air, and finally gets his one and only wish going up in a ridiculous "experimental" home-built plane when its builder begs him to try it out in the interest of science. This was the Southern "aristocrat" never known to read anything, the descendant of slave owners always contemptuous of the stage darkies Faulkner still amused himself with in *Sartoris* who live only to adore and serve him. The meaninglessness of life to Bayard Sartoris is the unexpected desolation his life now takes.

The lawyer Horace Benbow in *Sartoris* and *Sanctuary* is not "doomed," as Faulkner liked to say of the Sartorises and the Compsons in *The Sound and the Fury*. But being a lover of verse, genteel, and never combative (he was a YMCA worker in the Great War), he illustrates the weakness of his class when he comes up against the total, numbing decadence Faulkner described in *Sanctuary*. Faulkner seems to have been startled by his own achievement. In his preface to the 1932 Modern Library edition (the only one he ever wrote to any of his books) he said, "This book . . . is a cheap idea, because it was deliberately conceived to make money." It is actually one of his strongest books, and left such painful traces in Faulkner's mind that twenty years later he returned to Temple Drake in *Requiem for a Nun* (1951). The latter is a mess of a book, and not only because it is a historical narrative about the founding of Jefferson enclosing a play. In the play the cruelly nihilistic Temple, who in *Sanctuary* lied on the witness stand to get an innocent man executed for the murder committed by her "guardian" Popeye, now confesses all to the governor. Not in the hope of saving her black maid, Nancy, who murdered Temple's child to spare his suffering as Temple prepares to run off with another man, but to save her own soul.

Requiem for a Nun is another "cheap idea," a pseudo-moral one. With recognition at last of his genius—his books never earned him a living until then—Faulkner became respectable in his own eyes and hymned in his Nobel lecture "the old verities and truths of the heart, the old universal truths lacking which any story is ephemeral and doomed— love and honor and pity and pride and compassion and sacrifice. Until he does so, he labors under a curse." Faulkner had been called in *The New Yorker* "a Sax Rohmer for the sophisticated." His father pronounced anathema on his early stuff, and his mother would not read him (or was it the other way around?). He had certainly labored under a curse. *Sanctuary* gives us a really demonic urban South liberated from its old self-protective Christianity. No one ever forgets the witless, stunted egotism of Popeye, always threatening us with the automatic in his pocket as if it were the penis he cannot make love with or the static, airless, totally removed world of beds, beds in Miss Reba's Memphis brothel to which Popeye has delivered Temple. Her "sanctuary" indeed, in a ghastly world where in 1931 Faulkner saw none.

Mencken snootily labeled the "Bible Belt" the many plain Southerners who owned neither plantations nor slaves. Faulkner saw their lives reflected in the Old Testament's history of another pastoral people obedient to a God exclusively their own, the conqueror of inferior aborigines, and adamant on racial purity. Faulkner clearly lacked enthusiasm for religion but saw his native South reflected in the Old Testament. His first title for his projected epic of the Snopes family was "Father Abraham." The novel originally called "If I Forget Thee, Jerusalem" became at the publisher's insistence *The Wild Palms*. The last of his great novels was *Absalom, Absalom!* (1936). He was to tell students at the University of Mississippi that the four greatest influences on his work were the Old Testament, Dostoevsky, Melville, and Conrad.

Mississippi, the poorest state in the Union, remote, more haunted by race than any other (blacks outnumbered whites), and correspondingly more violent, was known as the "closed society"—i.e., it closed off its blacks. Mississippi refused to ratify the Thirteenth Amendment abolishing slavery, and was allowed back into the Union only when it ratified the Fourteenth and Fifteenth Amendments. In 1890 the Mississippi Constitution renewed with new vindictiveness the power of whites over blacks they had lost only in Reconstruction.

None of this was done without a firm belief in God. The piety supporting white supremacy was sanctioned by the exclusiveness depicted in the Bible. Religion and society were one, founded on innumerable restrictions and obligations ordered by the one God who, identifying with His creatures, appointed them His one and only holy nation, which certainly bolstered them in their own eyes. This God was more accessible than others in the Middle East. He was supercharged by his interest in human nature, was certainly not consistent but had made man in his own image so there would always be a bond between them. That bond, covenant, contract between creator and creature (eventually it turned into Father and Son) was ultimately His reason for being. Absurd, of course, to see the Creator of a limitless, ultimately imponderable universe as essentially friend, protector, confessor, beloved. Even His terrible status as unresting judge, looking into every heart, mindful of the tiniest slip away from His circumambient law, became a cosmic fairy tale long before one admitted the evolution of human beings in the animal kingdom. But the genius of this all-influential religion was that man had created a divinity who *cared*, who could no more do without man than man could do without Him (God even said this). They were positively related in a way that became the most natural relationship in the world—and the dearest of memories. Even His occasional bad temper and withdrawals proved and proved again how much He kept man in line—for His own sake, since there was finally no God conceivable to man who did not look out for man. They were as chained together as blacks and whites in a system—launched when the English first landed slaves in Jamestown, in 1619—that became an anachronistic horror supported by no Christian sentiment but its own, the harshest slave system in the Americas. The system succumbed in war—leaving an absolute belief in white supremacy—only by tearing the country apart in over two thousand battles and at the cost of almost a million deaths.

The race hatred never ends. Twenty-one blacks in recent years have been found dead by hanging in Mississippi jails. Some of them may be lynchings. Ben Chaney, younger brother of James Chaney, one of the three civil rights workers murdered near Philadelphia, Mississippi, in 1964: "This is a continuation, it's a revival, of the fear that existed in Mississippi prior to 1904."*

The "militant South" was the religiously traditional South, composing "generation after generation of the faithful heart." Man's dependence on God for his self-justification in all things was inherited, natural to a society more patriarchal than most. The slave owner's wife could say nothing as she moved among his bastards. It was from God as total sovereign (this told Calvinists at least man was never alone) that a stridently bossy type of man—he did not have to be a slave owner, the slightest contempt for blacks was enough—derived his authority over anybody lower on the chain that held them all. God could be hated but

---

*Neil McMillen at Mississippi State University: "We have historically been the state most haunted by race, and I think we are still the state most haunted by race." "It's this business of having two separate visions, this constant division between black and white, that's just so depressing to me. The gap has closed between Mississippi and the rest of the nation, not because we've moved so far, although I think we have moved considerably, but because so much of the nation seems bent on heading our way."

not missed. "And damn You, too, see if You can stop me," Jason Compson shrieks at God in *The Sound and the Fury* as he fruitlessly chases the niece who has stolen the money from him that is rightfully hers— "thinking of himself . . . dragging Omnipotence from His throne, if necessary, of the embattled legions of both hell and heaven through which he tore his way and put his hands at last on his fleeing niece."

No people in the officially democratic United States of America were so bossy, thrusting, and cocksure as a Southerner who thanked God every day he was not a "nigger." What not only permitted but positively encouraged a comfortably situated Christian to brand his name as owner on the forehead of a slave? The subjection of the slave was fundamental to this, but as Frederick Law Olmsted noted in his tours of the slave country in the 1850s, unbounded self-importance disregarded the actual inefficiency of slaves.

Olmsted as a reporter on the ground for *The New York Times* could see for himself, as abolitionists and Harriet Stowe could not, how the system distorted and degraded the black character. Toni Morrison, in *Playing in the Dark: Whiteness and the Literary Imagination* (1992), thinks that the "love" preached by Christianity saved the slave so far as anything could, and made for "one of the most resilient Africanist populations in the world." Olmsted, in *A Journey in the Back Country*, discounted the sainthood of Uncle Tom and the religious enthusiasm Mrs. Stowe was to see motivating her character Dred (based on the slave revolt leader Nat Turner). Olmsted found many blacks "are grossly ignorant and degraded in mind, with a crude, undefined, and incomplete system of theology and ethics, credulous and excitable, intensely superstitious and fanatical, what better field could a cunning monomaniac or sagacious zealot desire in which to set on foot an appalling crusade."

The Connecticut Yankee Olmsted was no friend to slavery but distinctly cool about it. Henry Raymond of *The New York Times* sent him to the South in the hope that war could be averted by an "objective picture of Southern life and manners." Olmsted in 1855 was to become editor of *Putnam's Magazine*, the first important national magazine to take a stand against slavery. A Free-Soiler, he published articles on the threat of slavery in Kansas and reviewed Frederick Douglass's autobiography and Melville's great story of black rebellion, "Benito Cereno," which he saw as an "allegory of American slavery against the stereotyped & false faces of black slaves." As Ahab said, "Strike through the mask!" Olmsted tried to do just that. The *Times*, January 12, 1854:

> The hopeless perpetuation of such an intolerable nuisance as this labor system . . . depends mainly upon the careless, temporizing, shiftless system to which the Negro is indebted for this mitigation of the natural wretchedness of slavery. The Southerner, if he sees anything of it, generally disregards and neglects to punish it. Although he is naturally excitable and passionate, he is less subject to impatience and anger than is . . . generally supposed, because he is habituated to regard him so completely as his inferior, dependent and subject.
>
> The direct influence of slavery is to make the Southerner indifferent to small things. . . . His ordinarily uncontrolled authority (and from infancy the Southerner is more free from control, I should judge, than any other person in the world) leads him to be habitually impulsive, imperious and enthusiastic. . . . Yet he seems to me to be very secretive. He minds his own business and lets alone that of others, not in the English way but in a way peculiarly his own; resulting, from want of curiosity, in part formed by such constant intercourse as he has with his inferiors (Negroes). . . . The Southerner . . . is greatly wanting in hospitality of mind, closing his doors to all opinions and schemes to which he has been bred a stranger, with a contempt and bigotry which sometimes seems incompatible with his character as a gentleman. He has a large but unexpansive mind. . . .
>
> He has the intensity of character which belongs to Americans in general. . . . But his want of aptitude for close observation . . . may be reasonably supposed to be mainly the result of habitually leaving all matters not of grand exciting importance . . . to his slaves and of being accustomed to see them slighted or neglected as much as he will, in his indolence, allow them to be by them.

It was against the long-dominant sense of privilege and importance that the god of defeat arose in the South to cloud Faulkner's early life as it mocked the old glory of the Falkners (he inserted the "u"). He took it all on—war, miscegenation, racial violence, exclusion, servitude, racial pride and humiliation, hatred and resentment of the rest of the country, delusions of racial grandeur on a mass scale unknown to the rest of the country. No wonder he sometimes looked haunted, and in a literary culture notorious for insatiable drinkers, he surpassed them all by sometimes turning to the bottle in the full flood of composition as well as in near-suicidal depressions.

"Blood, governors and generals," Jason Compson snarls to himself about his family's past importance and current pretensions, never failing to add that one brother is an idiot, another committed suicide, and that the sister whom all three brothers loved (Jason would never admit this) ran off after marrying a man who was not the father of the child she was carrying.

Faulkner's first offerings, slender sheaves of poetry influenced especially by poets of nostalgia like A. E. Housman, are crucial to the way his sensibility enveloped and enlarged scenes in his fiction with what one can only call his poetry of vision. "I'm a failed poet," he liked to say half-proudly, suggesting how much every instinct in him as a poet went into his fiction. He needed to invade the realistic scene with his own celebration, as a poet in love with language, of the Southern land as natural being. Truly, the land of milk, honey, and cotton was another country, and Faulkner was in love with it. His fervor would overflow the story, reaching in his great hunting story "The Bear" heights of rapture and bitter rumblings that erupted out of him like burning lava. Everything stretched out into life as an infinite present, filling the heart with its terrible immediacy. It is Faulkner's longing for the once "unstoried, uncorrupted" land, echoing his fury at being so knotted and reknotted as artist and man into a world without solution and redemption, that is behind a private world of imagination unparalleled by his contemporaries.

The thinking is black and white, like so much else in the South, but "it's all in the Bible." The creation was perfect until man—yes, and the woman along with him (Faulkner's misogyny is always in the picture)—muddied it by wanting "more and more," grasping more knowledge than they could deal with to dominate the earth and each other. Faulkner, a Calvinist without religion, sees nothing in life but human nature and the weather. The land, the hallowed, God-blessed land Ike McCaslin in "The Bear" sees poisoned by slavery, makes all the more vivid man's awfulness in desecrating it. The fall of man is his constantly intoned explanation of the Southern situation—the tangled history to which he is madly attached. "The voice that breath'd over Eden" is a sweet line from the Victorian poet John Keble's *Christian Year* that Quentin Compson in *The Sound and the Fury* heard so often in his childhood. It now comes back to haunt the Harvard student in Cambridge, Massachusetts, as he prepares to drown himself, June 3, 1910, because of his mad love for his sister Caddy which makes him feel that he has committed incest. He hasn't. Caddy was pregnant with another man's child when she married in late April.

It was thoughtful of Quentin to kill himself on Jefferson Davis's birthday, a Memorial Day in many Southern states. The Compsons sold their piece of long-cherished land to send him to Harvard. The tuition money has been wasted. This is only one of Jason Compson's many "outraged" (a favorite Faulkner word) complaints against his family. His father "drank himself into the ground" while showing off his classical education. His brother, born the idiot Maury Compson (after his genteel mother's forlorn pride in *her* family, and little to show for it), has had his name changed to Benjamin, now forever Benjy and "doomed" (another Faulkner favorite) never to cease seeking after the sister who has long disappeared. Jason had him castrated after he frightened some schoolgirls in a pitiful attempt to make contact with them. "I was trying to say, and I caught her, trying to say and she screamed and I was trying to say and trying and the bright shapes began to stop and I tried to get out." Like Joe Christmas in *Light in August*, he is all crucifixion, always at someone's mercy. Caddy, pregnant, was going to name her child after her brother Quentin even if it was a daughter. It was a daughter, and the money sent to Jason for her upkeep has been regularly secreted by him. He never stops telling you that he was never given the chance in life his brother Quentin forfeited, and has had to buy into the general store that employs him. He can never forgive anyone that Benjy is on the place along with the blacks he keeps—so he never stops complaining that he has to feed everyone. His mother's whining that the family has lost status heats up all his resentments. He is not a man one can love. His routine visits to Lorraine in Memphis are his only joy, but she always wants money.

Last time I gave her forty dollars. Gave it to her. I never promise a woman anything nor let her know what I'm going to give her.

That's the only way to manage them. Always keep them guessing. If you can't think of any other way to surprise them, give them a bust in the jaw.

Jason is a monster one comes to pity; he is so isolated by his rage when Quentin robs Jason of the money he has withheld and steals off with a man from the carnival who wears a red tie. Jason is shocked to think any man would wear a red tie.

Jason howling in pursuit, the third section of *The Sound and the Fury*, atrocious and comic at once, makes up one of the most extraordinary achievements in modern fiction. He is utterly beside himself, his maddened concentration on Quentin and companion astonishing everyone whose life he breaks into. First Benjy speaks in *The Sound and the Fury*, then his brother Quentin. Neither the idiot nor the imminent suicide, alone as each is, commands us as Jason does when he shuts himself off from everything and everyone, spewing hatred in every direction:

> I went on to the street, but they were out of sight. And there I was, without any hat, looking like I was crazy too. Like a man would naturally think, one of them is crazy and another one drowned himself and the other one was turned out into the street by her husband, what's the reason the rest of them are not crazy too. All the time I could see them watching me like a hawk, waiting for a chance to say Well I'm not surprised I expected it all the time the whole family's crazy.

By the end of April 6, 1928, Jason is cursing the whole living world. "And damn You, too," he yells, dreaming of taking "Omnipotence" down with him. April 8, two days later, Easter Sunday. Dilsey, the aged weathered black servitor to every member of the family, emerges at the opening of the fourth and last part of the novel to service the Compsons as usual before taking her family to church to hear a visiting preacher. This is where Faulkner takes over the narrative, after we have been listening so long to the voices of Benjy, Mr. and Mrs. Compson, Quentin, Jason, Caddy, and most of watchful Jefferson. I can never read it aloud without being affected by the exactitude of detail, the serene gravity of tone. But the essence is Dilsey herself, in effect still the Compsons' slave—a human being presented to us as a lifetime of toil and sacrifice.

The day dawned bleak and chill, a moving wall of grey light out of the northeast which, instead of dissolving into moisture, seemed to disintegrate into minute and venomous particles, like dust that, when Dilsey opened the door of the cabin and emerged, needled laterally into her flesh. . . . She wore a stiff black straw hat perched upon her turban, and a maroon velvet cape with a border of mangy and anonymous fur above a dress of purple silk, and she stood in the door for awhile with her myriad and sunken face lifted to the weather, and one gaunt hand flac-soled as the belly of a fish, then she moved the cape aside and examined the bosom of her gown.

The gown fell gauntly from her shoulders, across her fallen breasts, then tightened upon her paunch and fell again, ballooning a little above the nether garments which she would remove layer by layer as the spring accomplished and the warm days, in colour regal and moribund. She had been a big woman once but now her skeleton rose, draped loosely in unpadded skin that tightened again upon a paunch almost dropsical, as though muscle and tissue had been courage or fortitude which the days or the years had consumed until only the indomitable skeleton was left rising like a ruin or a landmark above the somnolent and impervious guts.

Easter Sunday begins for Jason Compson as another terrible day. He curses everyone in sight, as he curses God, for not helping him catch his runaway niece. For Dilsey it begins with her attending to Mrs. Compson's whining complaints and including Benjy in her family as they go off to church. "I wish you wouldn't keep on bringin him to church, mammy," her daughter says. "Folks talkin." "And I knows whut kind of folks," Dilsey retorts. "Trash white folks. Dat's who it is. Thinks he aint good enough fer white church, but nigger church aint good enough fer him." No room for a Christ always in the wrong place. The black children "in garments bought second hand of white people . . . looked at Ben with the covertness of nocturnal animals."

Frony tells a friend, "Mammy aint feelin well this mawnin." But is assured "Rev'un Shegog'll cure dat. He'll give her de comfort en de unburdenin." What happens now in church is extraordinary because Dilsey is. Her intensity of soul blazes out at us as she waits for the visiting preacher to tell her of the Resurrection. The others stare at him in consternation and unbelief. He is undersized, in a shabby alpaca coat. "He had a wizened black face like a small, aged monkey." " 'En dey brung dat all de way fum Saint Looey,' Frony whispered. 'I've knowed de Lawd to use cuiser tools dan dat,' Dilsey said."

And as she predicted, the visitor delivers. "Brethren and sisteren . . . I got the recollection and the blood of the Lamb!" His voice "consumed him, until he was nothing and they were nothing and there was not even a voice but instead their hearts were speaking to one another in chanting measures beyond the need for words. . . ."

" 'Breddren en sistuhn! . . . I got de ricklickshun en de blood of de Lamb!' They did not mark just when his intonation, his pronunciation, became negroid, they just sat swaying a little in their seats as the voice took them into itself. . . . 'Oh I tells you, ef you aint got de milk en de dew of de old salvation when de long, cold years rolls away.' " On their way from church her daughter is embarrassed. "We be passin white folks soon." Dilsey cannot stop weeping. She has had a vision. Everything will come down. "I've seed de first en de last. . . . Never you mind. . . . I seed de beginnin, en now I sees de endin."

The Sound and the Fury grows in emotional power from page to page, and ends in a visceral scream, poor Benjy howling for dear life as Dilsey's grandson Luster frivolously and perhaps vindictively (Benjy is always a bother) takes him home an unaccustomed way around the town square. But the four parts plausibly succeed each other only in theory— a story mounting from Benjy's primitive subconscious voice to the voice of Faulkner's own narrative authority, bringing the wretched Compsons to an end and closing the novel.

Light in August (1932) takes us into the heart of the South's obsession with race. It unifies itself around the finally coalescing stories of patiently loving Lena Grove, who gives birth as the murderer Joe Christmas is himself murdered. If ever Faulkner at the peak of his career—before he became a mere moralist—became interested in something like redemption, it was in the way he described not a resolution of good and evil but a balance in these two characters: one deliciously human and always faithful, the other never given a chance to become a human being.

The novel begins unforgettably with a pregnant young woman from

Alabama sitting beside a road in Mississippi, her feet in a ditch, her shoes in her hand, watching a wagon that is mounting the hill toward her with a clatter that carries for half a mile "across the hot still pinewiney silence of the August afternoon." She has been on the road for a month, riding a succession of farm wagons, walking the hot dusty roads with her shoes in her hand, trying to get to Jefferson. There she expects to find the father of her child working in a planing mill and ready to marry her. And there—in the big city—she will put on her shoes.

This opening scene, so dry and loving in its pastoral humor, centering on Lena Grove and her precious burden being carried in one wagon or another, by one farmer or another, ends sharply on the outskirts of Jefferson, where she can see smoke going up from a burning house. It is the house of Joanna Burden, who has just been murdered by Joe Christmas. What images have crowded us—the dust and heat of the unending road; the young woman continually amazed at how far "a body" can go; the serenity of her face, "calm as stone, but not hard"; the "sharp and brittle crack and clatter" of identical and anonymous wagons in "weathered and ungreased wood and metal"; the mules plodding in "a steady and unflagging hypnosis"; the drowsy heat of the afternoon; Lena's faded blue dress, her small bundle in which she carries thirty-five cents in nickels and dimes, the shoes she carries as soon as she feels the dust of the road beneath her feet. All these, we discover, provide that foundation in the local and the provincial, the earth and the road that man must travel, against which are set images of fire and murder, of aimless wandering and flight. These are embodied in the figure who soon enters the book and dominates it in his remorseless, gray anonymity.

Joe Christmas does not even have a name of his own, only a mocking label stuck on him at the orphanage where his grandfather Doc Hines deposited him one Christmas Eve because he was thought to have "black blood." "Joe Christmas" is worse than any real name could be. It indicates not only that he has no background, no roots, no name of his own, but that he is regarded as a nothing, a white sheet of paper on which anyone can write out an identity for him and make him live it.

It is the contrast of Lena Grove and Joe Christmas, of the country girl and the ultimate American wanderer, a stranger even to himself, that frames the book—literally so, since Lena Grove begins the book and ends it while Joe Christmas's agony and imminent crucifixion are enacted within a circle that he runs in an effort to catch up with himself. When he finds that he cannot run out of the circle and waits at last to die, the book comes back to Lena and ends on her deeply satisfying procession away from Jefferson with her baby and shyly loving Byron Bunch—Faulkner's version of the Holy Family. By the time we finish *Light in August*, we come to feel that the greatness of the book (and of Faulkner's unexpected compassion) lies in the amazing depth he brings to the contrast between the natural and the urban, between Lena Grove's simplicity and the way Joe Christmas walks all city pavements with the same isolation and indifference and eats at the usual "coldly smooth wooden counter." Faulkner leads up to a strange and tortured fantasy of Joe Christmas as Lena Grove's son. There is virtually an annunciation to Lena, in the moving last phase of the book, when Lena, delivered of her baby just as Joe Christmas is running for his life, hears Mrs. Hines, Joe's grandmother, call the baby "Joey"—a "nigger" murderer whom Lena has never seen. There is a new life in the world. But even Mrs. Hines's love for the grandson who never had a chance cannot make us forget that it was her own husband, maniacally obsessed against blacks, who cast off his "polluted" grandson in the name of religion.

Joe Christmas seeks the essence of Lena Grove all his life without knowing it, but runs full tilt into the ground. Lena Grove from Doane's Mill—the tiny hamlet too small for the post-office list that Lena, living in the backwoods, had not seen until her parents died—embodies, to the sound of the wagon wheel taking her away from it, the strength of soul that Faulkner so rarely finds among his characters. Lena is a kind of sacred grove, but the harshly Calvinist farmer McEachern, who takes Joey on after the orphan asylum, almost whips him to death for not obeying him to the letter. Joe runs away, only to fall in love with Bobbie the prostitute, is mocked by Mame the madam and beaten by Max the pimp. When Lena gets to Jefferson, we catch the dialectic of life and antilife on which the book is built in the way the slow, patient rhythm of Lena, the wagon, the road, is immediately followed by the whine of the saw in the planing mill, the reiteration of "smooth." The world is narrowing down to the contrast between Byron Bunch, the faithful workman and honest Christian, and "Brown," Lena's itinerant seducer back in Doane's Mill, who has coolly taken a name, "Brown," not his own, a name too conventional even to be *his* name. Joe Christmas never even had a name of his own.

Joe Christmas represents the horror of (supposed) miscegenation, of uprooting and the city man's anonymity in Southern lore. But Faulkner does not stop at the abstractness of the alien; he carries it on, he carries it out, to astonishing lengths. And it is this intensity of conception that makes the portrait of Joe Christmas so compelling in his strangeness; he is a source of wonder, of horror, even of pity, rather than a human being whose face we never really see. From the moment he appears, "there was something definitely rootless about him, as though no town nor city was his, no street, no walls, no square of earth his home." He comes to work in the sawmill in a serge suit and white shirt, the only clothes he has. Byron Bunch, watching him, knows that Joe Christmas "carried his knowledge always with him as though it were a banner, with a quality ruthless, lonely, and almost proud." Joe Christmas is only what others say about him. He is just a thought in other people's minds. More than this, he is looked at always from a distance, as if he were not quite human, which in many ways he is not.

We see Joe Christmas from a distance, and this distance is the actual space between him and his fellows. It is the distance between "Joe Christmas," which the orphan asylum thrust upon the foundling found on its doorstep Christmas Eve, and his actual suffering. He has to live up to the hollowness of his name, to the grandfather's mad suspicion that the baby had "some" Negro blood in him. Joe Christmas is "man" trying to discover the particular man he is. He is condemned by the race mania of his own grandfather, a former preacher who fanatically spends his life insisting that Negroes are guilty in the eyes of God. When his daughter ran away with a "Mexican" circus hand, Doc Hines killed the man, and after his daughter died in childbirth on Christmas Eve, he left the baby on the steps of an orphanage. He even became janitor in the place to make sure that the "nigger" would never be allowed to contaminate anyone.

This race madness goes hand in hand with a Calvinist belief in the elect and the hopeless sinfulness of others. It is found both in Joe Christmas's rigidly doctrinaire foster father, Calvin McEachern, and in his future mistress Joanna Burden, a descendant of New Hampshire Puritans who came to the South in order to change its ways. These torments about purity and guilt are to Faulkner the white Southerner the remains of an inhuman creed that added bigotry and arrogance to the curse of slavery. These are the fruits of a church that has lost its spiritual function and that has been deserted by the Reverend Gail Hightower, who spends his days in reveries of the Confederacy's irretrievable glory. The obsessions of the South have all combined to damn Joe Christmas, whose life is all flight from himself. Only his pursuers catch up with him, to murder and castrate him.

Joe Christmas is nothing but the man things are done to. He is treated even by his Negrophile mistress Joanna Burden as if he had no personality of his own, and is beseeched in her sexual transports as "Negro." He will kill her because she cannot stop praying over him. He is the most solitary character in American fiction, the most extreme phase conceivable of separateness in America. Joanna Burden tells her lover that the white babies forever coming into the world have "a black shadow already falling upon them before they drew breath. And I seemed to see the shadow in the shape of a cross . . . a black shadow in the shape of a cross. . . . And it seemed like the white babies were struggling . . . to escape from the shadow . . . as if they were nailed to the cross."

No help for Joe Christmas there, in a concern for the Negro that harbors dread. Compassion seems to be the essence of Faulkner's approach to Joe Christmas, and the triumph of the book as art is Faulkner's ability to show his violence always on tap yet to make us feel all his suffering. Faulkner, by a tremendous and moving act of imagination, has found in Joe Christmas the incarnation of "man" today—modern man, reduced entirely to his feelings. There are no gods in Faulkner's world—only "the Opponent" checkmating Lena's seducer and "the Player" who will idly move Joe Christmas's murderer toward the victim. There are only men—some *entirely* subject to their circumstances, like Joe Christmas. In his subjection, his distance from others, he is constantly trying to think himself back into life.

We hear him talking to himself and we follow his slow and puzzled efforts to understand the effect of his actions on others. We see him as a child in the orphanage, eating the toothpaste, frightening the dietitian who thinks he has seen her secretly making love. The boy is just staring straight at her, trying to understand what she is accusing him of. We watch him walking the path between his cabin and Joanna Burden's house for his meals, thinking between the four walls of her kitchen that he has never, anywhere, eaten a meal in peace. Finally we watch him running, and thinking deliriously as he runs, until, in that piercing scene near the end of his flight, he falls asleep as he runs. The pressure of thought, the torture of thought, is overwhelming—and useless. Joe Christmas does not know who he is and will never be given the chance to find out. But still he thinks, he broods, he watches, he waits. It is this brooding silence in him, fixed in attention over he knows not what, that explains why he is so often described as looking like a man in prayer— even like a "monk." There is a strange and disturbing stillness about him that eases him, more cruelly than other men, into the stillness of nonbeing. Faulkner has set him up for execution by a white supremacist and superpatriot whose misfortune it is not to have served in war. Faulkner was astonished to learn that in Percy Grimm he had created the premature American Nazi. As the fugitive comes into sight, Grimm's face had

> that serene, unearthly luminousness of angels in church windows. He was moving again almost before he had stopped, with that lean, swift, blind obedience to whatever Player moved him on the Board. . . .
>
> . . . He seemed indefatigable, not flesh and blood, as if the Player who moved him for pawn likewise found him breath. . . .
>
> It was as though he had been merely waiting for the Player to move him again, because with that unfailing certitude he ran straight to the kitchen and into the doorway, already firing . . . into the table. . . .
>
> But the Player was not done yet. When the others reached the kitchen they saw the table flung aside now and Grimm stooping over the body. When they approached to see what he was about, they saw that the man was not dead yet, and when they saw what Grimm was doing one of the men gave a choked cry and stumbled back into the wall and began to vomit. Then Grimm too sprang back, flinging behind him the bloody butcher knife. "Now you'll let white women alone, even in hell."

There was never any evidence that the "Mexican," Joe Christmas's father, was a Negro or part Negro. Joe Christmas lies on the floor, "empty of everything save consciousness. . . . For a long moment he looked up at them with peaceful and unfathomable and unbearable eyes. Then his face, body, all, seemed to collapse . . . and from out the slashed garments about his hips and loins the pent black blood seemed to rush like a released breath."

Black blood indeed. Just as Faulkner's style seems shaped by the fierce inner pressure of race problems that give no solution, so the texture of *Light in August* suggests, in the tension and repetition of certain verbal motifs, that man can never quite say what the event originally meant, or what he is to think of it now. Language never quite comes up to the physical shock of the event, the concussion to consciousness. The townspeople exist in *Light in August* as our chorus in life—they ask questions whose very function is to deny the possibility of an answer. Faulkner's grim, sarcastic asides show that he views language as in some basic sense unavailing. His repetition of certain key phrases and verbal rhythms shows that he returns back and back on the event he has described.

Call the event history, call it the Fall; man is forever engaged in bringing the past back so as to change it. That is why Joe Christmas's grandmother Mrs. Hines utters the most moving lines in the book when in the end she pitifully cries:

> I am not saying he never did what they say he did. Ought not to suffer for it like he made them that loved and lost suffer. But if folks could maybe just let him for one day. Like it hadn't happened yet. Then it could be like he had just went on a trip and grew man grown and come back. If it could be like that for just one day.

Afterword

Is it the gods who put this fire in our minds
Or is it that each man's relentless longing becomes a god to him?
VIRGIL, *Aeneid*, TRANS. ALLEN MANDELBAUM

MARCH 1851. In Pittsfield, Massachusetts, an excited Herman Melville (he was in the throes of finishing *Moby-Dick*) was in raptures at having found another genius in the Berkshires, Nathaniel Hawthorne. He wrote in homage to his idol six miles away that he, Hawthorne, surpassed all other men in his

> apprehension of the absolute condition of present things as they strike the eye of the man who fears them not, though they do their worst to him,—the man who like Russia or the British Empire, declares himself a sovereign nature (in himself) amid the powers of heaven, hell, and earth.

Melville, in the course of proclaiming Hawthorne "sovereign," slipped into writing "my sovereignty in myself." Obviously there was a lot of proud Captain Ahab in the thirty-one-year-old, still undefeated Melville, though he was overflowing in gratitude to Hawthorne for the man's very presence on earth. "Who's over me? Truth hath no confines," Ahab shrieks to the crew in the "Quarter-Deck" chapter, trying to make the "dolts" understand that what they are looking for in the white whale is not just blubber and oil but proof that he, Ahab, can take on anything and will conquer "the greatest animated mass since the Flood."

Comparing Hawthorne (really himself) to the great empires on earth, Melville's letter goes on to assert that such a man

> may perish; but so long as he exists he insists on treating with all Powers on an equal basis. If any of those other Powers choose to

withhold certain secrets, let them; that does not impair my sovereignty in myself; that does not make me tributary. And perhaps after all, there is *no* secret.

Melville is breaking out of his immense solitude. But why is he being so grandiose, magnifying Hawthorne by way of boasting about "Powers" who have no secrets for a "power" like himself? In his self-emergence as a great artist Melville boasts he can even take on God, who no longer has any "secrets."

"We incline to think that God cannot explain His own secrets, and that He would like a little information on certain points Himself. We must astonish Him as much as He us." Right after this boast Melville suddenly jumps into metaphysics:

> But it is this *Being* of the matter; there lies the knot with which we choke ourselves. As soon as you say *Me, a God, a Nature* so soon you jump off your stool and hang from the beam. Yes, that word is the hangman. Take God out of the dictionary, and you would have Him in the street.

Melville is exuberantly spreading himself. What he finally comes out with is that God is not a single entity to be taken seriously. It is not in "God" that we are immersed but in *being*, the actual flux and storm. We kill ourselves when we turn "God" from a word into an absolute separate power and then try to figure Him out. Useless. What counts is the positive action of American genius to deny and reject everything that affronts his sublime ego:

> There is the grand truth about Nathaniel Hawthorne. He says No! in thunder; but the Devil himself cannot make him say *yes*. For all men who say *yes*, lie; and all men who say *no*,—why, they are in the happy condition of judicious, unincumbered travellers in Europe; they cross the frontiers into Eternity with nothing but a carpet-bag—that is to say, the Ego.

Big deal. Hawthorne was hardly that "unincumbered traveller," and the wildly self-assured Melville of 1851 was soon to be the Melville who only a year later, with *Pierre; or, The Ambiguities*, was told by critics that it was "fit for Bedlam." In the marketplace of American letters Melville was to sink so far down that by 1866, back in his native New York (which he hated), he gave up trying to reach a public and privately wrote and published poetry paid for by an uncle. He now eked out a living as a customs inspector in New York Harbor.

Yet when Melville in his one and last moment of triumph so familiarly took on "God" as a power so like himself that He became a rival, Melville's radical individualism was in the American vein and spoke for more writers than he would ever know. Ahab finally admitted in his harangue to the crew,

> If man will strike, strike through the mask! How can the prisoner reach outside except by thrusting through the wall? To me, the white whale is that wall, shoved near to me. Sometimes I think there's naught beyond. But 'tis enough. He tasks me; he heaps me; I see in him outrageous strength, with an inscrutable malice sinewing it. That inscrutable thing is chiefly what I hate; and be the white whale agent, or be the white whale principal, I will wreak that hate upon him. Talk not to me of blasphemy, man; I'd strike the sun if it insulted me.

Melville was taking on Ahab's bravado, but many an American writer could have recognized himself in this speech. Just as Faulkner was to write as if he were taking on the South all by himself, so Melville invented a Hawthorne to rescue himself from the freezing depths of his solitude. The American writer was so self-sufficient that if his art was entirely his own, so (if he had one) was his religion.

Did Emerson recognize that his personal gift of faith was limited to himself when he complained that "the calamity is the masses"? This confession maliciously pleased Melville, who admired "all men who *dive*," but generally thought Emerson's rhapsodies innocent moonshine. Melville never mentioned his fellow New Yorker Whitman, but probably would have found his love-message not only too soft for words, but a case of another big American ego familiarly taking on God for himself. Thoughts of the divine never left Emily Dickinson's mind. But the fact that He was never there when you needed Him led her in so many directions peculiarly her own that what she came to *think* in a poem or a letter astonished her before it did everyone else.

Mark Twain, the first of the best-selling prima donnas of the modern

American novel, was in old age still trying to dispose of the Presbyterian God who like a bad fairy at his birth was to poison every success with guilt. William James believed so much in religion as therapy that for him, at least, it was no longer necessary to believe in God. T. S. Eliot, the anxious pilgrim who could not live without the authority and orthodoxy of the Church of England as the "Catholic Church in England," never recognized that in not coming close to the Father and the Son he was as much a "heretic" in the American style as the self-dependent writers of the "inner light" he condemned. Robert Frost was so triumphant in his own eyes that in his mental journey he generously included God as an *idea* intellectually (not devotionally) to be wrestled with.

If the American writer is usually alone in his imagination and in his devotions a secret to the rest of us, one reason is that religion is so publicly vehement, politicized, and censorious. The American writer has not been hostile to our periodic revivals and national "awakenings," just uninterested. Abraham Lincoln wordlessly turned away from the most elastic Baptist church on the Kentucky frontier to follow his own deciphering of human destiny. From Jefferson to Wallace Stevens, from Emerson "the father of us all" to "the fringe of reason" in many a New Age seer, that has been the usual path of the modern writer in America.

Still, so much radical individualism is bracing as opposition and innovation, never as belief in itself. There is no radiance in our modern writers, just stalwart independence, defiance of the established, and a good deal of mockery. Self-determination can also be the private reasoning from the heart which goes into belief. "But when you pray, go into your room and shut the door and pray to your Father who is in secret; and your Father who sees in secret will reward you" (Matthew 6:6).

Where with us is God the content and not just the message? It is impossible to imagine an American writer crying out, as the touching English poet Stevie Smith does in *The Holiday*,

> The soul does not grow old, the soul sees everything and learns nothing, and I say: How can we come back to God, to be taken unto Him, when we are so hard and separate and do not grow? And I say, if we are to be taken back, oh why were we sent out, why were we sent away from God?

George Orwell, the purest radical conscience of the totalitarian age, tossed off in a book review, "The problem of our time is to restore the sense of absolute right and wrong when the faith that it used to rest on—that is, the belief in personal immortality—has been destroyed. This demands faith, which is a different thing from credulity." Credulity serves doctrine. Faith is nothing but itself, is what remains within the anguish of seeing so many things destroyed in life—not least the belief in immortality, which has been submerged in American writing since the passing of Puritan theology. Though it pitifully rises again from the mass devastation and grief of war, it is soon lost again in our insistence on unlimited progress and prosperity as the goals of life.

Where genuine belief is lacking, "religion" as a social experience fills the bill. Religion is heritage, is institution, is teaching, company, and safety. It is where we are most at home and is always there when we need to go home again. The wonderfully harmonious Polish poet Czeslaw Milosz came out of the total infamy and horror of the Second World War to say in America, "Nothing could stifle my inner certainty that a shining point exists where all lines intersect." That is the European heritage from centuries of common worship in relatively homogeneous societies. The American writer lovingly reported in this book has (especially in our time) known no such heritage. In a very real sense he has no common religious heritage at all. Yeats the Irish Protestant not part of his country's religious majority was able to describe ("Two Songs from a Play") ancient beliefs in historical succession:

> *I saw a staring virgin stand*
> *Where holy Dionysus died,*
> *And tear the heart out of his side,*
> *And lay the heart upon her hand*
> *And bear that beating heart away;*
> *And then did all the Muses sing*
> *Of Magnus Annus at the spring,*
> *As though God's death were but a play.*

"The death of God" has not been a torment in America leading to a grand review of deities, as in Yeats's searing poem. Life even for the most religiously concerned has been more secular than not. Witness the exclusive triumph of realism in the American novel, the commercialism forever taking over the language, the endless whimpering of "feeling religious" without inner content. With us *now* everything, anything, is first seen as psychological. An honest believer is always on the couch. Thomas Pynchon in his wild, wonderful novel *Gravity's Rainbow* "courageously" explains religion. "It's a Puritan reflex of seeking other orders behind the visible, also known as paranoia." John Updike, modestly acquiescent to religious tradition, opens his novel *In the Beauty of the Lilies* with a minister's loss of faith, but never tells us what was lost—and why.

Starting from embattled lonely beginnings, each church in America was separate from and doctrinally hostile to others. The individual on his way to becoming a writer was all too conscious that it was *his* ancestral sect, his early training, his own holiness in the eyes of his church that he brought to his writing. He became its apostle without having forever to believe in it, in anything—except the unlimited freedom that is the usual American faith.

Index

PERMISSIONS ACKNOWLEDGMENTS

Printed in the United States
by Baker & Taylor Publisher Services